FATHERHOOD, AUTHORITY, AND BRITISH READING CULTURE, 1831–1907

During a period when the idea of fatherhood was in flux and individual fathers sought to regain a cohesive collective identity, debates related to a father's authority were negotiated and resolved through competing documents. Melissa Shields Jenkins analyzes the evolution of patriarchal authority in nineteenth-century culture, drawing from extra-literary and non-narrative source material as well as from novels. Arguing that Victorian novelists reinvent patriarchy by recourse to conduct books, biography, religious manuals, political speeches, and professional writing in the fields of history and science, Jenkins offers interdisciplinary case studies of Elizabeth Gaskell, George Meredith, William Makepeace Thackeray, George Eliot, Samuel Butler, and Thomas Hardy. Jenkins's book contributes to our understanding of the part played by fathers in the Victorian cultural imagination, and sheds new light on the structures underlying the Victorian novel.

T0304253

For Bobbie and Jaime

Fatherhood, Authority, and British Reading Culture, 1831–1907

MELISSA SHIELDS JENKINS
Wake Forest University, USA

Routledge
Taylor & Francis Group

LONDON AND NEW YORK

First published 2014 by Ashgate Publishing

2 Park Square, Milton Park, Abingdon, Oxon OX14 4RN
711 Third Avenue, New York, NY 10017, USA

Routledge is an imprint of the Taylor & Francis Group, an informa business

First issued in paperback 2016

British Library Cataloguing in Publication Data
A catalogue record for this book is available from the British Library

The Library of Congress has cataloged the printed edition as follows:
Jenkins, Melissa Shields.
 Fatherhood, authority, and British reading culture, 1831–1907 / by Melissa Shields Jenkins.
  pages cm
 Includes bibliographical references and index.
 ISBN 978-1-4724-1161-7 (hardcover: alk. paper)
 1. Fathers and daughters in literature. 2. Fathers and sons in literature. 3. Fatherhood in literature. 4. Authority in literature. 5. English fiction—19th century—History and criticism. I. Title.
 PR878.F36J46 2014
 823'.80935251—dc23

                                                                    2013039390

ISBN 978-1-4724-1161-7 (hbk)
ISBN 978-1-138-25784-9 (pbk)

Contents

Contents

Acknowledgments

I thank Leah Price, Elaine Scarry, John Picker, and Lawrence Buell, my advisers in the graduate program at Harvard University, for guiding me through the earliest stages of my interest in fatherhood. I would also like to thank the many generous colleagues and friends who have turned the project into what it is today. These individuals include Elaine Auyoung, Criscillia Benford, Karen Chase, Danielle Coriale, Debra Gettelman, Eileen Gillooly, Donald Hall, Anna Henchman, Anna Maria Jones, Catherine Keyser, Joshua King, David Latané, Julia Sun-Joo Lee, Allen MacDuffie, John Maynard, Maia McAleavey, Natalie McKnight, Andrew Miller, Rebecca Mitchell, Deborah Morse, John Plotz, Daniel Pollack-Pelzner, Matthew Rubery, Vanessa Ryan, Valerie Sanders, Kim Stern, Anne Stiles, and Lawrence Switzky. Audiences at the annual BAVS, NAVSA, and Victorians Institute conferences have been especially generous. I thank all of the individuals who participated in the National Humanities Center summer institute on *Jude the Obscure,* especially its gracious convener, Kate Flint. Thanks to Tom and Karen Dingledine, Nathan and Julie Hatch, Wake Forest's Office of the Provost, and the Mary Reynolds Babcock Foundation, for generous research and travel grants. My colleagues at Wake Forest University have provided the best environment in which to work. Special thanks to Michelle Balaev, Wanda Balzano, Bruce Barnhart, Rian Bowie, Anne Boyle, Mary Deshazer, Dean Franco, Susan Harlan, Omaar Hena, Sandya Hewamanne, Jefferson Holdridge, Claudia Kairoff, Scott Klein, Michael Klotz, Judith Madera, Barry Maine, William Moss, Gillian Overing, Jessica Richard, Gale Sigal, Randi Saloman, Ryan Shirey, Erica Still, Olga Valbuena-Hanson, and Elizabeth Way. I thank Ann Donahue for her faith in the project. I thank Rian Bowie, Patrick Smith, Jessica Richard, Katie Williams, and Anna Willis for readings and rereadings.

An early version of Chapter 1 appeared as "His Crime Was a Thing Apart: Elizabeth Gaskell Writes a Father's *Life*" in the *Victorians Institute Journal* 36 (2008). A portion of Chapter 2 appeared as "'Stamped in Hot Wax': George Meredith's Narratives of Inheritance" in *Victorian Literature and Culture* 39.2 (2011). A portion of Chapter 6 appeared as "You Are 'Father,' You Know: Hardy's Palimpsests" in *Fathers in Victorian Fiction,* ed. Natalie McKnight (2011). I thank these publications for the opportunity to revisit this material.

This book is dedicated to my extraordinary father, who, like Jane Austen's Richard Morland, "was not in the least addicted to locking up his daughters," and to my dear husband, the greatest companion for the work of life.

Introduction
Forms of Paternal Authority

In his 1831 essay "The Spirit of the Age," John Stuart Mill modestly proposes that "the nineteenth century will be known to posterity as the era of one of the greatest revolutions of which history has preserved the remembrance, in the human mind, and in the whole constitution of human society" (3). He presents his proposal at the eve of the 1832 Reform Act, an act meant to expand voting rights to male heads of households. The act was only part of Mill's envisioned revolution, in which the masses, having "awoke as from a dream" (3), discovered themselves to be "new men, who insisted upon being governed in a new way" (3). Mill wrote six years before the coronation of Queen Victoria, the matriarch who would give the era its name. He knew, however, that the coming age would be rocked by multiple challenges to traditional sources of authority. He proposes that "men are henceforth to be held together by new ties, and separated by new barriers; for the ancient bonds will no longer unite, nor the ancient boundaries confine" (3).

This book joins Mill's pronouncements with those by intellectual brothers and heirs such as Thomas Carlyle, Max Weber, Sigmund Freud, and Michel Foucault. The theorists offer overlapping models of what it means to be a "new man" calling for a new power structure within a new age. I focus on "paternal authority" and its more expansive cousin, "patriarchal authority."[1] This study does not offer a comprehensive overview of literary representations of fatherhood, nor does it tackle "fatherhood" solely as a monolithic construction via recourse to trans-historical cultural theory. Instead, I negotiate specific conflicting constructions of patriarchal authority within the marketplace for books. This interdisciplinary study entwines Victorian fiction with extraliterary modes that reinforce or challenge patriarchal authority. These modes include life-writing, conduct books, religious tracts, manuals, science writing, and history.

Each chapter of this study centers on a discovery by a Victorian novelist of another "way of writing"—a contested ground for paternal authority outside of fiction—that alters the nature of his or her literary output. Elizabeth Gaskell grapples with biography, and George Meredith revises the conduct book. W.M. Thackeray examines prayer books, and George Eliot channels political speeches. Samuel Butler joins the scientists, and Thomas Hardy the philologists and anthropologists. Each writer's method of "refiguring fatherhood" differs, since each draws on a different cultural source. However, all of the interventions share an imperative to reconsider the novel as a space for education: aesthetic, sexual, religious, civic, scientific, and historical.

---

[1]   When I refer to "paternal authority," I am speaking of specific powers attributed to the fathers of families, and when I speak of "patriarchal authority" I refer more generally to "male domination" (Mansfield 58) as it draws from the *idea* of fatherhood.

I do focus on years that correspond with the most dramatic changes in the culture's depictions of families within fiction. Growing fatigue with the family romance reflected tensions between print culture and lived culture. The rise of sensation fiction in the 1860s—with its thrilling tales of murder, bigamy, and betrayal within unstable homes—reflects eagerness to strain the bounds of propriety, at least in the safely carnivalesque spaces of literature.[2] The rise of adventure novels in the 1870s and 1880s, writes Charles Hatten in *The End of Domesticity* (2010), signals "a backlash that denigrated domesticity and sought a refuge from home and family" (30). The cultural myths of "home" clashed with the cultural myths associating the patriarch with heroism and adventure outside of the home. In *A Man's Place* (1999), John Tosh writes of the "tension between the qualities men need to sustain the routines of production and reproduction, and the qualities they might need if their community is threatened from the outside" (6). These cultural myths are created and perpetuated across fiction, drama, and poetry, but also across historical, political, religious, scientific, and didactic modes.

In the domain of the novel, however, the father is rarely given a chance to speak for himself.[3] This is a change from the literary landscape of the previous century. Feminist historians, argues Eve Sedgwick, find within the eighteenth century "a newly narrow focus on the nuclear family" and a "growing split between 'public' and 'domestic' spheres" (Sedgwick 135). As I will discuss at length in Chapter 2, the father's voice dominated conduct literature of the eighteenth century, with works such as James Fordyce's *Sermons to Young Women* (1766), John Gregory's *A Father's Legacy to His Daughters* (1774) and Lord Chesterfield's *Letters to His Son* (1774). By contrast, conduct literature in the nineteenth century was mostly written for women and by women (Warhol, *Gendered* vii).[4] The father who guided confessional Romantic lyrics such as Coleridge's "Frost at Midnight" (1798) and Wordsworth's "Anecdote for Fathers" (1798), or who exposed his flaws within the dramatic monologues of Browning and Tennyson, is silenced in many novels of the Victorian period.

---

[2]   See Anna Maria Jones, *Problem Novels: Victorian Fiction Theorizes the Sensational Self* (2007) and essays by Maia McAleavey: "The Plot of Bigamous Return" (2013), and "Soul-Mates: David Copperfield's Angelic Bigamy" (2010).

[3]   In *Victorian Masculinities* (1995), Herbert Sussman argues that first-person narration, especially expressive narration, was gendered female in the nineteenth century, as was the conventional marriage plot (35, 43). In addition, Jerome Buckley argues in *Season of Youth* (1974) that the bildungsroman, as a first-person mode, belongs to the child rather than the father.

[4]   Jacques Carré's essay collection, *The Crisis of Courtesy* (1994), ends with a bibliography of the most well-known conduct books of the sixteenth through twentieth centuries (183–93). Gender creates one clear divide between the eighteenth and nineteenth centuries. The eighteenth-century list is dominated by authors who present themselves as men, whereas the majority of the nineteenth-century list features titles presented as by women and for women.

In some ways, writes Andrew Dowling, "the novel was *made* masculine during the Victorian period, at least for its increasing number of male practitioners" (Dowling 39). Despite this, the novel's gaze at the patriarch becomes, if not hero-less as Thackeray posited in his subtitle to *Vanity Fair*, at least antipatriarchal. The fictional father's role becomes increasingly difficult to categorize. Novels centering on fathers are rarely narrated by them, and the few exceptions sell irony rather than sentiment. Exceptions are notable for their tendency for self-ridicule—see George Grossmith's *Diary of a Nobody* (1892)—or for the narrator's reluctance to define himself as a father figure, even when he has gained that status. Dickens's David Copperfield and Thackeray's Arthur Pendennis hide their newly established families from the reader until the concluding pages of their respective autobiographies. Instead, they offer "the *künstlerroman*, the novel about the making of a novelist," a mode "with an immense future" (Gross 31). Narrators focus on their past experiences as men of innocence rather than their present-tense status as men of experience. The biological father's present is secondary to the bildungsroman of his past. Yet these narrators participate in the connection of paternal power and authorial power.

Victorian novelists inherited from their predecessors an attraction to understanding the patriarch in writing, within a reassessment of the conventions of writing. In Jane Austen's *Northanger Abbey* (1818), Catherine Morland's biological father is too ordinary to produce a gothic heroine. In fact, he is almost too ordinary to mention. Richard Morland "was a clergyman, without being neglected, or poor ... he had a considerable independence besides two good livings—and he was not in the least addicted to locking up his daughters" (1). To make up for her inauspicious beginnings, Catherine imposes her gothic imagination on another father, General Tilney, whom she fails to understand because his crimes are economic, based in realism rather than in sensationalism. This novel emerges from the eighteenth century with discomfort about inheriting its father tropes. It asks, how does one write the newly "ordinary" father of realist narrative?

Fifty years later, George Meredith's protagonist in *The Adventures of Harry Richmond* (1871) has the opposite problem. His father, despite being ensconced in a realist novel, claims "that the entire course of his life was a grand plot, resembling an unfinished piece of architecture, which might, at a future day, prove the wonder of the world" (1.215). When Harry, deep in his metafictional meditations, concludes of his father, "Instead of a comic I found him a tragic spectacle" (2.199), he describes his father as a harlequin mishmash. He becomes the mad father in the attic who sets the ancestral home ablaze (2.342). These two novels, about failures to imagine sufficiently interesting fathers or contain excessively interesting ones, reflect a preoccupation within Victorian reading culture that has not been sufficiently explored. This book joins Claudia Nelson's *Invisible Men: Fatherhood in Victorian Periodicals* (1995) as a next step toward rectifying this deficiency. Nelson called for an analysis of how other extraliterary investigations of fatherhood, beyond the periodical, interact within Victorian literary culture. This book proposes a taxonomy—a working map—of forms of patriarchal authority during the transition from Victorianism to Modernism.

Increasingly, the subfield of masculinity studies has intersected with Victorian studies. Valerie Sanders' well-researched biographical sketches, in *The Tragicomedy of Victorian Fatherhood* (2009), build on John Tosh's ground-breaking historical study *A Man's Place* (1999). Lenore Davidoff and Catherine Hall's *Family Fortunes* (2002) offer to Victorian studies what Christopher Flint's *Family Fictions* (1998) and Ruth Perry's *Novel Relations* (2004) offer to studies of the eighteenth century. Charles Hatten's *The End of Domesticity* (2010) focuses on generic shifts in the last decades of the century. Matthew McCormack's *Public Men* (2007) attempts to remove the father's cloak of invisibility, by presenting masculinity as a "a tool of government" (5). Other critics have opted to tackle patriarchy through analyzing competing sources of power: motherhood, orphan-hood, surrogacy, and homosociality. After all, writes Foucault in *The History of Sexuality: An Introduction* (1976), "Where there is power, there is resistance, and yet, or rather consequently, this resistance is never in a position of exteriority in relation to power" (95). These studies have influenced me greatly. Donald E. Hall's *Fixing Patriarchy: Feminism and Mid-Victorian Male Novelists* (1996) puts the works of Dickens, Thackeray, Tennyson, and others into conversation with prominent feminist voices such as Harriet Taylor Mill. Eve Sedgwick's *Between Men* (1985) begins with the historical tension between patriarchy, which depends on heterosexuality, and homosocial alternatives (4). Herbert Sussman's *Victorian Masculinities* (1995) offers important feminist and queer interventions (Sussman 8). One of the texts in his analysis, Thomas Carlyle's lecture "The Hero as Man of Letters," is also a key text in this book. Sussman reads the lecture as an ode to homosociality, an attempt to wrest the writing world away from women in favor of "the masculinizing, or, more accurately, the re-masculinizing of literature itself, of its production, its function, its form" (Sussman 35). Carlyle writes this lecture, Sussman argues, in response to "the emerging opposition between the category of 'man' and the category 'writer,' the difficulty of affirming the manliness of letters in an utilitarian and commercial age" (37).

This book examines the effects of a decentralized, fragmented readership on a newly de-patronized, unmanned writer.[5] In turn, it connects the crises facing the author as authority with challenges to patriarchal authority. Consider the following exchange, recounted by George Henry Lewes in his 1847 essay, "The Condition of Authors in England, Germany, and France." Lewes was visiting a local registrar to record the birth of his son Herbert. Speaking of himself in the third person, within an essay that uses "we" in its discussions of the author's precarious economic and social state, he offers his own experience as a father as representative of the marginal status of authors:

---

[5]   In a note appended to his wife's essay "Reviewing" (1939), Leonard Woolf characterizes the eighteenth century as the source of "a revolution" within "the reading public and in the economic organization of literature as a profession" (Woolf *Collected* 2.215). He writes that the "expansion of the reading public" "killed the patronage system and eliminated the patron" (2.215). He agrees with Lewes and Carlyle in noting that the professional author, "if he wanted to make a living by writing, now had to write for 'the public' instead of for the patron" (2.215).

A convincing proof may also be seen in the unwillingness of literary men to own themselves professional authors; they almost all pretend to be barristers or gentlemen at large. An amusing incident happened to the present writer. He went to register the birth of a child. The registrar happened to know he was an author, and on taking down name, profession, and residence, he said,—

"I believe, sir, you are an author?"

Assent was signified by a bow.

"Humph!" said the registrar, deliberating. "We'll say, *Gent.*"

Accordingly he proceeded to inscribe "gent" in his best calligraphy; as he crossed the *t*, however, his mind misgave him, and, looking up with puzzled ingenuousness, he blandly asked,—

"I suppose, sir, *authors rank as gents?*"

His look spoke volumes! (294)

The statements reveal the "still uncertain social status of the literary profession: Is the author, or is he not, a gentleman?" (Peterson, *Becoming* 40). Lewes's status as "man" is threatened by his decision to perform intellectual labor at home rather than physical labor away from home, as was the status of contemporaries such as Thomas Carlyle (Picker 55). This was a new problem, since prominent male authors in the eighteenth century held titles other than "author": "Defoe, with many forms of employment; Fielding, a magistrate; Richardson, a printer; Smollett, a physician; Sterne, a clergyman" (Spacks 8). Those who braved writing as profession were wary to do so without looking for favor and financing to "men of rank" (Lewes, "Condition" 286). Lewes calls Samuel Johnson "the first professional author—the first who, by dint of courage and ability, kept himself free from the slavery of a bookseller's hack, and free from the still worse slavery of attendance on the great" ("Condition" 286).

Lewes's personal anecdote underscores the renewed social, professional, and gendered uncertainty ("I suppose, sir, *authors rank as gents?*") for the author seeking social recognition, and links several simultaneous threats to his authority. The occasion for his professional, social, and sexual "unmanning" was also the official action under which he could be recognized as a father. Later in his life, Lewes's decision to claim his wife's illegitimate children as his own would seal his inability to escape his adulterous marriage. He instead finds love, and an author to foster, with a woman whose chosen pseudonym, "George Eliot," pays tribute to George Lewes and to her vision of the proper, male, English author. Eliot's homage, in turn, underscores the authority that a masculine name can offer to a new novelist. The distinction between her name and her person reminds, again, that "authors" do not always "rank as gents." Finally, Lewes's anecdote also designates reading culture as a prominent ground on which to negotiate the performance of gender. As Harvey Mansfield writes in his unapologetically polemical study *Manliness* (2006), "The *word* stereotype came originally from printing: a stereotype is a kind of impression" (25). In this book, I offer six case studies, arranged into three categories. I derive the categories from "stereotyping" performed by John Stuart Mill and Max Weber during the transition from Victorianism to Modernism.

The Forms

John Stuart Mill (1806–73), the son of a prominent intellectual, and Max Weber (1864–1920), the son of a politician, offer startlingly similar categories when describing the "types" of authority prevalent in their respective nations, England and Germany. Both thinkers present their frameworks boldly, while acknowledging the limitations of what they offer. There is a touch of George Eliot's character Casaubon in each man's attempt to create a Key to Authority; indeed, each set of categories arrives in fragmented form. Mill's essay, "The Spirit of the Age" (1831) and Weber's multi-volume work, *Economy and Society* (1920), are incomplete, and both authors call for others to continue the pursuits. First, I will offer a visual shorthand of the categories. Then, I will describe each set of claims in more detail.

Mill's "The Spirit of the Age" (1831):

1. "eminent wisdom and virtue, real or supposed" (27), which evidences "the authority of superior minds" (28)
2. "power of addressing mankind in the name of religion" (27), held by "the interpreters of divine will" (28)
3. "worldly power" (27), held by "superiors in rank and station" (28).

Weber's Economy and Society *(1920):*

1. traditional authority" (1.215), which is "based on personal loyalty which results from common upbringing" (1.227)
2. "charismatic authority" (1.215), which is "sharply opposed to rational, and particularly bureaucratic, authority, and to traditional authority, whether in its patriarchal, patrimonial, or estate variants" (1.244)
3. "legal authority" (1.215), or a "belief in the legality enacted rules and the right of those elevated to authority under such rules to issue commands" (1.215).

I will argue, with Mill and Weber, for overlap as well as conflict between the three forms. For example, authority based in affect and authority based in social position, in their relations to the conventions of church and state, respectively, often absorb the language of patriarchy.

I want my pairing of these categories to be suggestive, but also open to emendation, revision, and discussion. I apply these three general categories to the special cases of paternal and patriarchal authority, although each writer designates only his first category ("eminent wisdom and virtue" and "traditional authority") as specifically patriarchal. The fathers I present in parts II and III of the book seem to turn to the second and third categories, "charismatic authority" and "legal-rational authority," as "traditional" authority and faith in "eminent wisdom and virtue" begin to wane. The fathers seem to seek new sources of authority as the oldest sources fail them.

I encourage others to add layers to this framework. In Mill's and Weber's categories, for example, some may see hints of Aristotle's categories of persuasion in *On Rhetoric*. His "three species" of persuasion are fueled by "the character [ēthos] of the speaker," or "emotion [*pathos*] by the speech," or persuasion via "the argument [*logos*] itself, by showing or seeming to show something" (*On Rhetoric* 1.2.2; pp. 37–8). "Ethos" resembles Mill's "eminent wisdom and virtue" and Weber's "traditional authority"; pathos, Mill's "power of addressing mankind in the name of religion" and Weber's "charismatic authority"; and logos, Mill's "worldly power" or Weber's "legal-rational authority." Others may look to Thomas Carlyle's (1795–1881) six categories in *On Heroes, Hero-Worship, and the Heroic in History* (1841). His "Hero as King" and "Hero as Prophet" resemble "eminent wisdom" and "traditional authority." His "Hero as Divinity" and "Hero as Priest" resemble influence in "the name of religion" and "charismatic authority." His "Hero as Poet" and "Hero as Man of Letters," in the focus on influence as a *profession*, resemble what Mill and Weber offer within "worldly power" and "legal-rational authority."

Sigmund Freud's *Moses and Monotheism* (1937) offers two categories of power wielded by "the great man"—"his personality" and "the idea for which he stands" (139)—that resonate with the distinction between "charismatic authority" and the authority gained from tradition or profession. Freud, with Mill, links the rise of the great man to the cravings of the masses: "This idea may lay stress on an old group of wishes in the masses, or point to a new aim for their wishes, or, again, lure the masses by other means. Sometimes—and this is surely the more primitive effect—the personality alone exerts its influence, and the idea plays a decidedly subordinate part" (139). The masses in their natural state, Mill suggests, "may at times be unhappy and consequently discontented, habitually acquiesce in the laws and institutions which they live under" (17). Why, asks Freud, do the masses long for "authority which they can admire, to which they can submit, and which dominates and sometimes even ill-treats them?" (140). Freud answers, "It is the longing for the father that lives in each of us from his childhood days, for the same father whom the hero of legend boasts of having overcome" (140). Freud accepts the definition of hero that defines him against his father, as "having been born against his father's will and saved in spite of his evil intentions" (9), since kings and queens "in dreams and fairytales always represent, accordingly, the parents" (10). Yet, the rebellion from the father, in favor of the "hero," creates a link between them. Freud finds it necessary to discuss the great man and the father at once: "now it begins to dawn on us that all the features with which we furnish the great man are traits of the father, that in this similarity lies the essence, which so far has eluded us, of the great man" (140). Foucault, in "The Subject and Power," attempts to define a form he calls "pastoral power" (782). In doing so, he evokes the other categories explored by Mill, Weber, Aristotle, Carlyle, and Freud before him: "certain individuals can, by their religious quality, serve others not as princes, magistrates, prophets, fortune-tellers, benefactors, educationists and so on" (783). This book seeks a fuller understanding of the forms of authority available to the patriarch as "Man of Letters," who attempts, in the eighteenth and nineteenth centuries, prominence equal to past divinities, poets, priests, and kings.

Modern theorists of authority assert that authority is not "an *entity*," especially not one "that came into existence in one historical era and disappeared in another," but is instead an "effect (and the perceived capacity to produce an effect) that is operative within strongly asymmetrical relations of speaker and audience" (Lincoln 116). Richard Sennett echoes Bruce Lincoln's formulation, stating that "authority is not a thing" but rather "an interpretive process which seeks for itself the solidity of a thing" (19). Authority, therefore, is dialogic. It is uncovered, reinforced, challenged, or vanquished though language exchange. Authority is also a social emotion, drawing on unequal power relations and reinforced via "assurance, superior judgment, the ability to impose discipline, the capacity to inspire fear" (Sennett 17–18). The loss of any of these qualities heralds the end of authority.

"Fatherhood" is a complex abstraction, as is "authority." James Joyce suggests as much in *Ulysses* (1922), when Stephen Dedalus receives a telegram containing one of George Meredith's aphorisms, "Fatherhood, in the sense of conscious begetting, is unknown to man. It is a mystical estate, an apostolic succession, from only begotter to only begotten … *Amor matris,* subjective and objective genitive, may be the only true thing in life. Paternity may be a legal fiction. Who is the father of any son that any son should love him or he any son?" (207). Joyce, too, touches on the different modes of authority I examine in this study—traditional ("estate"), charismatic ("apostolical"), and legal-rational ("legal")—but he strips the categories of their stability ("mystical," "unknown," "fiction"). He echoes Telemachus' cry in the epic on which his own modern intervention depends, "Who, on his own, has ever really known who gave him life?" (Homer 1.250–51). Joyce and Homer find it appropriate to look at fatherhood as "fiction." When Stephen's friends respond with skepticism—"What the hell are you driving at?" Stephens' friends ask, to which he responds, "I know. Shut up. Blast you! I have reasons" (Joyce 207)—he feels obligated to turn to his environment, the library, to justify his stereotyping. Through Shakespeare's Hamlet, and Shakespeare himself, Stephen encourages his hearers to consider ways in which all men are fathers of themselves, and all writers the fathers of men.

John Stuart Mill's Call

John Stuart Mill, who was born as Napoleon ascended to power and was a child when he was defeated, wrote "The Spirit of the Age," an incomplete series of short pieces for the *Examiner*, on the eve of the 1832 Reform Bill. In the series, Napoleon becomes a symbol for the darkest tyranny, "a man in whom all the evil influences of his age were concentered with an intensity and energy truly terrific" (35). Mill wrote "The Spirit of the Age" five years before the death of his domineering but influential father, James Mill, and at the end of a four-year period of emotional breakdown and recovery (Cazamian 115). Mill himself was ready for a change—ready, perhaps, to become one with those insisting on "being governed in a new way" (Mill, *Spirit* 3). Knowing that what he had written thus far would not be sufficient for the task ahead, he called for "a careful survey of the properties which are characteristic of the English national mind, in the present age—for on these the future fate of our country must depend" (40). Though he would not finish the essay series, his many writings on government and the individual, such as *On Liberty* (1859) and *Utilitarianism* (1861), would join with his continued interest in gender and power, manifested in the last book published before his death, *The Subjection of Women* (1869).

In Part IV of "The Spirit of the Age," Mill argues for "three distinguishable sources of moral influence:—eminent wisdom and virtue, real or supposed; the power of addressing mankind in the name of religion; and, finally, worldly power" (27). He gauges the state of a given civilization—gesturing expansively from the Dark Ages to Britain and America in the nineteenth century—based on the citizenry's belief in the legitimacy of its leaders within these three categories. At times, nations behave like dutiful children and "cleave with a strong and fervent faith to the doctrine which they have imbibed from their infancy" (28). At other times, the "three authorities are divided among themselves, or against each other," in which case "a violent conflict rages among opposing doctrines, until one or other prevails, or until mankind settles down into a state of general uncertainty and skepticism" (28). What is universal, Mill claims, is the general desire of individuals to cling to these three forms for as long as possible: "all bow down, with a submission more or less implicit, to the authority of superior minds, or of the interpreters of divine will, or of their superiors in rank and station" (28). This is not because men are improperly naïve, but because humans embed an innate longing for truth within specific people or institutions (14). Mill's first two categories point, straightforwardly, to the ancestor and the prophet/priest. Mill defines "worldly power" as distinct from "moral influence" in that worldly power is granted to those who, through filial inheritance or good fortune within the economy, hold a disproportionate amount of the world's goods. It is also the power given based on "rank and station" (27), on one's official title.

Part of the reason for the crisis in authority experienced in his age, Mill claims, is writing. Despite the truism that "there are things which books cannot teach" (31), he notes that "in an age of literature, there is no longer, of necessity, the same wide interval between the knowledge of the old, and that which is attainable by the young" as "the experience of all former ages, recorded in books, is open to the young man as to the old" (31). Later in the century, Mill reflects again on the role of print culture in destabilizing authority. This time, books themselves are in crisis. He writes in *On Liberty*, in a chapter that will inspire Sue Bridehead in Hardy's *Jude the Obscure* (1895),[6] "the mass do not now take their opinions from dignitaries in Church or State, from ostensible leaders, or from books. Their thinking is done for

---

6   As I discuss in Chapter 6 of this book, Hardy's character Sue quotes Mill's statement that "He who lets the world, or his own portion of it, choose his plan of life for him, has no need of any other faculty than the ape-like one of imitation" (Mill 86; Hardy *Jude* 234).

them by men much like themselves, addressing them or speaking in their name, on the spur of the moment, through the newspapers" (Mill, *Spirit* 92). In this, Mill is longing, with Carlyle, for a redefinition of the "hero." He does not ask for "the sort of 'hero-worship' which applauds the strong man of genius for forcibly seizing on the government of the world and making it do his bidding in spite of itself" (93), but rather for a man who can lead the masses to better things than they can choose for themselves. Such leadership, he thinks, requires a slower brand of reflection than what is available on the average newsstand.

Ten years after "Spirit of the Age," and almost two decades before Mill's melancholy reflections in *On Liberty*, Carlyle's *On Heroes, Hero-Worship, and the Heroic in History* (1841) makes a case for alternating periods in which authority is held by divinities, poets, priests, kings, and, most curiously, "the *Man of Letters*" (Carlyle 166). Carlyle, following Mill, characterizes his age as one that "denies the existence of great men," and also "denies the desirableness of great men" (13). His age, Carlyle posits, is more inclined to dissect the great man—to "account" for him and "take the dimensions of him" (13)—than to celebrate him (250). As with Mill, who began "Spirit of the Age" by describing the novelty of his title as a term—"a novel expression. I do not believe that it is to be met with in any work exceeding fifty years in antiquity" (3)—one of Carlyle's categories seems specific to the age in which he lives. He points to a new brand of hero in an age otherwise averse to them, one who "has hardly lasted above a century in the world yet" (166) but who should hold sway "so long as the wondrous art of *Writing*, or of Ready-writing which we call *Printing*, subsists" (166). He marvels at the sight of this new hero, considering his body beside his bodies of writing:

> Much had been sold and bought, and left to make its own bargain in the marketplace; but the inspired wisdom of a Heroic Soul never till then, in that naked manner. He, with his copy-rights and copy-wrongs, in his squalid garret, in his rusty coat; ruling (for this is what he does), from his grave, after death, whole nations and generations who would, or would not, give him bread while living,—is a rather curious spectacle! Few shapes of Heroism can be more unexpected.
>
>   Alas, the Hero from of old has had to cramp himself into strange shapes: the world knows not well at any time what to do with him, so foreign is his aspect in the world!" (183–4)

"The world knows not well … what to do with" the "inspired wisdom" of the "rusty coat" echoes Christ's apology for those who crucified him and cast lots for his garments,[7] and thus turns the writer into an "interprete[r] of the divine will" (Mill, *Spirit* 28). The Man of Letters's posthumous manner of "ruling (for this is what he does)" gives him a spark of "eminent wisdom and virtue, real or supposed" (27). In wielding his "copy-rights and copy-wrongs" he attempts to

---

[7]   "Father, forgive them, for they know not what they do. And they parted his raiment, and cast lots" (Luke 23:34). Oscar Wilde uses the same analogy for the same purpose in his poem "On the Sale By Auction of Keats' Love Letters" (1886).

gain a hold on "worldly power" (27). Carlyle seems to doubt that the prophets of his age will be recognized as such in their own time. It does not help that, by mid-century, the "Man of Letters" cramped himself into so many shapes; he and his kin were "poets, novelists, journalists, biographers, historians, social critics, philosophers, and political economists" (Liddle 17). How do these different kinds of men interact? How does the authority wielded—however tentatively—within each form relate to that within other forms? That is the major question that, with Weber's help, this book seeks to answer.

Max Weber's Response

Max Weber (1864–1920) lived during the rise of Germany into a world power, and then witnessed its initial decline after World War 1 (S.M. Miller 1). Having also watched Karl Marx turn economic class into the major engine of social interaction, Weber embarked on an expansive study of social relationships (10, 13). Weber had a special interest, as did Carlyle, in charismatic authority, as "part of his attempt to show the importance of the hero in history" (16). Much of Weber's work on authority in society is rooted in its smallest unit, the family. The authority that connects a family group, he writes, "is of two kinds: (1) the authority derived from superior strength; and (2) the authority derived from practical knowledge and experience" (Weber, *Economy* 1.359). In either case it is "the authority of men as against women and children; of the able-bodied as against those of lesser capability; of the adult as against the child; of the old as against the young" (Weber, *Economy* 1.359). Weber's other types of authority emerge from the family model: "The 'loyalty' [that unites a family] is one of subjects toward the holders of authority and toward one another. As reverence for ancestors, it finds its way into religion; as a loyalty of the patrimonial official, retainer, or vassal, it becomes part of the relationships originally having a domestic character" (Weber, *Economy* 1.359). "Household authority," he argues for his own age, is declining, as "the individual" gets pulled into, shall we say, the spirit of his age: "the individual becomes less and less content with being bound to rigid and undifferentiated forms of life prescribed by the group" (Weber 1.375). The pull away is due to the increased separation between home, workplace, and school, to the transition from familial to governmental protection, and to changes in the economic system that make it more profitable to focus on "a more intensive exploitation of the individual taxpayer" (1.375). The pull away is also biological, rooted in Fatherhood's status as, in Stephen Dedalus' words, "a legal fiction" (Joyce 207). Weber writes that without "the household as a unit of economic maintenance, the sexually based relationship between husband and wife, and the physiologically determined relationship between father and children are wholly unstable and tenuous" (Weber 1.357). The mother–child relationship is the only "natural" one, in that it is not dependent on market forces and collective social agreements (Weber 1.357).

Weber emerges with three categories, "pure types of legitimate domination" that he calls "traditional," "charismatic," and "legal-rational" (1.215). These pure types make appeals on objective grounds, such as external rewards, or subjective grounds that are "1. affectual: resulting from emotional surrender; or 2. value-rational: determined by the belief in the absolute validity of the order ... or 3. religious: determined by the belief that salvation depends upon obedience to the order" (Weber, *Economy* 1.33).

Weber's first category, "traditional authority," depends on "an established belief in the sanctity of immemorial traditions and the legitimacy of the status of those exercising power under them" (1. 215). Traditional authority draws on consensus that the individuals in charge embody the wisdom of the ages. The most important type of traditional authority, Weber writes, is "patriarchal domination," based "not on the official's commitment to an impersonal purpose and not on obedience to abstract norms, but on strictly personal loyalty ... grow[ing] out of the master's authority over his household" (Weber 3.1006). Weber's second category, "charismatic authority," "rest[s] on devotion to the specific and exceptional sanctity, heroism, or exemplary character of an individual person, and of the normative patterns of order revealed or ordained by him" (1.215). Charismatic authority is the least inherently "patriarchal" of the three forms, and the most revolutionary. Traditional and legal-rational authority are "everyday forms of domination" that are "bound to" rules, whereas charismatic authority, at least initially, is "foreign to all rules" (1.244). Yet traditional and charismatic authority overlap in their dependence on "a sense of loyalty and obligation which always has a religious aura" (3.1122). Thus, charisma's divergence from traditional and legal-rational forms is only temporary, Weber argues. For this personal, embodied authority to survive longer than the man who wields it, some apparatus for inheritance must be devised. Charismatic authority, embodied in "a savior, a prophet, or a hero" (3.954) becomes legal-rational or traditional when it is reintegrated into the economic considerations that it otherwise transcends. Weber writes, "it is the fate of charisma ... to recede with the development of permanent institutional structures" (3.1133). John Stuart Mill also registers the taming of "the power of addressing mankind in the name of religion" (1.27). He offers an extended description of the Protestant and Catholic churches, as systems, appropriating the influence of its prophetic voices and translating those voices into material gains. Connections between the church and patriarchy have since become commonplace. As Freud writes in *Civilization and Its Discontents* (1930), "the derivation of religious needs from the infant's helplessness and the longing for the father aroused by it seems to me incontrovertible, especially since the feeling is not simply prolonged from childhood days, but is permanently sustained by fear of the superior power of Fate" (19). Performative forms of authority may involve a paradoxical brand of obedience to the expectations of the waiting congregation. As John Galbraith writes in *The Anatomy of Power* (1983), authority figures can gain power from recognizing and exploiting the norm, as well as from establishing it. An individual may, for example, gain most from "his aptitude with the conditioned belief of his constituency," as with the "preacher who, correctly judging the rain clouds, proceeds to pray for rain" (Galbraith 44).

Legal-rational authority is based in "a belief in the 'legality' of patterns of normative rules and the right of those elevated to authority under such rules to issue commands" (1.215). As with Mill's "worldly power," then, which is based on rank, title, and wealth, legal-rational authority is externalized, based on social contracts. To discuss "worldly power" and "legal-rational authority" together, then, is to watch the patriarch grasp for renewed authority in the world of work, law, and "appointed" secular position. The distinction is that between "executive authority," or "the authority of those who are 'in authority'" and "epistemic authority," or the authority of "those who are 'an authority'" (Lincoln 3–4). In this third category, we transition from "I rule because I have done so" (traditional authority) and "I rule because I am" (charismatic authority) to "I rule because I adhere, or because I know" (legal-rational authority). Weber explains the difference between the first two forms and the third as related to "the struggle of the 'specialist' type of man against the older type of the 'cultivated man'" (3.1002). If traditional authority is the most explicitly patriarchal, legal-rational authority is most grounded in text. Weber writes, "administrative acts, decisions, and rules are formulated and recorded in writing, even in cases where oral discussion is the rule or is even mandatory" (1.219). Similarly, Michel Foucault types "the 'universal' intellectual, as he functioned in the nineteenth and early twentieth centuries" as "the man of justice, the man of law, who counterposes to power, despotism and the abuses and arrogance of wealth the universality of justice and the equity of an ideal law" (*Power* 128). This mystical figure "finds his fullest manifestation in the writer, the bearer of values and significations in which all can recognize themselves" (128). In legal-rational authority we find the last stand of the hero as man of letters.

The Chapters

Part I of this book combines Mill's category of "eminent wisdom and virtue, real or supposed," and Max Weber's category of "traditional authority." This is the only category of the three that is specifically patriarchal, though, I will argue, it has become commonplace to understand all three via recourse to the family. Mill's essay discusses ancestor worship as a key example of this type of authority, and books as a threat to it (*Spirit* 29–31), and Weber turns to "the sanctity of immemorial traditions" (Weber 1.215). In Chapter 1, "Elizabeth Gaskell Writes a Father's *Life*," and Chapter 2, "A Father's Conduct: George Meredith and the Book-within-a-Book," I track real and fictional fathers who gain and lose power via recourse to conventions. In the first chapter, I claim that Manchester novelist Elizabeth Gaskell changed her novelistic practice after responding to Patrick Brontë's claims about genre—about the moral differences between the writers of novels, and the writers of pamphlets, poems, and biography. In the second, I describe George Meredith's enduring fascination with the conduct book, especially distinctions between conduct books written by fathers and the lives lived by sons and daughters.

Part II of this book pairs the second of Mill's "distinguishable sources of moral influence" (27) with Weber's second "pure type" of authority, linking "the power of addressing mankind in the name of religion" with "charismatic authority." Chapter 3, "'An Attitude of Decent Reverence': Thackeray and the Father at Prayer," and Chapter 4, "'Lay Hold of Them by Their Fatherhood': George Eliot, Persuasion, and Abstraction," turn to the shaping power of appeals to sentiment. Weber uses this category to discuss religious authority as well as political authority (3.1163–4; 1173–6) and Part II of this book follows his lead. Thackeray's recuperation of the father at prayer, and Eliot's turn to "fatherhood" as political ideal, show both authors subject to the form of authority they test in their respective works. The patriarch, as cultural construct, draws cultural capital from shaping feeling as well as shaping thinking. Thackeray and Eliot draw attention to the performative, and temporally bound, aspects of this form of authority, especially as it comes under threat from an increasingly secular state.

Part III examines Mill's category of "worldly power" alongside Weber's category of "legal-rational authority." Chapter 5, "Samuel Butler at the Museum," surveys Butler's appropriation of the authority of the historian and scientist as he refigures the shape of his life, texts, and career in response to his father's demands. Ultimately, Butler's seeming aversion to patriarchy becomes a radical method of appropriating its forms. Chapter 6, "'Preserve the Shadow of the Form': Hardy's Palimpsests," analyzes Thomas Hardy's interest in the palimpsestic text—the manuscript that makes its own inheritances visible, despite attempts at erasure by the text's youngest handlers.

In the book's conclusion, I examine one more act of refiguring the father, Edmund Gosse's 1907 work *Father and Son.* In this novelistic combination of biography and autobiography Gosse self-consciously categorizes his father as Victorian and himself as Modern. He draws on a strict psychological typology that is as novelistic as the texts to which he responds, especially as he rewrites Charles Dickens's *Dombey and Son* (1848) and *David Copperfield* (1850). Gosse's biography also incorporates the extraliterary sources of authority analyzed in my other chapters—science writing, life writing, conduct literature, historical writing, the sermon, and the speech. It is a final reminder that father-based fictions are not the only texts within which we can analyze the power wielded, negotiated, lost, and regained by the patriarch's pen.

Gosse's analysis takes us back to Lewes's crisis within the Registrar's Office, in which he was being assessed as father, gentleman, and author. Lewes sought tenuous, and conflicting, sources of authority loaned to him by church, state, social convention, and the market for books. When asked to "sell himself" to the skeptical registrar, he seemed to fall short on all counts. No wonder, then, that the registrar's look "spoke volumes."

PART I
Traditional Authority

"eminent wisdom or virtue, real or supposed …"

Chapter 1
Elizabeth Gaskell Writes a Father's *Life*

Although many scenes in Elizabeth Gaskell's works resemble moments in Patrick Brontë's writing, I begin with one key scene that illustrates the crucial distinctions between the two writers' views on patriarchal power. In *The Maid of Killarney* (1818)*, Patrick Brontë's patriarch fires a pistol into the Irish moors for romantic emphasis, to impress upon his visitors the sublime effects of the echoing hills in his native land (84). His guns come in handy later, as the Captain defends his home from a band of robbers at the novel's climax (107). Patrick Brontë's armed patriarch protects his family and conveys the glory of his country. In Elizabeth Gaskell's hands, the armed father symbolizes more sinister forces. The father figure who shot his pistol for romantic effect becomes an image of uncontrolled, nonverbal wrath. In her biography of his daughter, Charlotte, Gaskell argues that Patrick Brontë "did not speak when he was annoyed or displeased, but worked off his volcanic wrath by firing pistols out the back door in rapid succession." She portrays a father whose anger is so primal and pre-verbal that, regardless of how it is manifested—in breaking furniture, cutting dresses, or shooting pistols—it "still was speechless" (*Life of Charlotte Brontë* 42).

Gaskell's presentation is ideologically charged, and inflected by her approach to novel-writing. The libel accusations Gaskell faced after the first edition of the biography left her stunned and chastised (L. Miller 85–6). Servants in the Brontë household felt they had been improperly characterized, and the married Lady Scott objected to Gaskell's unflinching portrayal of Branwell Brontë's indiscretions while working in her household. After Lady Scott's objections, the *Athenaeum* retracted early praise of the biography. Gaskell complained to George Smith in early August 1857, "Every one who has been harmed in this unlucky book complains of something" (Gaskell, *Letters* 463). On the worst of the charges, Patrick Brontë defended Gaskell (J. Barker, *Brontës* 804–5). As a nod to this favor, she wrote to George Smith to "take out the pistol shooting" (*Letters* 467–8) in the subsequent edition, to remove the story of Patrick Brontë firing his pistol to work "off his volcanic wrath" (*Life* 42).

Some accounts of Elizabeth Gaskell's composition process declare that Ellen Nussey commissioned the work, while others focus on Elizabeth Gaskell's personal determination to compose the biography (Hughes and Lund, *Victorian Publishing* 125; Peterson, *Becoming* 134). Christine Krueger's feminist reading suggests that Gaskell hatched the plan herself, "fearing only the wrath of Patrick Brontë" (Krueger 221). In fact, Charlotte Brontë's father was an essential part of the conception and execution of the biography. He shared materials with Gaskell, and offered editorial advice—some solicited, some unwelcome. So far, however, critics have overlooked his influence on Gaskell, and thus overlooked an aspect of her responses, across her career, to patriarchal authority.

Spooked by a pamphlet that sensationalized his daughter's home life, Patrick Brontë had a specific request for Gaskell as she wrote. In an anxious letter written to Gaskell in November 1856, he wrote that he had "no great objection" to "[t]he book-making gentry" who made him into a "somewhat extraordinary and eccentrick personage ... admitting they can make a penny by it" (Lock and Dixon 503). Here, he argues that "book-makers" of all kinds borrow from the conventions of fiction. Pamphleteers, like novelists, know which "characters" sell books. In describing hopes of a more sympathetic characterization from Gaskell, Patrick Brontë shows his awareness of Gaskell's novels:

> But the truth of the matter is—that I am, in some respects, a kindred likeness
> to the father of Margaret, in "North and South"—peaceable, feeling, sometimes
> thoughtful—and generally well-meaning. Yet unlike him in one thing—by
> occasionally getting into a satirical vein—when I am disposed to dissect, and
> analyze, human character, and human nature, studying closely its simples and
> compounds, like a curious surgeon—And being in early life thrown on my own
> resources ... I may not be so ready as some are, to be a follower of any man,
> or a worshipper of conventualities or forms, which may possibly to superficial
> observers, acquire me the character, of a little eccentricity. (P. Brontë, *Letters* 249)

Patrick Brontë requests a formal intervention. He feels misrepresented by pamphleteers who profess to write fact, and appeals to a fiction writer for a more accurate representation. He asks Gaskell to recast him as one of her characters. He feels an affinity to her literary father figures, men who are invariably misunderstood and ostracized within her novels.

One objective of this chapter is to track Gaskell's response to his request, as she creates a pivotal role for the fiery Irishman in her biography, and re-creates him again in her final, unfinished novel *Wives and Daughters* (1865), which features a surgeon of Scottish heritage as the father of her motherless heroine. The first portrayal is a replica of the pamphleteer's slander; the second portrayal is a recuperation. Another objective of the chapter is to understand one of Gaskell's most pervasive responses to a father's traditional authority. Despite calling himself no "worshipper of conventualities or forms" (P. Brontë, *Letters* 249), Patrick Brontë approached Elizabeth Gaskell in hopes of imposing system and order. He wanted her to create a coherent story out of the letters, clippings, and scraps of juvenilia he had collected. Gaskell could not comply with his request for a seamless story, however, without playing against her narrative tendencies. What Patrick Brontë sought to pull together, Gaskell sought to break apart. Patsy Stoneman argues that Gaskell's works "show in sensational terms the devastating effects of fathers who try to control their sons without cultivating personal bonds" (Stoneman, "Gaskell" 137). Similarly, Jenny Uglow calls Gaskell's fathers "ambivalent figures, whose strength conceals weakness and who are viewed by their children—especially their daughters—with mingled tenderness and resentment, longing and anger" (54). In Stoneman's response, we see Gaskell's enduring interest in the father as villain. In Uglow's recourse to paradoxical phrases ("tenderness and resentment, longing and anger"), she registers Gaskell's creation of fictional fathers who are in themselves fragmentary.

The fragmentation of Gaskell's father figures is intimately connected with the most common subject within her works—the relationship between a daughter's life narrative and a father's intervention in it. One would be hard-pressed to find a text by Gaskell in which the patriarch is not a narrative problem that needs to be solved—an incomplete personage who fuels narrative by his very incompleteness. Gaskell's pervasive technique is not unchanging, however. Writing *The Life of Charlotte Brontë* (1857), and dealing with its generic challenges, and its legal ones, forced Gaskell to reconsider the nature of her own narrative authority. The biography becomes an important hinge on which an entire career turns.[1] She reconsiders the relationship between fact and fiction within literary culture, and reconsiders how the child's story should respond to paternal demands for "system." Across her oeuvre, Gaskell makes new decisions about how a father's life (or *Life*) should be arranged.

The first two chapters in this book, united under the header "traditional authority," tackle a father's presence as character, but also as author and editor. Max Weber's category of "traditional authority"—as distinguished from charismatic authority and legal-rational authority—discusses allegiance and obedience to "the *person* of the chief who occupies the traditionally sanctioned position of authority and who is (within its sphere) bound by tradition" (Weber 1.216). One element that renders such authority tenuous is that "the obligation of obedience is a matter of personal loyalty" (1.216), and this personal loyalty is a result of "a common upbringing" (1.227). In Weber's three categories of "pure types of authority," then, traditional authority is the most straightforwardly patriarchal. This form of domination is often embodied in "gerontocracy" and "patriarchalism" (1.231), or power based in age and lineage.

As I outlined in the book's introduction, John Stuart Mill writes in "Spirit of the Age" (1831) that in a time of stability all tend to "bow down, with a submission more or less implicit, to the authority of superior minds, the interpreters of divine will, or of their superiors in rank and station" (27). As with Weber, Mill connects his first category with age, his second with charisma, and his third with wealth and office. The latter two categories are the subjects of parts II and III of this book. In Part I, I interrogate what Mill means by "the authority of superior minds,"

---

[1]   Aina Rubenius's *The Woman Question in Mrs. Gaskell's Life and Works* (Harvard, 1950) was one of the first works to claim *The Life of Charlotte Brontë* as a turning point in Gaskell's career. The tendency, writes Christine Krueger, is to claim that Gaskell's "newly awakened feminist consciousness released her from the obligation to write social problem novels ... and write art for art's sake" (Krueger 227). I join Krueger in defining the shift differently. Krueger claims that Gaskell is still writing against patriarchal authority, in books that "fracture or deny the recuperative closures by which challenges to patriarchal authority could be domesticated" (228). I argue instead Gaskell is attempting reconciliation and closure, both in her past treatments of patriarchs, and in her treatment of the limitations of past narrative approaches.

alongside Weber's category of traditional authority.[2] Stable societies revere ancestors and bow to the wisdom derived from experience on earth; an age of transition shows "disregard of the authority of ancestors" (29). Mill looks to the Victorian era to come as an important period of transition in which "Mankind will not be led by their old maxims, nor by their old guides; and they will not choose either their opinions or their guides as they have done before" (Mill 5).

Books, Mill writes, are the greatest threat to authority based on age and generation, since the knowledge within books is "open to the young man as to the old" (Mill, *Spirit* 31). Gaskell unmasks the role of tradition in the perpetuation of literary conventions as well as domestic ones. Gaskell does so by refiguring fiction and biography.

Patrick Brontë's Plotting, and Gaskell's Plots

The last decades have led critics to reconsider Gaskell's version of Patrick Brontë. John Lock and W.T. Dixon's *A Man of Sorrow* (1965) was the first work in a series of attempted recuperations.[3] For example, Frances Beer describes Juliet Barker's 1994 biography as the opposite of Gaskell's biography, claiming that the former idealizes the patriarch while the latter vilifies him (77). Others reinsert Patrick Brontë into the story of his daughters via a focus on his writing life. His first purchase after taking the A.B. degree, Walter Scott's *The Lay of the Last Minstrel* (1805), is mentioned by every modern critic who wants to find traces of the father's imagination in the daughters (Barker, *Brontës* 13). Robert Polhemus argues in *Lot's Daughters* (2005), for example, that "the key to understanding the soul that generated his daughters' genius is to see that he loved the world of secular education, politics, and military power; loved the flesh of erotic life, and loved the dazzling, dangerous words of profane literature" (143). This vision of Patrick Brontë startles when contrasted with the comparatively staid content of his writing. Patrick Brontë left a handful of poems, two novels—*The Maid of Killarney* (1818) and *The Cottage in the Wood* (1815)—and many religious writings. Since all of these works were in the family library ("Haworth" 24), they are occasionally connected to specific works by the Brontë sisters. Polhemus calls *The Cottage in the Wood* "virtually unreadable" and "banal," but says that it is "a key source for *Jane Eyre*" (144). His 1818 novel *The Maid of Killarney* is widely

---

[2]   Patrick Brontë was an "interpreter of divine will" in his office as Anglican minister. However, in this chapter I am most interested in the tools he used to assert his influence over his daughters and over Gaskell, as opposed to over his congregation; those tools were secular as much as spiritual. The categories, of course, overlap and affect each other, as I will discuss in detail in the book's conclusion. Mill's categories reinforce or undercut each other: "When an opinion is sanctioned by all these authorities, or by any one of them, the others not opposing, it becomes the received opinion" (Mill, "Spirit" 27).

[3]   Other pivotal continuations that I will discuss in this chapter include Juliet Barker's *The Brontës* (1994), Lucasta Miller's *The Brontë Myth* (2003), and Robert Polhemus's chapter on the Brontës in *Lot's Daughters* (2005).

discussed as an influence on Anne Brontë's *Agnes Grey* and *The Tenant of Wildfell Hall* (Barker, *Brontës* 78; Barker, "Haworth" 24–5; Chitham 118, 122).

Patrick Brontë's works are rarely studied today, but they provide insight into Gaskell's particular challenges when writing his daughter's biography. Warnings about the fantastical novel—the novel that entertains more than instructs, and has grounding in the world of the imagination more than the world of the real—fill his volumes of poetry and fiction. Most of his comments about writing support assumptions about his aversion to the sensational, romantic, or improbable. The prefatory notes of *The Cottage in the Wood: Or, The Art of Becoming Rich and Happy* (1815) criticize the "sensual novelist" for replacing "probability" with the "*miraculous*" (102). He calls these novelists, and their readers, "beings of depraved appetites and sickly imaginations" who "are diligently and zealously employed in creating an imaginary world, which they can never inhabit, only to make the real world, with which they must necessarily be conversant, gloomy and insupportable" (104). His various commentaries about writing emphasize order. He calls for a simple moral message, a clear and accessible style, and minimal rhetorical flourishes. His preface to *Cottage Poems* (1811) characterizes them as "not above the comprehension of the meanest capacities" (vii). He claims to have "aimed at simplicity, plainness, and perspicuity, both in manner and style" (viii). His stance in the prefatory materials extends to the works themselves. "The Happy Cottagers" describes the relationship he sees between fact and the novelist's art:

> I sing of real life;
> All else, is empty show:
> To those who read, a source
> Of much unreal woe:
> > Pollution, too,
> > Through novel-veins,
> > Oft fills the mind,
> > With guilty stains. (21)

Brontë presents the epic "I sing" only to deflate it. He sings not of "a man," "wrath," or of "arms," but of "real life." His speaker fears fanciful writing because "empty show" can be dangerous. The reader of immoral novels absorbs their taint passively and unconsciously, as she takes in polluted air or acquires an infection of the blood. Brontë imagines a coven of melancholy readers washing imaginary spots off of soiled hands. He sees his own writing as a corrective and a warning.

Gaskell reinforces this image of caution crushing creativity. The father of writers seems, to Gaskell, unimpressive as a writer and unaware of his children's talents. Patrick Brontë's admiration for Gaskell's writing was not matched by her feelings about his use of words. Of his failure to penetrate his children's inner lives, Gaskell says, "He says now that he suspected it all along, but his suspicions could take no exact form, as all he was certain of was, that his children were perpetually writing—and not writing letters" (Gaskell, *Life* 250). At first, she saw Patrick Brontë as a useless correspondent. She wrote to George Smith, explaining why she was requesting the publication date of *Jane Eyre* from him rather than from the patriarch, "her father both did not know of it till much later (though he does not want to have this said) and dresses up facts in such clouds of vague writing, that it is of no use to apply to him" (Gaskell, *Letters* 424). Whereas Patrick Brontë characterized his own writing as focused on fact rather than fancy, Gaskell criticizes Patrick Brontë for "dress[ing] up facts." She was equally unimpressed by his speech, despite his vocation. She criticized him for the coldness of his formal exercises, as seen in her account of his interrogation of his masked children (Gaskell, *Life* 42–3). His aversion to artful communication, according to Gaskell, stands in ironic contrast with the literary gifts of his children. Her separation of his writing life from theirs frees their stories from the father's influence.

Yet a closer look at Patrick Brontë's oeuvre complicates this vision. Brontë published his most fanciful novel, *The Maid of Killarney*, anonymously. The novel, of which extant copies have almost disappeared, flirts with the very attractions his poetry condemns. The story of Flora; her father, Captain Loughlean; and her suitor Albion resembles a Highland adventure by Sir Walter Scott. The characters' commentaries often become a self-conscious self-critique. When a didactic character describes the proper speaking style of a minister, his sister replies, "he seems to me to deal out pretty liberally those tropes and figures he so much condemns" (132). Yet, his characters find more value in certain texts than in others. As with Mary's limited reading in *The Cottage in the Wood* (she avoids novels in favor of the Bible), Flora's reading is carefully monitored. Captain Loughlean says, proudly, that his daughter "reads nothing ... but what first passes through my hands, and meets my approbation"; he allows for some novels "which are not only harmless, but very entertaining and instructive" (60–61). Loughlean prefers a seamless style, "an unbroken narrative" that allows one to "have the whole picture, at once, in view" (66). The fragment holds no attraction for him.

Patrick Brontë's preferences mirrored his Captain's. He sought a writer who could present clear moral messages in simple language, and who could achieve wholeness in representation. He left evidence that he would have written his daughter's biography himself had he not found a satisfactory alternative (Lock viii). When he wrote to Elizabeth Gaskell in September 1853, he praised her "able, moral, and interesting literary works" (Lock and Dixon 465). He appreciated her preference for tales of workers and cottagers. Gaskell's first publication, "Sketches among the Poor" (1837), which she composed with her husband, resembles *Cottage Poems*. The worldview of Patrick Brontë's *The Cottage in the Wood* mirrors that in *North and South* (1854).[4] Both writers presented patriarchs whose religious faith was tested, but not destroyed, and did so by a focus on the cottage rather than the manor. However, the motivating factor in Patrick Brontë's writing—relating the book's content, clearly and didactically, to "real life"—is not friendly to Elizabeth Gaskell's primary strategy when writing fathers. Her goal seems to be turmoil rather than reconciliation, as I will unfold in the readings that follow.

---

[4]   For example, Patrick Brontë's favorite Gaskell patriarch, Mr. Hale (from *North and South*), has a discussion about faith with an alcoholic unbeliever. In *Cottage in the Wood*, a cottager tries to convince a dissolute drunkard that the Bible is not just "idle fable" (107–8).

Elizabeth Gaskell structures her novels around conflicts with the father. It is easy to overlook this emphasis, because the heroine-centered marketing of her novels masked her original intentions. In letters, Gaskell expressed frustration about the shift by the publishers of *Mary Barton* (1848) away from the father. She wrote to Miss Lamont in January of 1849, "'John Barton' was the original name, as being the central figure to my mind." John Barton was her "hero," but "it was a London thought coming through the publisher that it must be called *Mary B*" (Gaskell, *Letters* 70). She continues, "So many people overlook John B or see him merely to misunderstand him, that if you were a stranger and had only said that one thing (that the book sh[oul]d have been called *John B*) I should have had pleasure in feeling that my own idea was recognized" (Gaskell, *Letters* 70). The common story that Gaskell wrote the novel on her husband's urging, as she mourned the death of her son, was another way to feminize both Gaskell and her novel (Cazamian 213; Krueger 169–70).[5] The absence of a pivotal father figure in *Cranford*, her domestic novel about a community of "Amazonian" women, was also determined by external forces rather than by Gaskell's choice. Gaskell wrote to John Ruskin about the early exit of the patriarch Captain Brown, "The beginning of 'Cranford' was *one* paper in 'Household Words'; and I never meant to write more, so killed Capt. Brown very much against my will" (Gaskell, *Letters* 748). As with *Mary Barton*, it was marketplace expectation, rather than her "own idea," that downplayed the father figure within her design. Publishers led readers to expect less engagement with the patriarch than appears within the books themselves.

In the father-centered pages of her books, as opposed to their child- or place-centered title pages, children negotiate the patriarch's crimes. In a startling number of cases, Gaskell's father characters are responsible for another's death, either through premeditated murder (*Mary Barton*), crimes of passion ("A Dark Night's Work" [1863], "Doom of the Griffiths" [1858], "Libbie Marsh's Three Eras" [1847–1848]), or a crippling moral harshness ("The Half-Brothers" [1859], "Lizzie Leigh"[1850]).[6] When Gaskell's fathers are not causing another's death,

---

[5]   Gaskell contributed to the conservative packaging of *Mary Barton,* which made an otherwise subversive literary debut. As she wrote to her friend Miss Lamont about the controversy it incited, "Some people here are very angry and say the book will do harm" (*Letters* 70). Gaskell considered several male pseudonyms for herself before deciding to publish *Mary Barton* anonymously (Lenard 114), and the novel's epigraph from Carlyle about the limits of authors, and her preface claiming no expertise in politics, were additional corroborating gestures (Hughes and Lund, *Victorian Publishing* 36).

[6]   "Lizzie Leigh" begins with a father's deathbed repentance for turning out his daughter three years before (Morse, "Lizzie" 39). Then, when the drunk father of Lizzie's friend contributes to the early death of Lizzie's child, the text gestures back to Lizzie's father, connecting his neglect to the second crime (Morse, "Lizzie" 40). Felicia Bonaparte's 1992 work *The Gypsy-Bachelor of Manchester: The Life of Mrs. Gaskell's Demon,* adds "Morton Hall" to this list of fiction involving children who have to atone for a father's sins (32). Sometimes, as in the bigamy tale "The Manchester Marriage" (1859), a father will take responsibility for another's death even when ignorance is his only crime. In this story, the second husband blames himself for the first husband's suicide.

they are committing other economic or social crimes, as with the transported criminals in "Sin of a Father" (1858) and "The Heart of John Middleton" (1850). "The Poor Clare" (1856) features the ominous biblical refrain "The Sins of the fathers shall be visited upon the children" (363), and the narrator of "The Heart of John Middleton" begins, "I was the son of John Middleton, who, if he were caught, would be hung at Lancaster Castle ... The son of the overlooker at the mill never ceased twitting me with my father's crime" (*Works* 1.182). In all of these texts, the plot consists, primarily, of the child's struggle to redeem the family name. The children are split between their desires for independence and their duty to family.

Felicia Bonaparte's *The Gypsy-Bachelor of Manchester: The Life of Mrs. Gaskell's Demon* (1992) divides the writer herself into two beings—a social conformist and a social rebel (127, 130). The doubleness of Gaskell, Bonaparte argues, appears everywhere in her texts, even at the level of the sentence; she notes Gaskell's emphasis on "seeming words" (168), conditionals that tame the demon of didactic certainty (144). The "id" of the artist, she claims, is a root of the fragment aesthetics that characterize Gaskell's work. Gaskell checks and polices her own authority.

Her "eccentric" fathers are similarly split in two. Gaskell's supernatural tales exploit the uncanny effects of the gothic double. She bookends 1851's "Disappearances" with two stories about missing fathers; in the second, the father is living a double life as the head of two families. Shirley Foster describes "Disappearances," a short story that Gaskell presents as nonfiction, as "typical of the liberties Gaskell takes with the (his) stories she claims to have heard" (S. Foster 119). In *Ruth* (1853), the father of the heroine's child has two names. In the first portion of the novel he goes by "Bellingham," and he becomes "Mr. Donne" after he has gained respectability. Ruth herself becomes "an icon, the subject of patriarchal misreadings" (Krueger 171).

Directly before Ruth's sexual fall, the failures of a constellation of fathers—her dead biological father, her substitute guardian, and her paternalistic lover—blend into one image of fading power.[7] As Deborah Morse describes it, the "power of the father, as embodied by Mr. Hilton, seems to be merely static image, which is strangely evoked in Ruth's memory when, in the company of Bellingham, her gentleman seducer, she sees a spiderweb across the front entrance of the house at Milham Grange" ("Stitching" 54). The front door announces encroaching solitude, overlooked well-being, and a family falling into disrepair. Gaskell encloses her heroine within domestic space, only to make that space threatening and stagnant. The failures of the father figure are invariably failures to communicate. "Old

---

[7]   Similarly, Ruth's dream about her infant son becomes a gothic nightmare of doubling: "she dreamt that the innocent babe that lay by her side in soft ruddy slumber, had started up into man's growth, and, instead of the pure and noble being whom she had prayed to present as her child to 'Our Father in heaven', he was a repetition of his father; and, like him, lured some maiden (who in her dream seemed strangely like herself, only more utterly sad and desolate even than she) into sin, and left her there to even a worse fate than that of suicide" (136–7).

Thomas," who was "like a father" (44) to Ruth after her own father's death, failed to protect her from Mr. Bellingham because he could not access the words he needed:

> He longed to give her a warning of the danger that he thought she was in, and yet he did not know how. When she came up, all he could think of to say was a text; indeed, the language of the Bible was the language in which he thought, whenever his ideas went beyond practical every-day life into expressions of emotion or feeling. (45)

The Bible verse he quotes fails Ruth because it "fell on her ear, but gave no definite idea" (45). Ruth's salvation is instead assisted by alternatives to paternalistic ways of writing and speaking. Aid first comes from Miss Benson, a young woman with a self-proclaimed "talent for fiction"(126), who tells the Bradshaws that Ruth is the widow of a "young surgeon" (126) in order to improve her reputation. Miss Benson excuses the falsehood this way:

> it is so pleasant to invent, and make the incidents dovetail together ... [a]nd, Thurstan—it may be very wrong—but I believe—I am afraid I enjoy not being fettered by truth. Don't look so grave. You know it is necessary, if ever it was, to tell falsehoods now; and don't be angry with me because I do it well. (126)

Thurstan, the dissenting minister, is able to reach Ruth because his draw is not paternal. Miss Benson, in reflecting on her brother's fanciful nature, decides that she "was a more masculine character than her brother" (170), and that he, despite the eloquence of his sermons, needed her "clear, pithy talk" to recall "his wandering thoughts" (170). Perhaps Gaskell intuited the "patriarchal" reaction to this second novel about a fallen woman redeemed, in recruiting alternative voices to support her heroine. In early February 1853 she wrote to Eliza Fox about two "very anxious father[s] of a family" who burned the first volume of her novel, and "a third" who "has forbidden his wife to read it" (Gaskell, *Letters* 223). Her "'Ruth' fever," she writes, is partly due to "how 'improper' I feel under their eyes" (223).

Mr. Bradshaw, a benefactor for Ruth until he learns of her sexual sin, is the novel's embodiment of traditional paternal authority. One can certainly imagine Mr. Bradshaw burning the novel that contains him. He claims, strictly and paradoxically, "All children were obedient, if their parents were decided and authoritative; and every one would turn out well, if properly managed" (175). His children feel the oppression, and in their faults become models of his failures (as will Meredith's Richard Feverel, to be discussed in the next chapter). "Father" cannot be everything and everywhere, and he cannot have full control over his creations. Mr. Bradshaw claims that his wife "is in the habit of repeating accurately to me what takes place in my absence" (184) and that he has "trained her in habits of accuracy very unusual in a woman" (184). Yet, Richard chafes at "the monotonous regularity of his father's household" (270), which even includes the policing of fatigue and illness (223), and Ruth says to young Mary and Elizabeth, "All that your papa wants always, is that you are quiet and out of the way" (219). Ruth's nightmare of her son's character repeating his father's bears out in Mr. Bradshaw's life rather than her own. Richard's crime of forgery (327, 329–33) becomes a grotesque expansion of his father having "more than tacitly sanctioned bribery" (253). His authority fades when it is exposed as hypocrisy. Bradshaw "always disliked going to church, partly from principle, partly because he could never find the places in the Prayer-book" (229). Yet, his self-righteous response when he discovers Ruth's sin—"he was absolutely choked by his boiling indignation" (277)—is the first strong moment of his daughter's resistance to him.

In her first full-length fiction, *Mary Barton*, her narrator describes the dual "love" and "horror" the heroine comes to feel for her father, John Barton. The conflicting emotions "seemed to separate him into two persons—one, the father who had dangled her on his knee, and loved her all her life long; the other, the assassin, the cause of all her trouble and woe" (346). Disembodied voices and disconnected body parts characterize the reader's experience of John Barton, as in the ominous scenes of his associates invading the sanctity of Mary's home:

> Strange faces of pale men, with dark glaring eyes, peered into the inner darkness, and seemed desirous to ascertain if her father was at home. Or, a hand and arm (the body hidden) was put within the door, and beckoned him away. He always went. And once or twice, when Mary was in bed, she heard men's voices below in earnest, whispered talk. (118)

Here, John Barton loses his individual outline and becomes one in a crowd of shadowy men synecdochized into faces, eyes, limbs, and voices. The dispersal of one presence into many poses a mortal threat to the girl forced to engage with them unprotected.

The father's destructiveness, and destruction, hinge upon scraps of paper. After drawing lots with Harry Carson's torn caricature of the workers, John Barton is forced to become Harry's murderer. He says, "I cannot be still at home, I must be moving" (198). But, in an episode that reinforces his doubleness, John Barton pauses during his errand. He is temporarily waylaid by one more "fatherly" act that is the polar opposite of his murderous quest. Gaskell writes of his assistance to a lost child, "With beautiful patience he gathered fragments of meaning from the half-spoken words which came mingled with sobs from the terrified little heart. So, aided by inquiries here and there from a passer-by, he led and carried the little fellow home" (198). In his kindness to the child, John Barton recalls interactions with his own "lost" son, "little Tom ... the dead and buried child of happier years" (198). In continuing his mission, he reinhabits his murderous second self. The "old" John Barton helps the child find his home, while the new John Barton declares "I cannot be still at home, I must be moving" (198). One John Barton pauses to gather "fragments of meaning" from a panicked child, while the other takes a torn piece of a son's drawing as a command to blow a hole in that son's body.

Elizabeth Gaskell approaches Patrick Brontë, and the task of writing his daughter's story, having honed her skills in writing Janus-faced, murderous fathers. She wrote to John Forster of meeting Patrick Brontë, "He was very polite and agreeable to me ... but I was sadly afraid of him in my inmost soul; for I caught a glare of his stern eyes over his spectacles at Miss Brontë once or twice which made me know my man" (Gaskell, *Letters* 245). She comes to "know" Patrick Brontë as double, as inspiring both love and fear. As with her fictions, the biography depends on the intrigue created by the difference between the father's private and public faces. His public face, Patrick Brontë feared, was dirtied by the gossip mill surrounding his newly famous daughters. Elizabeth Gaskell combined these voices with the conventions that fueled her novels. Juliet Barker writes that Gaskell "too easily identified what she perceived to be the facts of Charlotte's life with the themes of her own novels: Charlotte and her sisters thus became the dutiful, long-suffering daughters and Branwell the wastrel son of a harsh, unbending father" (Barker, *Brontës* 829). In this vision, the goal of the biography is to resist patriarchal authority. The father, as writer, becomes the father as tyrant.

The "doubleness" in Gaskell's depiction of Charlotte Brontë—as writer and as woman—has received ample critical attention.[8] In the biography, Gaskell uses a painting by Branwell Brontë to set the visual scene.[9] A pillar separates Charlotte from her sisters, and covers Branwell Brontë's initial attempt to include himself in the image. Gaskell also separates Charlotte Brontë into her professional and personal selves, moving back and forth between "the literary opinions of the author" and "the domestic interests of the woman" (354). But Gaskell's separation of Charlotte Brontë into two people creates clarity rather than confusion.

Less explored is how, from the beginning of the biography, Patrick Brontë is, both physically and intellectually, a man apart. The opening description of the home describes the "family sitting-room" on the left, and the patriarch's study on the right (39). In having personal space away from the "family sitting-room," Patrick Brontë separates himself from the most representative of domestic spaces.[10] His performance of mental tasks in isolation from the family comes in stark contrast with the writing lives of the Brontë children, who composed collaboratively. In Gaskell's subsequent sweep of the churchyard, she reminds readers that only the

---

[8]   In addition to the work by Peterson (2007, 2009) and Bonaparte, several articles have discussed Gaskell's depiction of Charlotte Brontë in the *Life*, most notably Pamela Parker's "Constructing Female Public Identity: Gaskell on Brontë" (2000), and Dierdre d'Albertis's "'Bookmaking out of the Remains of the Dead': Elizabeth Gaskell's *The Life of Charlotte Brontë*" (1995). Both articles describe a mother–daughter relationship between author and subject. Yet Lock and Dixon's biography of Patrick Brontë, Lucasta Miller's *The Brontë Myth*, Patsy Stoneman's article of the same name, and Polhemus's *Lot's Daughters* still stand alone as extended meditations on Gaskell's portrayal of the patriarch in the biography. Each work focuses on modern critics' recognition of the flaws in the biography, but not on Gaskell's technique in writing the biography and the influence Patrick Brontë might have had on her.

[9]   This 1834 painting was purchased by London's National Portrait Gallery in 1914. As the poorly mixed paint fades, Branwell's ghostly image becomes visible underneath the pillar.

[10]   For a general meditation on the study as paternal space, and on the separation of the father from the rest of the family in the design of Victorian homes, see Judith Flanders's *Inside the Victorian Home* (2004).

"childless and widowed father" (14) remains above ground. Whereas Charlotte Brontë is set apart from Emily and Branwell by the inches that divide them in the family plot, or by a small block of light on a painting, Patrick Brontë is set apart by the feet that separate the family room from his study, and by the vast expanse that separates life and death. Patrick Brontë becomes a walking contradiction, a childless father who is unnatural in outliving his wife and all of his children.

In a triumphant declaration against tidy representation, Gaskell writes, "I do not pretend to be able to harmonize points of character, and account for them, and bring them all into one consistent and intelligible whole" (43). Instead, Patrick Brontë is consistently inconsistent. Despite his request that Gaskell *counter* pamphleteers who made him into an "eccentrick" personage, the word "eccentricity" becomes a refrain. The sin of Haworth's town magistrates is that they "were most of them inclined to tolerate eccentricity" (*Life* 22); those living in more isolated homes "sufficiently indicate what strange eccentricity—what wild strength of will—nay even what unnatural power of crime was fostered by a mode of living in which a man seldom met his fellows" (*Life* 23). The progression of this latter sentence—"eccentricity" to "wild strength" to "unnatural power of crime"— makes the qualities of criminality and lawlessness seem to follow naturally from eccentricity. The equation of eccentricity with crime recurs throughout Gaskell's depiction of Patrick Brontë in the biography. Yet there is more than one use for the doubled father in Gaskell's work. We will see how the father set apart from his family can also be set apart from his crimes.

"Not Writing Letters": Fiction and Fact in *Cranford* and *The Life of Charlotte Brontë*

In the biography, Gaskell lingers on an early lesson about the relationship between life and the writing of a life. She describes M. Heger's method of "synthetical teaching," in which he read opposing accounts of a historical figure to the Brontë sisters, and "[w]here they were different, he would make them seek the origin of that difference by causing them to examine well into the character and position of each separate writer, and how they would be likely to affect his conception of truth" (173). One can imagine Gaskell asking herself how the biography would fare under Heger's exacting standards.

Cranford (1853), the novel that preceded *The Life of Charlotte Brontë*, anticipates some of the challenges she would face. The novel thematizes the difficulty of understanding people through the writing they leave behind. In *Cranford*, itself based on previously published true accounts,[11] Matty describes

---

[11] Gaskell's "The Last Generation in England," published in July 1849 as a reminiscence in *Sartain's Magazine* and not identified as Gaskell's until 1935, is later fictionalized as *Cranford* (*Works* 2.89–91). It begins, "I must however say before going on, that although I choose to disguise my own identity, and to conceal the name of the town to which I refer, every circumstance and occurrence which I shall relate is strictly and truthfully told without exaggeration" (*Works* 2.91).

an exercise that her father used to teach the divide between fact and fiction. The exercise resonates with M. Heger's instructions to the Brontë sisters. Matty was told to "keep a diary in two columns," and explains that "on one side we were to put down in the morning what we thought would be the course of events of the coming day, and at night we were to put down on the other side what really had happened" (107). The thought of separating one life into "ideal" and "real," and then documenting that separation on paper, leads Matty to remark, "it would be to some people rather a sad way of telling their lives" (107). The father's life in letters reiterates that sad distinction. As *Cranford*'s narrator helps Matty to read and then destroy her father's letters, she remarks, "I never knew what sad work the reading of old letters was before that evening" (42). The "sad work" recalls the exercise that he taught Matty—the "sad way of telling" one's life in competing columns of *is* and *could have been*. The pathos comes from the urge to turn messy lives into easily digestible textual experiences—to create an equation that adds up to something important. The difference between the internal aspiration and the external final summary throws shortcomings into strong relief.

For *Cranford*'s narrator, there is a painful connection between the words describing the life and the life itself. In burning the father's letters—"watching each blaze up, die out, and rise away, in faint, white, ghostly semblance, up the chimney" (44)—the women conjure up the ghostly body of the lost writer. The "destruction" of the letters interests Mary Smith because they were vessels "into which the honest warmth of a manly heart had been poured forth" (44). The narrator of Herman Melville's "Bartleby the Scrivener," first serialized in the same year as *Cranford*, says of the irony of fading into oblivion while working in a "dead letter" office, "Dead letters! Does it not sound like dead men?" (46).[12] *Cranford*'s engagement with letters presents the same macabre thoughts. The language chosen by Mary Smith—"honest warmth," "poured forth," "die out," and "rise away"—underscores how the person's continued presence on earth, however ghostly, depends on the fate of his written remnants. In contemplating the father's remains in this novel, Gaskell implies that if the father of children resembles the author of texts, his authority is based on quite fragile materials.

Gaskell's father-based negotiations of fact and fiction raise larger questions about reader expectations. As with Patrick Brontë, who moved self-consciously between poetry, romance, didactic fiction, and sermons, the writing of the biography led Gaskell to new thoughts about novels. In May of 1855, Gaskell, already a celebrated novelist, was looking for her next writing challenge. She wrote to F.J. Purnivall, "I doubt if I shall ever write again for publication; but nobody knows; not I, certainly, whether I shall keep to this idea, or write a Dictionary, or some other good sensible voluminous work" (Gaskell, *Letters* 341). After beginning her first foray into biography, she wrote to Harriet Anderson:

---

[12]   A similarly literal reading of the "Dead Letter" designation appears in a pivotal moment in Gaskell's "The Crooked Branch" (1859), when a father and daughter frantically interpret this message on a returned letter as a sign that the family's prodigal son has died (*Works* 4.92).

> I don't exactly know how to set about it; you see you have to be accurate and
> keep to facts; a most difficult thing for a writer of fiction. And then the style too!
> that is a bugbear. It must be grander and more correct, I'm afraid. (Uglow 397)

As she began the biography, she was thinking about being "sensible," "accurate,"
"grand," and "correct," and contrasting everything she knew and loved about fiction
with those tendencies. James Fitzjames Stephen argued, in "The Relation of Novels
to Life" (1855), that a novel, at its base, is "a biography—an account of the life, or
part of the life, of a person." The failure to craft fiction as if it were biography leads
to a "tiresome" text that is a "mere string of descriptions" (95–6). The difficulty,
however, is in the fact that the novel must be "expressly and intentionally fictitious"
(95–6). Gaskell was fully aware of the "contract" between writers and readers in
regards to the line between fact and fiction. The process of writing the biography
would clarify, and, in many ways, transform, her sense of that line.

Her characters argue that reading a father's writing is quite different from
reading that of a mother or a child. When a letter from Mary Smith's father
interrupts her story of the Amazonian Cranford women, she relates that it "was just
a man's letter" (119). "Just a man's letter," she explains, means that it was "very
dull, and gave no information beyond that he was well, that they had a good deal
of rain, that trade was very stagnant, and there were many disagreeable rumours
afloat" (119). Mary Smith is fascinated by the "honest warmth" of Matty's dead
father, as conveyed through his letters, but is bored by what her own living father
offers in his letters. Her father's letter gets in the way of the story she wants to tell.
The "dullness" of the father's fact-based approach is matched in its faults, though,
by the excessive didacticism of Miss Deborah Jenkyns's letters. A father's letter
may be very "dull" in its focus on facts, but the letters of an unattached spinster
lead Mary Smith to exclaim, "Oh dear! How I wanted facts instead of reflections,
before those letters were concluded!" (47). In comparing the letters of Matty's
father, her own father, and Deborah Jenkyns, we find that Mary craves texts that
lie between dull fact and florid, biased, didactic "reflection." She finds this balance
in the unsorted artifacts left behind from the dead rector's romantic past—from
the opportunity to reveal a side rarely seen of an extinguished life. One wonders,
however, if Mary Smith would be as enchanted by the rector's letters were he still
living—were his body there to contradict her imaginative recreation of it.

One could contrast Gaskell's disdain for the Rev. Brontë's "vague writing"
(Gaskell, *Letters* 424) with Mary Smith's enchantment with the letters she
ceremoniously burned: "They were full of eager, passionate ardour; short, homely
sentences, right fresh from the heart; (very different from the grand Latinized,
Johnsonian style of the printed sermon…)" (43). Patrick Brontë also scorned the
printed sermon. He preached without notes because, he explained, "extempore
preaching … is more likely to be of a colloquial nature, and better adapted, on the
whole, to the majority" (P. Brontë, "Funeral" 253). Yet, Gaskell's experience with
his letters was more like Mary Smith's with her own father than Mary Smith's
with Matty's father. Mary Smith's impatience with her father's letter resembles
Gaskell's disdain for Patrick Brontë's "clouds of vague writing."

In her own correspondence, Gaskell describes eagerness to read the letters of others and an urgent need to protect her letters from unintended readers. In March of 1854 she writes to her daughter Marianne, "I am always afraid of writing much to you, you are so careless about letters (Gaskell, *Letters* 274).[13] To George Smith she writes, in December 1856:

> please when I write a letter beginning with a star like this on its front [drawing of a star], you may treasure up my letters; otherwise, please burn them, & don't send them to the terrible warehouse where the 20000 letters a year are kept. It is like a nightmare to think of it. (*Letters* 426)

In this letter—often quoted by twenty-first-century critics— Gaskell struggles with competing desires to present and protect her true self. In May of 1854 she wrote to John Forster, "Don't you like reading letters? I do, so much…" (*Letters* 289). The thought about the vicarious pleasures of reading letters leads her, immediately, to anxiety about her own letters. She adds, "Please do read my letters instead of *Mary Barton* one morning at breakfast, & then return all three to me. Oh! Mr Forster if you do not burn my own letters as you read them I will never forgive you!" (*Letters* 290). Here, Gaskell equates her letters with her novel, seeing them both as pleasant breakfast table reading. However, she acknowledges a key difference between the freedom with which one can handle fiction, and the care that should be taken with letters. Her work with Brontë's biography underscored this distinction for her.

Patrick Brontë hoped that the biography would focus on Charlotte Brontë's writing rather than on her personal life, yet Linda Peterson argues that "literary professionalism is underplayed" by Gaskell, as she "suppresses or minimizes aspects of [Charlotte] Brontë's letters to George Smith, Thomas L. Newby, and even herself that dwell on professional aspects of authorship" (Peterson, *Becoming* 147). According to Peterson, despite moments in which Gaskell describes Charlotte Brontë's negotiations with publishers, as in the final chapter of volume 1 of the biography, she does much more to emphasize the tortured genius, an *artist* rather than a workmanlike professional writer.[14] Hughes and Lund similarly argue that Gaskell domesticates Charlotte Brontë's genius, just as the marketplace domesticated the authority of "Mrs. Gaskell" (*Victorian Publishing* 137). Charlotte Brontë certainly wanted to be considered as a "professional" writer. She embarked upon the *Poems* collection that preceded her novels by purchasing *The Author's Printing and Publishing Assistant* (Peterson, *Becoming* 1), and in her juvenilia she imitated the title pages, content tables, and popular typefaces of print. Yet the romantic mythology that Gaskell created persisted into the twentieth century. Virginia Woolf writes, for example, that Charlotte Brontë "owed nothing to the

---

[13]   Marianne was the only Gaskell daughter who ignored her mother's requests to burn letters (Bonaparte 4).

[14]   This is in line with Gaskell's sense of Charlotte Brontë's precedents for authorship; she saw them as "Romantic, her impulses for writing linked to inspiration, imagination, and genius" (Peterson, *Becoming* 141).

reading of many books. She never learnt the smoothness of the professional writer, or acquired his ability to stuff and sway his language as he chooses" (*Collected Essays* 1.187). Such perceptions explain why so many, Gaskell included, have trouble separating Brontë's writing life from her personal life.

Gaskell's insistence on the intimate connection between Charlotte Brontë's feelings and the content of her books is part of why she ignores Patrick Brontë's request to shield the most intimate details of her life from public view. In discussing Charlotte Brontë's novels, she assumes a one-to-one correlation with her life. This strategy indicates a sense of Charlotte Brontë as a naïve writer (a belief that she must write what she knows in order to write at all), but is also a method for bolstering Gaskell's authority beyond the materials provided by publishers and patriarchs. She hoped that by stressing the known, Charlotte Brontë's writing, she could claim access to the unknown, the private details of Charlotte Brontë's life.[15] Gaskell calls Helen Burns "as exact a transcript of Maria Brontë as Charlotte's wonderful power of reproducing character could give" (*Life* 56) and writes of *Shirley* that "the real events which suggested it took place in the immediate neighborhood" (76–7). She writes that "Shirley herself, is Charlotte's representation of Emily" (*Life* 299), and writes to Charlotte Brontë's friend Ellen Nussey, "Are not *you* Caroline Helstone?" (Gaskell, *Letters* 378).[16]

Gaskell expressed the intent to handle Charlotte Brontë's letters with care, recognizing the intrusion involved in writing a biography. She wrote, "I HATE photographs & moreover disapprove of biographies of living people" and called "writing 'notices' or 'memoirs' of living people" an "objectionable & indelicate" practice (*Letters* 760–1). She accepted the biography with the caveat that "a good deal of detail as to her home, and the circumstances, which must have had so much to do in forming her character," can "be merely indicated during the lifetime of her father, and to a certain degree in the lifetime of her husband" (*Letters* 349). The excitement of writing, though, would loosen her reservations. She told George Smith that "it would be a shame, not to express everything tha[t] can be, in her own words," but promised that letters would not "assume a prominent form in the title or printing" within her "very careful" inclusion choices (*Letters* 370, 404–5). Gaskell still encountered several problems with the inclusion of the letters. First, she experienced a temporary refusal from Charlotte Brontë's widower, Mr. Nicholls, who had legal control over the letters. Then, she had to justify her

---

[15]   Critics and biographers in the early and mid-nineteenth century shared a tendency to read literary work as an "illustration" of the author's life, especially in the case of otherwise mysterious figures such as Shakespeare. See Richard Altick, *Lives in Letters: A History of Literary Biography in England and America*, 97.

[16]   In *Fraser's Magazine*, a reviewer praised the biography on grounds that implied Gaskell was correct in connecting life and novels, and in smoothing over seeming inconsistencies: "[Brontë's] life is transcribed into her novels ... When you read her life, you read *Jane Eyre*, *Shirley*, *Villette* in fragments. The separate parts have simply to be taken out, arranged, riveted together, and you have the romance. But what in life is fragmentary and incomplete ... is by the artist's insight cast into dramatic sequence" (Shirley, "Charlotte Brontë" 570).

inclusion of intimate details by promising Smith that she would mark out sensitive parts later (*Letters* 421–2, 429).

When Gaskell turned away from the *Life*, it was with some dismay about the results of her style of truth-telling. To William Fairbairn she wrote, "for the future I intend to confine myself to lies. It is safer" (Gaskell, *Letters* 458). As Marion Shaw puts it in her post-*Life* overview of Gaskell's writing, "In the years to follow, a kind of compromise was reached in which she was to keep to fiction, but fiction spliced with historical events of sixty years or more ago" (Shaw 78). Of *Sylvia's Lovers* (1863), Shaw writes that "[t]here is a palpable feel of actuality to the story" due to her consultation of historical records (85). In other ways it is a return to form. The crisis within the novel is the arrest, trial, and execution of Sylvia's father, Daniel, an unjust fate that spins the daughter's life into a spiral of misery. Sylvia's mother falls ill and dies, and her husband, exposed in concealing Kinraid's survival in order to marry Sylvia, leaves in disgrace, leaving Sylvia to be "both feyther and mother to my child" (367). Throughout the text, Gaskell's narrator consciously records shifts in the reputation of the town, and also the patriarch's status within it. Sylvia's father, for example, was "a sort of fellow possessed by a spirit of adventure and love of change, which did him and his own family more harm than anybody else" (33). Her father is another walking contradiction, "just the kind of man that all his neighbours found fault with, and all his neighbours liked" (33).

Hughes and Lund argue that Gaskell's early narrators deferred to inherited forms—"other social problem novels" as well as "letters, court papers, newspapers" (*Victorian Publishing* 48)—while the narrator of *Sylvia's Lovers* gained "narrative strength" from "history (a Victorian perspective on the time of the French Revolution), feeling (respect for the 'strange mystery of Sylvia's heart'), and nature (especially the sea)" (*Victorian Publishing* 60). They suggest that her narrators gained authority as her works progressed because Gaskell became less self-conscious about adapting existing forms. Yet moments of reflection in the same novel seem to announce that Victorian narrative will be, to a modern eye, *less* authoritative than what preceded it. The novel's narrator reflects:

> In looking back to the last century, it appears curious to see how little our ancestors had the power of putting two things together, and perceiving either the discord or harmony thus produced. Is it because we are farther off from those times, and have, consequently, a greater range of vision? (63)

She then retreats from this supposed superiority, dripping irony into the claim that "such discrepancies ran though good men's lives in those days. It is well for us that we live at the present time, when everybody is logical and consistent" (63). In fact, she acknowledges that the past is only clear to those who fail to see the lack of clarity in their own present moment. In my reading of her final novel, I argue that Gaskell continued to respond to inherited forms, this time, her own. I read the final novel as a self-conscious reworking of her approach to fathers, authors, and authority. Work left unfinished in the biography was still on Gaskell's mind as she returned to the supposedly freer terrain of fiction.

The Father Refigured: Wives and Daughters

Gaskell's final, unfinished novel, *Wives and Daughters,* is the culmination of a career spent writing about fathers. It stands apart, though, as "the first full-length novel in which the education of daughters becomes the focus of attention" (Stoneman, "Gaskell" 143). It also stands apart as a retrospective of Gaskell's career. The novel encourages readers to follow sly references to different texts. In "The Life of Charlotte Brontë and the Death of Miss Eyre" (1995), Leah Price sees one such allusion in a brief reference to a retiring governess named "Miss Eyre." Jane Austen's *Mansfield Park* (1814) may occur to the reader when Roger says to Molly Gibson of her place in the family, "Have you noticed that she [Mrs. Hamley] sometimes calls you 'Fanny'? It was the name of a little sister of ours who died. I think she often takes you for her" (*Wives* 210). The similarity between Molly and "Fanny" extends to their books. As with Austen, Gaskell's novel centers on two brothers, who have been discouraged from falling in love with a lowly visitor. In both works, one brother makes a scandalous match. This "Fanny," this sister in situation to Molly Gibson, has died, which emblematizes Gaskell's relationship with prior texts. In her final novel, she tests whether, and how, dead things can be improved in the reincarnation. I will argue that *Jane Eyre* and *Mansfield Park* are not the only echoes detectable within the work.

Robert Gibson, as described by Elizabeth Gaskell in her final novel, bears much more than a passing resemblance to the "character" of Patrick Brontë in Gaskell's biography. Patrick Brontë has a waning relationship with his Irish heritage; one finds "no trace of his Irish origin remaining in his speech" (*Life* 33). Robert Gibson has a waning relationship with his Scottish heritage, in that his voice maintains only a "slight Scotch accent" (*Wives* 30). Patrick Brontë is a widower whose wife was named Maria; Robert Gibson is a widower whose wife was named Mary. Gaskell writes of Patrick Brontë that he had "something of an Irishman's capability of falling easily in love," and that when he fell for Maria Branwell, "*this time* [he] declared that it was for life" (*Life* 35, emphasis Gaskell's). In *Wives and Daughters,* Robert Gibson twice muses about his wife, Mary, Molly's mother, that she was not even his third love (48, 148). These circumstantial connections, while interesting, are secondary to the larger ideological connection between the two texts. When read beside *The Life of Charlotte Brontë, Wives and Daughters* becomes a correction.

A brief analysis of source material demonstrates Gaskell's evolution. First, compare how Patrick Brontë describes himself in a letter, and how Elizabeth Gaskell describes him in the biography. Edward Chitham notes in *The Brontës' Irish Background* (1986) that "Mrs Gaskell's account of Patrick Brontë's birth and ancestry was exceedingly sparse and relied entirely on what the old man wished to tell her" (64). In his June 20, 1855, letter to Gaskell, Patrick Brontë gives Gaskell her first pieces of source material:

> For the gratification of those who might be desirous of knowing anything of me—I will, in as few words as I can, gratify their curiosity. My father's name was Hugh Brontë—He was a native of the South of Ireland, and was left an

orphan at an early age—It was said he was of an Ancient Family. Whether this was, or was not so, I never gave myself the trouble to inquire, since his lot in life, as well as mine, depended, under providence, not on Family De[s]cent, but our own exertions. (P. Bronte, *Letters* 233)

Patrick Brontë's version of his life focuses on his "own exertions" to gain a quality education. The narrative that follows describes his "early fondness for books" and the gumption he showed in starting a successful school at 16, "Knowing that my Father could afford me no pecuniary aid" (P. Bronte, *Letters* 233). The sentences read like a passage out of Samuel Smiles's *Self Help* (1859), which would become a bestseller in England four years later. Granted, if Patrick Brontë cared nothing for lineage he would have omitted the "Ancient Family" possibility entirely (and would not have seen fit to change the family name from "Brunty" to "Brontë"). Yet, in the act of redirection, he attempts to derive a moral from his life story and his father's, arguing for a judgment of them based on good works rather than on "Family de[s]cent."

Gaskell makes selective and strategic use of this material. She adds "facts" that Patrick Brontë's "clouds of vague writing" seem to have left out. She borrows his phrasing (sometimes verbatim), but rejects his moral:

The Rev. Patrick Brontë is a native of the County Down in Ireland. His father, Hugh Brontë, was left an orphan at an early age. He came from the south to the north of the island, and settled in the parish of Aghaderg, near Loughbrickland. There was some family tradition that, humble as Hugh Brontë's circumstances were, he was the descendent of an ancient family. But about this neither he nor his descendants have cared to inquire. (*Life* 32)

In Patrick Brontë's account, the rumors belong to society at large ("it was said"), but in Gaskell's account, noble lineage is a "family tradition" made improbable, "humble as Hugh Brontë's circumstances were." In Patrick Brontë's account, his story is one of self-help, and he "never gave [himself] the trouble to inquire" about any other path. In Gaskell's account, Hugh Brontë and "his descendents" have not "cared to inquire," and she offers no reason why. A story of individual exertion becomes a story of collective indolence.

Gaskell does, however, go on to compliment the family on an impressive physical pedigree:

He [Hugh Brontë] made an early marriage, and reared and educated ten children on the proceeds of the few acres of land which he farmed. This large family was remarkable for great physical strength, and much personal beauty. Even in his old age, Mr Bronte is a striking-looking man, above the common height, with a nobly-shaped head, and erect carriage. In his youth, he must have been uncommonly handsome. (*Life* 32)

Elsewhere in the biography, Gaskell's focus on Patrick Brontë's physical health becomes an accusation. She claims, for example, that Patrick Brontë's rash choice to settle in Haworth led to the deteriorating health of his wife and children. "One wonders how the bleak aspect of her new home," Gaskell writes of Maria Brontë, "struck on the gentle, delicate wife, whose health even then was failing" (31). She describes his destruction of the children's rainboots, despite the dampness of the moors, because "they were too gay and luxurious for his children, and would foster a love of dress" (42). Most damningly, after describing appalling living conditions at Cowan's Bridge School, she asks why Charlotte "did not remonstrate against her father's decision to send her and Emily back to Cowan's Bridge, after Maria and Elizabeth's deaths" (57). This is a false claim, as Patrick Brontë withdrew Emily and Charlotte from the school (Gaskell, *Life* 462n5). Lucasta Miller criticizes Gaskell for using as source material "the tall tales, picked up by Lady Kay-Shuttleworth, of an ex-servant who had been dismissed from the Brontë household and whose testimony was thus extremely suspect" (L. Miller 41). Gaskell used the material she had to tell the story she wanted to tell, one that fit her preconceived notion of Patrick Brontë's wrath and Charlotte Brontë's genius. She saw her final novel, however, as an opportunity to rethink the relation between fiction and fact.

Next, let us compare Gaskell's "introduction" to the father in chapter 3 of *The Life of Charlotte Brontë* to our introduction to Mr. Gibson in chapter 3 of *Wives and Daughters*. The latter is strongly metafictional and self-conscious—revealing, and critiquing, the source material used to compile it. As she reaches the portion of her novel that mirrors the same moment in her biography, she rethinks both works:

> And "who was this Mr. Gibson?", they asked, and echo might answer the question, if she liked, for no one else did. No one ever in all his life knew anything more of his antecedents than the Hollingford people might have found out the first day they saw him: that he was tall, grave, rather handsome than otherwise; thin enough to be called "a very genteel figure," in those days, before muscular Christianity had come into vogue; speaking with a slight Scotch accent; and, as one good lady observed, "so very trite in his conversation," by which she meant sarcastic. As to his birth, parentage, and education, —the favourite conjecture of Hollingford society was, that he was the illegitimate son of a Scotch duke, by a Frenchwoman; and the grounds for the conjecture were these: —He spoke with a Scotch accent; therefore, he must be Scotch. He had a very genteel appearance, an elegant figure, and was apt—so his ill-wishers said—to give himself airs. Therefore, his father must have been some person of quality; and, that granted, nothing was easier than to run this supposition up all the notes of the scale of the peerage ... (*Wives and Daughters* 30)

Let us see what questions "echo" might answer for us. Patrick Brontë, who was of Irish birth and heritage, is described as "a striking-looking man, above the common height, with a nobly-shaped head, and erect carriage." The narrator concludes, "[i]n his youth, he must have been unusually handsome" (32). The narrator of *Wives and Daughters* describes Mr. Gibson as "tall, grave, rather handsome than otherwise, thin enough to be called 'a very genteel figure" (30), adding a joke about "muscular Christianity" that is more fitting to discussing a clergyman than a surgeon. In the two descriptions, we move from the effusive to the tentative. "Above common height" becomes "tall," "striking looking and once unusually handsome" becomes "rather handsome than otherwise." "Nobly shaped head and erect carriage" shifts to the second-hand quoted report of "a very genteel figure."

Robert Gibson's lineage is no more certain than Patrick Brontë's, but the narrator is more aware of her limitations. In contrast to the population of Haworth, the gossips of Hollingford embellish rumors about Mr. Gibson; some say that his father "must have been some person of quality," and others that the son is "the illegitimate son of a Scotch duke, by a Frenchwoman" (30). The speculation, Gaskell proclaims, is baseless: "No one ever in all his life knew anything more of his antecedents than the Hollingford people might have found out the first day they saw him" (30). As we recall, Gaskell worried, in moving from novel to biography, that her approach had to be "accurate" and her style "grander and more correct" (Uglow 397).[17] Patrick Brontë suggested that he is prone to "getting into a satirical vein" and "to dissect and analyze human character and human nature ... like a curious surgeon" (P. Brontë, *Letters* 249). In *Wives and Daughters*, "one good lady" circulates gossip about the surgeon Mr. Gibson; she says that he is "'so very trite in his conversation,'" which, the narrator explains, "meant sarcastic" (28). Gaskell uses these gossips, even the "one good lady," to show how a "grander style" does not necessarily hold "more correct" conclusions.

Readers looking to characterize her biography as novelistic can point to the elaborate panorama with which it begins, the sweep from town to churchyard to house to gravesite. Within the survey of the landscape, she plants the seeds of the family's pending doom. She writes of the "slow and sluggish stream" (11) that follows the railway, the "hard" and "discordant" voices of the inhabitants, and the "dim and lightless" air as one approaches Haworth (12). Gaskell satirizes such openings in the first lines of *Wives and Daughters*:

> To begin with the old rigmarole of childhood. In a country there was a shire, and
> in that shire there was a town, and in that town there was a house, and in that
> house there was a room, and in that room there was a bed, and in that bed there
> lay a little girl; wide awake and longing to get up. (5)

Instead of sweeping us from town to house to church to graveyard, to rest at the grave of a dead girl, she sweeps us to the bright room of a living girl. When we

---

[17]   It is certainly possible, especially given the conversations about "a man's letter" within *Cranford*, that Gaskell gendered this distinction in the way we might expect. It is a commonplace to think about masculine writing as "closed" in form and feminine writing as "open" in form, masculine writing as straightforward and feminine writing as fragmentary. In *Victorian Publishing and Mrs. Gaskell's Work*, Hughes and Lund quote Estelle Jelinek's collection *Women's Autobiography* (1980) on "feminine, as opposed to masculine, autobiographies" (108), and quotes Margaret Beetham's essay in *Investigating Victorian Journalism* (1990) on the "closed" versus "open" distinction (108). The most famous essays supporting this formal divide between men and women as writers is Helene Cixous's "The Laugh of the Medusa" (1976) and the tradition of *écriture feminine.*

peek into Molly's bedroom, we find not darkness, sickness, and gloom, but instead that "the room was full of sunny warmth and light" (5). The change foreshadows the novel's rethinking of the family fatalism, the theme of the child in peril, upon which Gaskell relied so heavily in the *Life of Charlotte Brontë*. Her use of Patrick Brontë as a model, in the story where she rethinks family fatalism and the child in peril, underscores her dedication to reinvention.

Both the *Life of Charlotte Brontë* and *Wives and Daughters* feature a young man who is called by his mother's maiden name—Branwell Brontë in the biography and Osborne Hamley in the novel. In both the biography and the novel, she uses these young men, who both meet tragic ends after ill-fated clandestine love affairs, to reconsider theories about the workings of inheritance. The novel also asks the same practical questions about single parent households that one finds in the biography. Should fathers rear daughters? To what, or to whom, should one attribute a child's failings, when the father is the primary shaper of the child's early experience? In the biography, Gaskell not only blames Patrick Brontë for the death of his wife (in the ill-advised move to unhealthy Haworth), but also blames him for the girls' isolation from consistent and positive female influences. By contrast, Mr Gibson's remarriage and strategies for incorporating Molly Gibson into society means that her community of women becomes even stronger after her mother's death (Hughes and Lund, *Victorian Publishing* 26).

In the *Life of Charlotte Brontë,* Gaskell turns to phrenology. She writes of the doomed Branwell Brontë, "the nose … is good; but there are coarse lines about the mouth, and the lips, though of handsome shape, are loose and thick, indicating self-indulgence, while the slightly retreating chin conveys an idea of weakness of will" (138). The *Life of Charlotte Brontë* also depends on a stark contrast between "Brontë" blood and that of the maternal line, laying all of the family's brutality at the father's door. While Patrick is an eccentric man within a negligent, lawless society of men, in the Branwells "the violence and irregularity of nature did not exist" (35). In contrast with the inscrutable Patrick, the Branwells are characterized by a "gentle and sincere piety" that "gave refinement and purity of character" (35). There is wholeness to the blood of the Branwells that does not exist in the blood of the Brontës—a purity of character in a literal and narrative sense—and a related inevitability in Gaskell's romantic depiction of the doomed mother and son.

In the novel, Osborne Hamley stands in Branwell Brontë's position as the eldest son who takes his mother's characteristics along with her maiden name. We are told that Osborne's "appearance had all the grace and refinement of his mother's. He was sweet-tempered and affectionate, almost as demonstrative as a girl" (40). In contrast, Roger, his father's namesake, is seemingly in consequence "clumsy and heavily built, like his father" (40). *Wives and Daughters* leaves contradictory messages about whether a child's fate is determined by qualities inherited from either parent.[18] Squire Hamley says:

---

[18]   In fact, when one looks beyond the physical inheritances, both Osborne and Roger can be seen as partly feminized. As Hughes and Lund write in *Victorian Publishing and Mrs. Gaskell's Work,* "If Osborne perpetuates his mother's aesthetic and physical delicacy, Roger perpetuates her genius for comfort and conciliation" (29).

> [H]ere am I, as good and as old a descent as any man in England, and I doubt if a stranger to look at me, would take me for a gentleman, with my red face, great hands and feet, and thick figure ... and there's Osborne, who takes after his mother, who could not tell her great-grandfather from Adam, bless her, and Osborne has a girl's delicate face, and a slight make, and hands and feet as small as a lady's ... Now Roger is like me, a Hamley of a Hamley, and no one who sees him in the street will ever think that red-brown, big-boned, clumsy chap is of gentle blood. Yet all those Cumnor people, you make such ado of in Hollingford, are mere muck of yesterday. (74)

The inheritance plot of *Wives and Daughters* is meant to be frustrating. Throughout, the gossips of Hollingford are deemed foolish for trying to distinguish between worker and gentleman through physical cues alone. The "faith in long descent" instilled in Mrs. Gibson by Osborne hides the social secret of a marriage that undercuts inheritance (240), while Roger, the overlooked son, emerges as the primary preserver of the family line. The public makes "much ado" of the wrong people based on a false sense of their bloodlines.

An opposing story of genetic probability appears at the end of *Wives and Daughters*, when the editor, Frederick Greenwood, provides a coda to the novel left unfinished by Gaskell's sudden death. Whereas Gaskell's ending rejects determinism, Gaskell's editor recovers it as he completes the narrative and eulogizes its author. He sees the "likeness in unlikeness" of the two brothers as Gaskell's greatest triumph:

> She began by having the people of her story built up the usual way, and not built up like the Frankenstein monster; and thus when Squire Hamley took a wife, it was then provided that his two boys should be as naturally one and diverse as the fruit and the bloom on the bramble. "It goes without speaking." These differences are precisely what might have been expected from the union of Squire Hamley with the town-bred, refined, delicate-minded woman whom he married; and the affection of the young men, their kind-ness (to use the word in its old and new meanings at once) is nothing but a reproduction of those impalpable threads of love which bound the equally diverse father and mother in bonds faster than the ties of blood ... (688)

This level of completeness and naturalness, the assumption that "brotherly kind-ness" is "nothing but a reproduction" of its source, is the editor's dream. It runs counter to Squire Hamley's incredulous statement about the workings of inheritance; it is a neat ending to a messy novel. Gaskell does not write in the "usual way," but instead invests much energy in the depiction of difference and divergence in families. In the early novels, Gaskell continuously understood her fathers by splitting them in two, and in the *Life* she refuses to reconcile Patrick Brontë's contradictions. The closest she gets to making him into a "coherent whole" is in showing another side of a related "character" through fiction. *Wives and Daughters* becomes a novel *about* revision, written at the end of a career characterized by pattern and reiteration. The jarring experience of "sing[ing] of real life," as Patrick Brontë phrased it in his early poem, had a measurable effect.

Collecting the Fragments

In July of 1856, Elizabeth Gaskell borrowed Charlotte Brontë's unfinished story *Emma* from Ellen Nussey. An excited Gaskell, who was researching and writing the *Life of Charlotte Brontë* at the time, wrote to a friend to describe her impressions:

> This fragment was excessively interesting: a child left at school by a rich flashy man, who pretended to be her father; the school-mistresses' deference to the rich child ... the non-payment of bills, the enquiry—no such person to be found, & just when the child implores mercy and confesses her complicity to the worldly and indignant schoolmistress the story stops—for ever. (*Letters* 409)

The outline was "excessively interesting" to Gaskell for a number of reasons— for the uncertainties of the family dynamic, for its status as a newly discovered Brontë orphan narrative, and for how the text's incompleteness encourages links to other Brontë works or to her life. Gaskell's version of Charlotte Brontë was equally disadvantaged, and Gaskell's version of Patrick Brontë was equally unknowable. She wanted to know how the fragmented story ends, and how she could use it to reflect upon its author.

There is another fragment by Charlotte Brontë that ends where "The Last Sketch" began. Charlotte Brontë's unfinished *Mr. Ashworth and His Son* shows her own deep investment in the concept of writing fiction in the form of a recovered life, foreshadowing her first major literary success, *Jane Eyre: An Autobiography*. The narrator of the fragment wants to record a father's life that has "formed the theme of many anecdotes communicated in the evening talk" (1),[19] but has not yet found the proper form. The story follows a man named Mr. Ashworth whose "public exploits were performed" in Yorkshire but whose "private history remains to this day in a great measure a mystery" (1). This young man goes bad, partly due to the failures of his "almost ... unnatural father" (2) and partly due to an attraction to society with which "crime [is] often connected" (4). And here we get our third version of the father as gunslinger. Unlike the Captain, whose gunshots were the shots of romance, or the patriarch in *The Life of Charlotte Brontë*, who shot his pistol out of preverbal rage, Charlotte's protagonist is a manic preacher who likes to "discharge fire arms at random over his own dining table" and "fling about shovels full of hot coals" during his "Yorkshire sprees" (9–10). The passage ends with a situation much like Charlotte Brontë's "Last Sketch"—a daughter brought to a London school, and a headmistress impressed enough by her bearing to overlook the uncertain identity of her father (20).

It is tempting to see continuity between this fragment about a tyrannical father and a vagrant son and Brontë's own father and brother. But, the fragment resists this interpretation—the narrator is, after all, writing a biography rather than a novel. This means a necessary decrease in seamless narrative structure: "were I

---

[19] My page references refer to an undated manuscript copy of the story available in Harvard's Houghton Library.

writing a novel I would not have it so I would—select my Sir Hargrave Pollexfen & my Sir Charles Grandison—& give inferior talent and bad luck to the former while the latter should be clad with gifts & graces utterly irresistible—However I am now speaking of real events and as a faithful chronicler I must say [the] tale as it was said to me" (4).[20] But in the end, biography is also an insufficient category. While chapter 1 ends with Ashworth's "Birth, His Bridal, and His Bankruptcy" (13), the narrator begins chapter 2 by insisting that this is not a biography after all. She writes, "Biography is not my forte and especially the biography of such a man" (13). This man makes biography difficult because of his inexplicable moral flaws. Instead, the biography of the man becomes the story of his daughter. When the narrator enters the school, she says, "We have had enough of narrative and Didactics—I must now come more closely to the point and endeavour to illustrate character by the occasional introduction of scenes and Dialogue" (21). What began as a biography of a man becomes a novel about a young woman, the pattern we saw with Brontë's biographer.

I have argued that Gaskell comes to revise the rigor with which she judged her sinning father figures, and in the process grappled with the conventions that appear and reappear in her novels. *A Dark Night's Work* (1863) depicts a disturbing relation between a beloved daughter and widowed father. The daughter takes the mother's place at the dinner table: "It was half pitiful, half amusing to see the little girl's grave, thoughtful ways and modes of speech, as if trying to act up to the dignity of her place as her father's companion" (*Works* 4.215). Mr. Wilkins "liked to feel his child dependent on him for all her pleasures. He was even a little jealous of any one who devised a treat or conferred a present, the first news of which did not come from or through him" (*Works* 4.216). He was very reluctant to allow his daughter to marry and indeed, his crime leads to a broken engagement. This daughter, like Mary Barton, must decide whether or not to reveal her father's crime of murder (S. Foster 122). The key difference between *Mary Barton* and *A Dark Night's Work* is that Mary is sheltered from the body of her father's victim, but Ellinor helps to bury it (*Works* 4.xvii). A review of *A Dark Night's Work* in *The Reader* laments:

> it is impossible not to regret the increasing tendency, which Mrs. Gaskell's later works display, to a depth of wholly unrelieved melancholy. Formerly she was content with killing off most of the collateral or subordinate characters—now, in addition to this, she makes her principal characters so miserable that it would be a charity to treat them after the same fashion ... Will she never give us another Margaret Helstone? (May 9, 1863, pp. 450–51; qtd. in *Works* 4.xxii)

Due to the heightened darkness in her story, the child's act of forgiveness becomes more pronounced and forceful. When the father says, "No, Nelly, you

---

[20] Compare to Patrick Brontë's digression about heroes and heroines in *The Maid of Killarney*. Flora and Albion have their own (albeit minor) moral flaws, to counter "our writers of novels and romances," who "either because they are unwilling or unable, seldom give us a genuine picture of real life" (91).

must never kiss me again. I am a murderer," she replies, vehemently kissing him, "But I will, my own darling papa ... I love you, and I don't care what you are, if you were twenty times a murderer, which you are not; I am sure it was only an accident" (*Works* 4.250). The scene replays *Mary Barton*, but this new daughter is sure of her father despite his crime, and refuses to stand in judgment of him: "It was not for her to undo what was done, and to reveal the error and shame of a father" (*Works* 4.258).

Mary Barton's path to forgiveness is more tortured, but even here the fear inspired by her father is largely resolved: "All along she had felt it difficult (as I may have said before) to reconcile the two ideas, of her father and a blood-shedder. But now it was impossible. He was her father! ... His crime was a thing apart, never more to be considered by her" (354). If separation, being a "man apart," begins as a source of anxiety in Gaskell's works, it ends as a vehicle to separate a father from his crimes. Gaskell's 1858 story "The Sin of a Father" nears its end with the frightened cry of the disgraced son who has just discovered his father's criminal past: "I shall lose all my practice. Men will look askance at me as I enter their doors. They will drive me into crime. I sometimes fear that crime is hereditary!" (560). Gaskell presents, and then resists, this anxiety. When she reprints the story in 1860, it is titled "Right at Last," shifting the reader's emphasis from the crime to the redemption (*Works* 3.107).[21] Deborah Morse, in her reading of both *Mary Barton* and *Ruth* as biblical parables that overturn patriarchal readings of the old stories ("Stitching" 63), says specifically of *Mary Barton* something that applies also to "Lizzie Leigh" and *A Dark Night's Work*, "The father's house must be transformed from the Old Testament place of Judgment that it has been to the New Testament place of forgiveness" ("Stitching" 48). As with John Barton, of whom we wonder "how body and soul had been kept together" (Gaskell, *Mary* 354) only to find that they are two parts of the same man, Gaskell's strategy, drawn from the strategies of the compilers and recorders that so captured her imagination, is to take her subject apart in order to reconsider the whole.

Ultimately, we find more engagement with Patrick Brontë's way of thinking and writing than even Gaskell could have expected. The version of him as the antithesis of his artistic children is too simplistic, as is the view of the nonverbal, aggressive patriarch who, according to an early reviewer, "like a mad dog ought to have been shot" (Lock and Dixon 516). There are as many versions of Patrick Brontë as there are of the anecdote about the pistol-packing papa, as critics remind us when they return to explain this strange detail from the Brontë biography. Robert Polhemus, for example, argues that Patrick Brontë was proud of Emily for learning to shoot (Polhemus 177, 192). Barker attributes his keeping a loaded pistol in the house overnight to the 1812 Luddite uprisings, and says that he discharged the bullet in the morning, "a ritual which aroused much further comment," because

---

[21]	Gaskell wanted the title "Right at Last," but Dickens thought that "The Sin of a Father" would be more attractive (Bonaparte 55). She restored her original intentions when given the opportunity.

this was the only way to disarm safely (J. Barker, *Brontës* 47, 844n62). These interpretations match Patrick Brontë's explanation in *The Maid of Killarney* for the gun echoing through the hills, but Elizabeth Gaskell and Charlotte Brontë's echoing guns must be heard, too.

This study of one writer's engagement with fatherhood—and, by extension, with competing models of authorship and textual authority—reveals much about the role of fatherhood more generally in the Victorian marketplace. First, we realize, through Gaskell's example, that the father is, as Valerie Sanders notes, a Janus-faced figure on stage, wearing the masks of comedy and tragedy. We also realize that he pulls strings backstage. The most dramatic "characters" may also be aggressive editors, or secret authors. It is tempting to join modern critics in denying Patrick Brontë's influence on Gaskell's biography, just as, in the biography, Gaskell downplays his influence on his daughter's creativity and writing life. Felicia Bonaparte argues that in writing about the Brontës, Elizabeth Gaskell is really writing about herself (Bonaparte 232). Gaskell is, certainly, aware of writing within a male tradition, writing under the thumb of Dickens as editor and model, and with her husband's firm hand on her shoulder. She is also aware, in part through Charlotte Brontë's example, of how one can absorb the conventions of literary tradition and still, simultaneously, find ways to subvert them. When Gaskell writes about fathers, she is also writing about writing, and in the process making important changes to the ultimate shape of the Victorian novel.

Elizabeth Gaskell and George Meredith were both thoughtful readers of Charlotte Brontë's writing. Both novelists respected her attempts to find a specifically female voice within a masculine literary tradition, foreshadowing the assessments of Virginia Woolf early in the twentieth century and Gilbert and Gubar near the century's end. In the August 1887 *Fortnightly Review*, George Meredith lists Charlotte Brontë's description of Vashti as one of the great passages in English literature (*Miscellaneous Prose* 159–60). In *Villette* (1853), Charlotte Brontë's narrator, Lucy Snowe, describes the actress Rachel ("Vashti") as embodying, in her demonic power and fury, "something neither of woman nor of man" (247). Brontë's mesmerized protagonist contrasts the Vashti's powerful self-fashioning with a bloated, sedentary Cleopatra, as rendered by a male artist: "Where was the artist of the Cleopatra? Let him come and sit down and study this different vision. Let him seek here the mighty brawn, the muscle, the abounding blood, the full-fed flesh he worshiped: let all materialists draw nigh and look on" (247). George Meredith's writing expands upon Brontë's rebellion from a limiting portrait of female agency and human sexuality.

George Meredith's novels—and his engagement with a different extraliterary source of paternal authority, the conduct book—take us even deeper into the father's library. Meredith, too, engages with acts of revision and reinterpretation. He finds that when a child, rather than an interested outsider, assesses the father as writer, the father's authority is even more difficult to shake.

Chapter 2
A Father's Conduct:
George Meredith and the
Book-within-a-Book

George Meredith connected his interests in gender, genre, and generations. Oscar Wilde notes all three preoccupations when his speaker reflects, in his commentary about George Meredith within "The Decay of Lying" (1898), "whatever he is, he is not a realist. Or rather I would say that he is a child of realism who is not on speaking terms with his father" (976). The father fuels Meredith's thoughts about writing because of the patriarch's connection with the author role. The rebellious children and dictatorial fathers who captured his imagination were writers, battling each other through opposing texts. His thematic questions about fathers and children always, as in Wilde's quotation, give way to formal questions about genre and authority.

Many of Meredith's novels center on texts-within-texts, often works written by, or consulted by, fathers and father figures. In *The Egoist* (1879), the "Book of Egoism" guides Sir Willoughby Patterne as he lobbies to transform Crossjay Patterne into a gentleman. The title character's father in *Harry Richmond* (1871) consults the elocution manual *The Speaker*, and the heroine's father in *The Amazing Marriage* (1895) composes *Maxims for Men*. To this list of "tutelary books" Gillian Beer adds Diaper Sandoe's volume of verses in *The Ordeal of Richard Feverel* (1859), and *The Rajah of London* and Colney Durance's serial "the Rival Tongues" from *One of Our Conquerors* (1891). Beer argues that Meredith uses the tutelary book to "intensif[y] the cerebral effect of his novels; his people live not only in a world of ideas but of books and writing" (81). Meredith was equally interested in the "tutelary book" itself, and his novels become testing grounds for patriarchal authority as performed within the literature of conduct. This chapter will begin with Meredith's first full-length novel, *The Ordeal of Richard Feverel*, which explores a son's sexual reproduction as a by-product of his father's textual production. The chapter will end with Meredith's final novel, *The Amazing Marriage*, which duplicates the aims and objectives of the first work, but with the sex/text narrative focused on daughters rather than sons.

My analysis of paternal authority will again lead us in several related directions—alternatives to such authority, the domains in which this power is best employed or most often tested, and ways in which book-based battles demand formal transformations. On this latter point, Meredith's modern critics frequently note his unorthodox style. His works negotiate several modes at once—the bildungsroman, the satire, the autobiography, the social problem novel, and the romance (Williams 190–91). Meredith connects psychic conflicts with representational difficulties, and uses psychic breakdowns as opportunities for formal ones. Not for nothing did an 1894 *Punch* cartoon show him as a human-faced bull destroying china vases labeled "grammar" and "syntax."[1] Not for nothing did Virginia Woolf write of *Feverel*, "He has been, it is plain, at great pains to destroy the conventional form of the novel ... he has destroyed all the usual staircases by which we have learnt to climb. And what is done so deliberately is done with a purpose" (*Collected Essays* 1.226). Meredith decenters his place within the literary canon, writes Ioan Williams, by "confusingly distribut[ing] various of the elements at work in life in general among characters in the action" (192). Richard Stevenson connects Meredith's penchant for metacommentary with his "stylistic incongruities" (41) and occasional "stylistic disaster[s]" (50). He writes that confusion emerges from "Meredith's wish to write a new form of novel combined with his uncertainty about exactly what that form was or how to go about achieving it" (41). Meredith's obsession with writing about fathers and children battling over books connects the power dynamics within families to those within communities of writers. The tensions between Meredith's characters embody the ambiguous relationship between writers and readers, as well as between writers, editors, and printers.

Conduct Unbecoming: Richard Feverel's Literary *Ordeal*

Before turning to George Meredith's engagement with the conduct book mode, I will describe the conventions that most captured his imagination. In the conduct book tradition, there were few contemporaries for Meredith to look to in the nineteenth century. In the few conduct books written for men by men in the nineteenth century, the status of the book, and its author, are much diminished, and the social functions performed by the conduct book are appropriated by other literary forms (Carré, Introduction 2). Holistic systems of courtesy had devolved, by the Victorian era, into mechanical rules of etiquette (8). For example, even the earliest readers of Lord Chesterfield's *Letters* excerpted and anthologized the work into a to-do list (8). The mode of authority on display within conduct literature also underwent a transformation. Writes Jacques Carré in his introduction to the book *Crisis of Courtesy*, "in the Augustan age, conduct literature was still about authority," whereas afterwards "[t]he often modest status of the writers on conduct as fathers, mothers, tutors, clergymen or simply persons of experience, offered them sufficient justification for giving advice, without recourse to social eminence" (3). Even aristocrats such as Lord Chesterfield, he writes, "nevertheless insist on their fatherly care for the welfare of their children rather than on their authority as grandees" (4). It is important, however, to note that Chesterfield appeals to traditional sources of authority where necessary. At one point he writes, "Do not think that I mean to dictate as a parent; I only mean

---

[1]   E.T. Reed, "Meredith Destroying Literary Form." *Punch* July 28, 1894. Reprinted on page 220 of Stewart Marsh Ellis, *George Meredith: His Life and Friends in Relation to His Work*.

to advise you as a friend" (Chesterfield 14). Moments later, however, he feels the need to bolster his claim on his work-in-progress: "I do not, therefore, so much as hint to you, how absolutely dependent you are upon me; that you neither have, nor can have a shilling in the world but from me; and that, as I have no womanish weakness for your person, your merit must, and will, be the only measure of my kindness" (14–15).

Although fathers were no more likely to die than mothers—to the contrary, maternal mortality rates soared due to complications with childbirth—paternal authors of conduct books often described the book as a substitute for the father's physical presence. Allusions to the father's mortality served as powerful rhetorical flourishes. As mentioned, the most famous examples of conduct books written by fathers *as* fathers belong to the eighteenth century, so eighteenth-century predecessors are particularly important to Meredith's imaginings of conduct. William Penn's widely printed *Fruits of a Father's Love* (1727) is typical of the mode in beginning, "My dear children, Not knowing how long it may please God to continue me amongst you, I am willing to embrace this opportunity of leaving you my advice and counsel" (3). His opening raises the status of his words to deathbed wisdom, and justifies the publication of the book as more than a vanity project. Lord Chesterfield's *Letters to His Son and Others* (1774), one of the most reprinted, and parodied, conduct books from the eighteenth century, circulated despite Chesterfield's lack of explicit intention to publish the work (v).[2] His letters, composed while he was away for business or leisure, or while his son was away at school, underscore the virtual, and sometimes one-sided, nature of their exchanges. He commonly offers statements such as, "Adieu! Do not write to me; for I shall be in no settled place to receive letters while I am in the country" (7). In other letters, Chesterfield reminds his son that his impressions of the boy are text-dependent and virtual. In one instance, he turns his son into a text authored by himself. After receiving a report of his son's fine new apparel, he writes:

> The natural partiality of every author for his own works makes me very glad to hear that Mr. Harte has thought this last edition of mine worth so fine a binding; and, as he has bound it in red, and gilt it upon the back, I hope he will take care that it should be *lettered* too. (25)

To find conduct literature by men and for men in the Victorian era, one must look to religious texts printed for the benefit of congregations, to political

---

[2]   Two verse parodies—*The Graces* (1774) and *The Fine Gentleman's Etiquette* (1776)—argue that Chesterfield's advice is superficial and that he fails to acknowledge wealth as his true source of authority over his son. For example, the speaker of *The Graces* promises to "teach thee, with a sire's concern, / All that is proper for a son to learn: / In pleasing segments how to pare your nails, / Segments must please, as long as taste prevails" (Gulick 11). *The Fine Gentleman's Etiquette* performs an additional attack on Chesterfield's paternal authority by advertising itself, on its title page, as having been "versified by a Lady" (Gulick 13).

speeches, and to illustrative biographies.[3] In addition, Victorian books of conduct tend to include admonitions against turning to books as models for conduct. Samuel Smiles's *Self-Help* (1859) borrows from biography to distinguish itself from its eighteenth-century predecessors. It displays the declining deference to the author on the part of the reader. Though each man is his own best model, Smiles argues, "Biographies of great, but especially of good men, are, nevertheless, most instructive and useful, as helps, guides, and incentives to others. Some of the best are almost equivalent to gospels—teaching high living, high thinking, and energetic action for their own and the world's good" (19). Within the biographical sketches, Smiles privileges industry over art, and workers over writers.

His chapter on painters and musicians, entitled "Workers in Art," follows chapters about the titans of industry, invention, science, and the professions. Scattered references to Alexander Pope, Shakespeare, and Sir Walter Scott appear throughout, but his closest approximations of Carlyle's "Hero as Man of Letters" do not appear until chapter 11. Here, Smiles discusses writers, academics, and publishers, but to highlight their efforts towards self-education rather than to celebrate the end products of their intellectual labors. For example, Smiles quotes "a well-known author and publisher, William Chambers, of Edinburgh" (357) to *discourage* reading as the primary mode of education: "I assure you that I did not read novels; my attention was devoted to physical science, and other useful matters" (358). Smiles quotes Thomas Carlyle to the same end, as Carlyle advises a young man that "It is not by books alone, nor by books chiefly, that a man becomes in all parts a man" (Smiles 329). Finally, Smiles downplays his own authority as complier and presenter of the advice. He does not appear in the first person to discuss his role as a shaper of his readers, and he figures reading itself as a poor substitute for physical exercise and effort in the world. "The multitude of books which modern readers wade through," he writes, "may produce distraction as much as culture … reading is often but a mere passive reception of other men's thoughts; there being little or no active effort of the mind in the transaction" (Smiles 328). He culminates the critique by layering the problems of printing on top of the problems of reading, writing that "the multiplication of books and newspapers by means of steam-engines and printing machines" is "not altogether an unmixed good" since they encourage readers "rather towards superficialism than depth or vigor of thinking" (Smiles 337–8). He expresses the fear that "our life, like our literature, is becoming more mechanical" (338). George Meredith's first novel, published in the same year as *Self-Help*, dramatizes the conclusions Smiles describes. Meredith's

---

[3]   In Chapter 1, and in the book's conclusion, I discuss the patriarch as relates to the conventions of biography. In chapters 3 and 4, I discuss the patriarch's "charismatic" authority, as embodied in sermons, religious treatises, and speeches. One prominent author of religious conduct literature, from earlier in the century, is John Angell James. In books such as *The Family Monitor: or, A Help to Domestic Happiness* (1828), he discusses the duties of "parents" to children, and vice versa, without drawing distinction between fathers and mothers in parenting duties. James, too, is wary about an overemphasis on reading over doing: "A very undue importance has been attached in our schools to polite literature, to the neglect of science and commercial knowledge" (*Family* 84).

patriarchs seek the confidence of the previous century's patriarchs, but within an age that is moving away from confidence in patriarchal authority.

The Ordeal of Richard Feverel (1859) centers on a conduct book written by a father, Sir Austin, to outline the system used to raise his son, Richard. Along with this document, "The Pilgrim's Scrip," Sir Austin has drafted a marriage manual and a "Manuscript 'Proposal for a New System of Education of our British Youth'" (157). Like a modern Walter Shandy, the patriarch of Sterne's mock-autobiography *Tristram Shandy* (1759–1767), Feverel attempts to write his son's life as it is lived. Walter Shandy and Sir Austin Feverel hope that writing the lives of their sons in real time will offer models for others to emulate, as well as guides to living for their sons. Problems abound, however, for the *Pilgrim's Scrip* and the *Tristapaedia*. If the son's life is meant to both model and follow the conduct book, the books become, in a way, authorless, or at least composed by competing authors (father and son). Another difficulty is temporal. Can one follow one's own guide to life while it is being written? Another problem is the unpredictable nature of reader response. What if the tomes are misread, misquoted, or revised in unauthorized ways by their subjects? Rejecting his father's *Tristapaedia* alongside Horace's recommendations for narrative epic or tragedy, Tristram declares, "in writing what I have set about, I shall confine myself neither to his [Horace's] rules, nor to any man's rules that ever lived" (8). In the battle between Sir Austin's clear, printed aphorisms and the half-illegible scrawl of his son's wild cursive writing, Meredith's novel pits the easily reproducible and transportable text against the first blushes of original expression.

Sir Austin's child-rearing manual and his son grow up together, but not without difficulty. In his early adolescence, Richard feels "insulted" by his father when he undergoes a mandatory physical examination (38). When the doctor presiding over the examination asks Sir Austin "whether it was good for such a youth to be half a girl?" he is not referring to any visible physical abnormality. Instead, he refers to the father's tendency to create a "half-man" by mixing his clichés, by describing his son as both timid, "a shamefaced girl," and spunky, "a headlong boy" (40). The *Pilgrim's Scrip*, this novel's text-within-a-text, serves as another way to expose Richard's private self and ensure his "reproductive" health. Richard's health will determine the health of the book—its ability to produce more copies, and thus to influence more young men. The book becomes a protective barrier for the developing "corpus" of the son. The System "hung loosely on his limbs at first" and Richard wore its edicts "unconscious of the tight jacket he was gathering flesh to feel" (35). As Richard ages, though, Sir Austin loses control over his System, and the boy it was meant to rear. Since Sir Austin's plan does not allow for marriage until his son's twenty-fifth (121) or thirtieth (40) year, the book and the boy break ranks when Richard reaches puberty. In the first of the novel's three editions, Sir Austin tries to marry Richard to a descendent of Sir Charles Grandison, and thus to put him into a literal relation with Samuel Richardson's paradigmatic fictive model gentleman. The reference to Richardson's *Sir Charles Grandison* in the first edition of *Feverel* is more than a consideration of a young man's journey from innocence to experience. Richardson's protagonist stood as a model of noble chastity (in contrast to a promiscuous hero such as Fielding's Tom

Jones), and the novel *Grandison* stood as a model of the moral, instructive text. Meredith evokes Richardson's eighteenth-century novel at the start of his own so that his revisions stand out starkly. The text becomes a "Shandean" rejection of Richardsonian systems.[4]

The father tries to cast the son into a time in literary history when, writes Clifford Siskin, the novel and the system were complementary genres.[5] When Sir Austin tries to write his son into the eighteenth-century didactic novel, however, Richard is drawn only to the youngest Grandison daughter, a tomboy who asks Richard to call her Carl. Richard rebels, instead living all of the clichés of texts that do not suppress the details of reproduction. He marries a buxom young maiden against his father's will (courting her in a chapter whose title, "Ferdinand and Miranda," alludes to Shakespeare's problem play), commits adultery with a kept woman, fights a duel for his wife's honor, and then becomes a "broken man." This novel debuts a writer who tackles genre conventions as he dismantles gender norms.

Meredith revised *The Ordeal of Richard Feverel* twice, in 1875 and 1896, and in each revision retreats from the first edition's pointed critique of writing itself. The first version of *The Ordeal of Richard Feverel* asks whether literature should direct a young man's education in sexual practice—whether pornography (represented by the imaginary text *The Adventures of Miss Random*) is "an Establishment, and Wild Oats an Institution" (330), or whether boys should write poetry as a "safety-valve" (123) to curb desire. As cynical Adrian Harley says (in a later deleted line), the poet "to avoid more punishable transgressions, must commit verse" (236). In his subsequent revisions of the novel, Meredith preserves hints of Richard's homosexual attractions.[6] His edits instead remove arguments against the manufactured page as a proper space to dictate matters of human development.

---

[4]   The reviewer in *The Critic* (July 2, 1859) writes, "The adventures of his [Richard's] early years are very various, and are related with something of Shandean humour, and, indeed, the whole book forcibly reminds us in various ways of Sterne's remarkable work" (Review of *The Ordeal of Richard Feverel* 6).

[5]   Quoting Anna Barbauld in 1810, "Let me make the novels of a country, and let who will make the systems," Siskin begins an article that argues that "system, like the novel, is a genre and not just an idea" and "a form of writing that was crucially important to the eighteenth and early nineteenth centuries" (202). Johnson's *Dictionary* defines system against essay, as the "'reduct[ion]' of 'many things' into a 'regular' and 'uni[ted] combination' and 'order'" (Siskin 204). Richardson's rival, Fielding, proclaims in *Tom Jones*, "I am not writing a system, but a history" (Siskin 203).

[6]   The opening sections of *Feverel* contain several not-so-subtle references to Richard's unregulated sexuality. For example, Adrian Harley mutters after the episode in which Richard and his friend Ripton burn Farmer Blaize's property, "Ripton and Richard were two pretty men"; the nursery rhyme fan familiar with "Robin and Richard" would know that the next line is "They lay in bed till the clock struck ten" (94, 502n2). When young Ripton is sent away for being a bad influence on Richard, we are told that Richard "had no special intimate of his own age to rub his excessive vitality against, and wanted none. His hands were full enough with Tom Bakewell" (105), his new male companion. The young hero's homosocial attractions are stated most clearly by his disappointed cousin in her diary—"Richard was not sorry to lose me. He only loves boys and men" (444).

Only the first edition of the novel contains the episodes in which Sir Austin tries to transform his son into the heir of *Sir Charles Grandison*. And only the first edition opens with chapters in which a female court gathers around Sir Austin to alternately praise and condemn his depiction of women in "The Pilgrim's Scrip."[7] (Perhaps Meredith realized that readers were willing to attend to the social matter of the novel or to its form, but not both at once.) The deletions reveal Meredith's awareness of these "metafictional" scenes as a special category within his novel. In his debut as a novelist, Meredith seems especially invested in deciding what novels can or should do. It has been easy to read the novel for its discussions of sexuality. Only with the new privileging of the first edition of the novel have critics started to understand the importance of *text* to Meredith's vision of this father–son struggle.

Sir Austin says of his son, the "systematized youth" (137), that a father should gain a level of knowledge of the workings of his child so that "all its movements— even the eccentric ones—are anticipated by you, and provided for" (139). His quest to turn Richard into a standard, reproducible product is so pronounced that Adrian looks at the adolescent and says, "He isn't a boy, or a man, but an Engine. And he appears to have been at high pressure since he came to Town—out all day and half the night" (284). Adrian registers the artificial origins of Richard's desires (managed by his father, and running automatically in response to his pressure), and the speed at which the mechanism set into motion by Sir Austin can run awry.

Bella Mount, the androgynous temptress who draws Richard away from Lucy with her "man-like conversation" (397), again tests reader expectations for what it means to write like "a man." The double meaning of "conversation"—discourse and sexual intercourse—becomes clear when Bella takes on a persona she names "Sir Julius" in order to capture Richard's attention. Meredith's contemporary reviewers did not know what to make of this unconventional love interest. The *Saturday Review* called her a "much naughtier woman" than Richard's wife (Review of *Ordeal* 49), and *The Critic* deemed her a "temptress and an enchantress" and chastised Meredith for the warmth of the seduction scene that "betrays a fondness for gloating over what had better be only hinted at" (Review of *Ordeal* 7). Samuel Lucas's review in *The Times* turns her presence into a *formal* problem. He writes that "the winning of the hero under such circumstances revolts our notions of consistency and drags us from the sphere of harmonious art into the chaos of caprice" (5). Lucas phrases his objection in aesthetic terms. The seduction seems wrong "in an artistic sense" (5)—it threatens harmonious narrative systems as much as harmonious moral systems. In eliding Bella's status as a masculinized woman, and focusing instead on her disruption of the fabric of a literary representation, these reviewers begin the transference of Bella Mount from social to artistic challenge. Similarly, modern critics look at Bella Mount and see not literal androgyny, but a search for a "fully integrated male personality" (Stevenson 60), or for "frank" female sexuality (M. Jones 157). Literal readings of her make

---

[7]   To see the variations between the different editions of *The Ordeal of Richard Feverel*, consult George Meredith, *Bibliography and Various Readings*, Volume 27 of the Memorial edition of Meredith's *Works*.

her into a lesbian (Horne 43), which comes from her statement to Richard, "You are as tempting as a girl" (469). In putting the divergence from the sexual norm at her door, critics ignore her role as a reflection on Richard's uncertain sexual status. These readings also fail to recognize that Richard's attraction to Bella is as radical as Bella herself.

For Meredith, linguistic distinctions between genders occasionally eclipse physical differences. In his poem "Marian"—a poem probably inspired by his first wife, the daughter of T.L. Peacock, who had "the full freedom of her father's library" (Stone 11)—the speaker characterizes his heroine as fascinatingly transgressive by noting that she "can talk the talk of men" (l.7). The poem connects this masculine speech with the ability to wield unusual power as a writer: "She can flourish staff or pen, / And deal a wound that lingers" (ll.5–6). The pen's potentially phallic power, when wielded by a woman, imparts a strange masculinity. Yet it is also possible for a man to brandish a feminized pen. Sir Austin is "just like a woman" (367) in temperament, but also profession. As mentioned, he writes conduct books at a time in which most advice manuals were written by and for woman.[8] In Victorian periodicals, more articles were dedicated to the fear of masculinized mothers than to the fear of feminized fathers (Nelson *Invisible* 16), so Meredith's focus is unique. In the opening chapters of the 1859 edition, we learn that Sir Austin "was melting to Woman. Woman appreciated his Aphorisms, and Man did not" (15). "Melting to Woman" means both that he is warming to their company, *and* that he is shifting his own shape to match theirs. In Meredith's pages, all authors are described as hermaphroditic: the Griffin crest on Sir Austin's title page leads the women to call him a "double-animal" (10), and the woman writer is described as "the half-man" (13, 154).

The new technologies of printing created a complicated relationship between an author and his work. In his study of the years 1840–1890, Allan Dooley argues that during the transition from hand-press to plates, "authorial control was entwined with the processes of printing" (Dooley 5). For example, "each impression from stereo plates might present a chance to correct textual errors," but "publishers and printers discouraged a degree of revision which might require the casting of new plates" (Dooley 5). The popularity of a printed book increased the speed and frequency of the printing, which meant that, for the most popular titles, "the actual amount of time during which an author could ask for changes might be quite brief" (Dooley 5). High-speed printing machines meant that the authors produced copy more slowly than it was being reproduced; attempts to catch up led to errors at both the composition stage and the production stage (Dooley 84). After the type was set, the manuscript was "dead copy" and often "simply discarded by printers" (18–19). Even before this moment, the printer felt at liberty to make "deliberate deviations from an author's approved text … particularly in the magazines" (54).

---

[8]   Robyn Warhol's *Gendered Interventions: Narrative Discourse in the Victorian Novel* (1989) argues that earnest and direct didactic address in novels is gendered female at this time, whereas irony and distance were reserved for male narrators.

Victorian theorists had differing opinions about "the application of machinery to the printer's art" (Knight 2.367). On the one hand, according to an 1845 assessment of English innovation, the advent of printing meant that authors no longer had to find "encouragement from the ranks of the upper-classes, who alone were regarded as the intelligent and educated orders" (2.367). Instead, the "judges and patrons of literature" become "not the few but the many" (2.367), democratizing the literary marketplace. This has its benefits and its risks. It means that readers "purchase for pence more and better literature than our grandfathers bought for shillings—better in point of authorship, of morality, of practical sense and educational value" (2.367). Yet, the name of "author" loses its potency. An author is no longer "tolerably successful" if he sells five hundred copies (2.367). Yet another downside to the democratization of the reading public was strongly on Meredith's mind—the loss of control over who consumes books, and the resulting need to avoid offending the general and/or "gentle" reader. At times, no limitation annoyed Meredith more. He wrote to Augustus Jessopp on September 20, 1864, "A man who hopes to be popular, must think from the mass, and as the heart of the mass. If he follows out vagaries of his own brain, he cannot hope for general esteem; and he does smaller work" (qtd. in G. Beer, 35).

If acts of writing can threaten stable gender identity, and acts of publishing threaten an author's control over his creations, what happens to any traditional notion of a father's authority? By imposing a system onto Richard, and elevating his manuscript into a System, Sir Austin forfeits some control over his book and his boy, just as the innovations of printing can supplant the authority of the writer in the publication process, Reprinting, on the other hand (available for books but not for boys), was seen by authors as a chance to reconsider and revise, sometimes extensively, especially when the reprinting was from serial to volume form (90, 94). Sir Austin's major tool of control, the aphorism, fails to contain his boy-engine. Sir Austin concludes, ironically in proverb form, that "a proverb is the half-way house to an Idea … and the majority rest there content" (476). In *The Egoist*, Willoughby Patterne (of the telling surname), concludes, "There are people who do *not* know themselves, and as they are the majority they manufacture the axioms" (245). In both aphorisms, the "majority" is worthy of disdain. Suspicion of mechanism ("manufacture") in Meredith's works applies to multiple forms of mass production and consumption. For example, early critics of *The Egoist*, led by Robert B. Mayo, quickly noted the similarity between Sir Willoughby's name and the popular "Willow Pattern" of china en vogue at the time of composition.[9]

---

[9] Samuel Smiles's *Self-Help*, his celebration of the lives of great men, begins with "Leaders of Industry—Inventors and Producers" (40). Its first extended portrait is of James Watt, seminal in "the invention of the working steam-engine—the king of machines" (41–2). Josiah Wedgwood, so important for porcelain manufacture, is also featured in the chapter. Smiles's placement of the inventors as the first in his line of great men runs counter to the aversion to the regular productions of machinery evidenced in Meredith's novels. Remember, for example, that his heroine in *The Egoist* rejects "Patterne" and rejects her appellation as a "dainty rogue in porcelain" (36).

Just as Richard cannot escape System entirely (he rejects his father's conduct book but still imitates inherited literary forms), Sir Austin's system imposes itself on its author. We are told early on of Sir Austin, "he had written a book; he had made himself an object" (12). The phrase means that Sir Austin has become a target for critics, but the phrase also becomes literalized. The narrator calls Sir Austin "the PILGRIM" (384), as if he has become a walking version of his book. So, what happens to a chastened authority? When Sir Austin's system fails, he retires with a blank notebook, and suddenly the Aphorist becomes impossible to read. His sister, who "pierced into the recesses of everybody's mind, and had always been in the habit of reading off her brother from infancy ... confessed she was quite at a loss to comprehend Austin's principle" (370–71).

If the father has failed as both author and text, what of his son's attempt to become an author rather than just a text? It takes time for the father to discover that his son also writes. Sir Austin is surprised to see in his son's room, "the forsaken couch, a picture of tempest: the papers, with half-written words ending in reckless tails and wild dashes, strewn everywhere about, blankly eloquent" (124). In the "blankly eloquent" poetic scribbles of his son, Sir Austin finds movements that aren't accounted for in his System. An optimistic reader may see this scene as a sign of Richard's impending liberation from the *Pilgrim's Scrip*. The question remains, though, how to reconcile Richard and Lucy's idealistic valuation of Richard's poetry with its low, amateurish quality. The young Richard ultimately cannot escape the influence of prior models. Though these poems are not copies of his father's writing, they are poor copies of Petrarchan love poetry. Although Richard's poetic effusions begin as a way to rebel against his father's structured plan for his sexual life, Adrian Harley criticizes the way Richard's clichéd poems render the object of desire as only partial: "Lips, eyes, bosom, legs—legs?" he says, "I don't think you gave her any legs. No legs and no nose. That appears to be the poetic taste of the day" (235). He adds, "I'm aware that you've had your lessons in Anatomy, but nothing will persuade you that an anatomical figure means flesh and blood. You can't realize the fact" (235). In his essay "Criticism of Female Beauty," from *Men, Women, and Books* (1847) Leigh Hunt makes a similar statement about the male poet's inability, or refusal, to depict a whole woman. Hunt assesses poetic descriptions of feet, bosoms, teeth, and waists, and wonders about the dearth of references to legs. Of the nose he writes that "[i]n itself it is rarely anything. The poets have been puzzled to know what to do with it" (153).[10] Leigh Hunt's essay and Meredith's cynical character offer humorous parallel commentaries about the illusion of realism within poetry.

Richard's attempts to write himself away from his father lead him to clichés that he inherited unconsciously but no less directly. As with biological inheritance,

---

[10]   For more on the Petrarchan blazon's tendency to leave things out, see Nancy Vickers, "Members Only: Marot's Anatomical Blazons" (1997) or her article "The Blazon of Sweet Beauty's Best': Shakespeare's Lucrece," (1985). In *S/Z*, Roland Barthes writes of the blazon, "once reassembled, in order to *utter* itself, the total body must revert to the dust of words, to the listing of details, to a monotonous inventory of parts, to crumbling: language undoes the body, returns it to the fetish" (113).

literary inheritance can be beyond the author's conscious control. Sir Austin, seeing his son's poetry as a waste of paper at best and at worse a sign of degeneracy, is pleased to know that Richard has "done what no poet had ever been known to be capable of doing," burning his own manuscript, or as the narrator puts it, "Killing one's darling child" (113).[11] The attempted destruction of Richard's poems (bastard grandchildren that Sir Austin is reluctant to own), leads directly to an enactment of what the poetry depicted. Richard's secret love affair with the rustic girl Lucy Desborough begins when he rescues one of his own poems from a volume that Lucy has dropped into the water (131). By forcing his son to adhere to a "Scrip," Sir Austin reared a son unable to develop beyond his predecessors. His father's story ends with a failed recovery—the son's "smaller work" has supplanted the father's.

"The reason why men and women are mysterious to us, and prove disappointing," we read in Sir Austin's *Pilgrim's Scrip*, "is, that we will read them from our own book: just as we are perplexed by reading ourselves from theirs" (287). The romantic, didactic, or poetical narratives of sexuality are problematic, but so is, Meredith concludes, the seductive depiction of sexuality in *The Adventures of Miss Random*. The problem with both overly didactic and overly explicit literature, Meredith argues, is that the audience automatically sorts itself along gender lines. Authors who seek to speak to all speak to some or none. Feverel Version 1.0 was banned by the largest circulating library for its "generic unorthodoxy" (Roberts 8), and the *Saturday Review* declared "It is quite right that there should be men's novels, if only it is understood at the outset that they are only meant for men … *The Ordeal of Richard Feverel* is entirely a man's book" (Review of *Ordeal* 49).

Across his career, Meredith draws distinctions between a "father's book" (didactic, focused on good conduct, meant for wide audiences) and a "man's book" (subversive, focused on pleasure, meant for select audiences). In his first novel, Meredith introduces the category of the "son's book" (subversive, focused on personal expression, meant as a direct response to the father's book). In breaking down categories for both gender and sexuality, Meredith fragments one's sense of the literature that describes or polices the body. As I will argue in the chapter's next section, Meredith's novels offer a trial run for a different kind of narration— narration that would live out Coleridge's statement in *Table Talk* that "a great mind must be androgynous" (188). Meredith agrees, arguing in his 1877 "Essay on the Idea of Comedy" that the entire category of text called "Comedy" cannot exist when men and women are not treated as equals (15, 31).

Feverel's Daughters

Meredith's heroines are usually orphans (Lucy, Diana, Aminta, the adult Carinthia) or motherless with "fathers who are either tyrannical or else ineffective

---

11   The life of the ever-secretive Meredith parallels Richard's on this point. He tended to burn manuscripts once his works went into print, and, as Gillian Beer has noticed, many of Sir Austin's aphorisms originated in a Meredith chapbook.

and unhelpful" (M. Jones 144).[12] Often the father must perform the roles of both father and mother. This is the case for Sir Austin, the man who is "like a woman" (367), but also for Sir Willoughby Patterne in *The Egoist*, who "womanized his language" (31) when necessary, and wants to raise little Crossjay in the absence of his sailor father. In *The Amazing Victorian*, Mervyn Jones explains the lack of mothers in Meredith's novels as allowing Meredith to "highlight the predicament of girls deprived of sympathy or good advice" (Jones 144).

The *Ordeal of Richard Feverel* offers daughters as a special case, though Meredith saves his extended meditation on daughters for later novels. His narrator is interested in the cutting power of careless words about gender difference, as when, in a comic scene, the drunk Ripton toasts Mrs. Berry with "La'ies and gen'l'men!," thus "splitting the solitary female who formed his audience into two sexes" (301). Words emaciate the sentimentalized woman, as when Richard watches Lucy eat "dewberries." The "[f]astidious youth, which shudders and revolts at woman plumping her exquisite proportions on bread-and-butter," says the narrator, "would (we must suppose) joyfully have her quite scraggy to have her quite poetical" (127). Finally, words can erase her body if there are literally no words for her, as Mrs. Berry remarks of one famous eighteenth-century text's inadequacies. She says of her status as an abandoned wife, "they haven't got a name for what she is in any Dixionary ... Johnson haven't got a name for me!" (272). Here, Mrs. Berry comments on the limits of text when asked to catalog or define unconventional female bodies, in her case, that of "a widow and not a widow" (272). Similarly undefinable bodies may be elderly, hermaphroditic, disabled, deformed, hypersexual, or asexual. They might be the bodies of widows, or spinsters, or women who otherwise fail to fit into standard narratives of birth, marriage, and death. What to do with a woman whose sexual or social status does not correspond with anything listed in "official" texts? The objection of the women who read the "Pilgrim's Scrip"—"You make dolls of us! puppets! Are we not something—something more?" (13)—resonates with the way that words can distort and fragment real human bodies.

One of Meredith's most popular novels, *Diana of the Crossways* (1884), offers an extended feminist meditation on the relationship between writing, parenting, and gender. The discussion emerges from Meredith's work with fathers and *sons* in his previous novels. At one point, Lady Dunstane thinks about her distant relation Mrs. Cramborne Wathin in literary terms:

> She was a lady of incisive features bound in stale parchment. Complexion she had none, but she had spotlessness of skin, and sons and daughters just resembling her, like cheaper editions of a precious quarto of a perished type. You discerned the imitation of the type, you acknowledged the inferior compositor. (151)

---

[12] Meredith's motherless heroines include Emilia, the Fleming sisters, Renée and Cecilia in *Beauchamp's Career*, Princess Ottilia in *Harry Richmond*, and Clara and Laetitia Dale from *The Egoist* (Jones, *Amazing* 144).

The Darwinian pun ("type") again links biological inheritance to literary production. The inferior parent is like the inferior author, who, in setting the type poorly, guarantees inferior offspring.

The heroine of *Diana of the Crossways*, an aspiring writer who proofreads her manuscript as she faces charges of adultery, finds that different strategies for telling her life story mean the difference between social slavery and social freedom.[13] When *Feverel's* Bella Mount, says, "Wasn't it a shame to make a woman of me when I was born to be a man?" (398), she refers to the sexual assertiveness denied to her gender, but also to her inability to "make" herself against the will of an unnamed creator. *Diana of the Crossways* similarly bemoans the heroine's "misfortune of … not having been born a man" (186). Diana, however, is more aware than Bella Mount of the role that writing plays in her inability to "make" herself. She writes, "We women are the verbs passive of the alliance … We are to run on lines, like the steam-trains, or we come to no station, dash to fragments. I have the misfortune to know I was born an active" (75–6). Here, Diana describes the struggle of the woman using the terms of the woman writer. Her misfortune of being an active verb trapped in a passive construction—in other words, her status within a written text—parallels her laments about her gender status as a man's soul in a woman's body. If she refuses to "run on lines," to follow the conventions of the literature into which she was born, then she is destined to "dash to fragments."

Diana sees her father's library as a sacred space, but still tries to escape his influence through her own writing. She competes against the reputation of her father, the "legendary improvising songster … the convivial essayist, the humorous Dean, the traveled cynic" (191). With every encounter with the daughter, the public hopes to answer the question, "Is genius hereditary?" (192). Diana is burdened by the lack of attention paid to her as subject rather than object. When she goes to see a publisher to sell her suitor's secret to the newspapers, "Men passed her, hither and yonder" and "[s]he lost, very strangely to her, the sense of her sex and became an object—a disregarded object" (374). Meredith connected her situation as an author stifled by the example of a literal father with his own status as an author grappling with inherited literary conventions. To channel her, he had to become her. In a letter to D.H. Anders on November 9, 1907, he wrote, "In *Diana of the Crossways* my critics own that a breathing woman is produced, and I felt she was in me as I wrote." He added that he "treated [his] books of prose as the mother bird her fledglings" (*Letters* 3.1577–8). He found a space for connecting his writing life with Diana's by embracing a brand of literary androgyny.

Meredith begins his engagement with realist fiction with a novel about a spectacularly failed heterosexual union, poorly plotted by a father's conduct book and the conventions of multiple outdated literary genres. In his last complete prose

---

[13]   Diana's life is based on that of Caroline Norton (1808–1877),whose famous and public disagreement with her abusive husband led to reforms of Victorian marriage and custody laws. Importantly, Norton was also known as a writer (supporting herself through fiction when her husband could not or would not) and an advocate for a woman's freedom in life and the writing life.

work, *The Amazing Marriage* (1895), the union is similarly ill fated, but the heroine gains strength through her capacity to translate paternal advice to her own situation. In this final novel, the conduct book was discovered *by* the child and was not written *for* her. Carinthia, deemed another one of Meredith's "triumphant androgynes, a wonderful girl with a man's heart" by a contemporary reviewer (Wells 842),[14] crosses gender lines in consulting her dead father's *Maxims for Men*. Meredith's narration attempts the same feat, as the text alternates between the voices of a restrained male narrator and a chatty woman nicknamed "Dame Gossip."

The novel begins, as with *The Ordeal of Richard Feverel*, with a father who has written a conduct book. The battling male and female narrators have different degrees of receptiveness to this text-within-a-text; the philosopher speaks of Dame Gossip's "detestation of imagerial epigrams" (319). Of the "Maxims for Men," Dame Gossip writes, "I shudder at them as if they were muzzles of firearms pointed at me" (6). Though they were "not addressed to [her] sex," the aphorisms do give her "an interest in the writer," who she imagines must be "a truly terrible man" (6–7). To some extent Dame Gossip is absolving herself of blame for her inability to decipher the patriarch's aphorisms. After quoting one of the Old Buccaneer's statements verbatim ("Old Buccaneer" is the patriarch's nickname), she writes, "I give it to you as it stands here printed. I do not profess to understand" (9). Similarly, of men's erroneous "readings" of women, based on facts they often gain from untrustworthy sources, Dame Gossip laments, "The truth is, they have taken a stain from the life they lead, and are troubled puddles, incapable of clear reflection" (71). The men and women of *The Amazing Marriage* have difficulty reading each other, as when, one thinks, upon hearing of Countess Fleetwood's disappearance, that women "were an illegible manuscript, and ladies a closed book of the binding" (249).

Into this clouded atmosphere enter various texts by fathers and mothers, left to be deciphered by later generations of daughters and sons. It is notable, when thinking about *The Ordeal of Richard Feverel* and the battle between the easily reproducible conduct book and the only manuscript copy of the son's scribbled poetry, that the preference for the rare and original found in many of Meredith's novels extends to the work that steers *The Amazing Marriage*, the Old Buccaneer's book of aphorisms. Dame Gossip relates that the limited edition *Maxims for Men* "fetches a rare price now wherever a copy is put up for auction" (6). Perhaps its rarity combines with its status as *found* object, rather than imposed one, to make it more attractive (at least initially) than the average "tutelary book" in Meredith's oeuvre.

Carinthia and her brother Chillon are embodiments of their father's greatest sayings, as when Chillon says "a better lantern we left behind us at the smithy," and Carinthia immediately exclaims, "Father!" because the final word in the phrase "was one of the names he has used to give to her own home" (55). Brother and sister become interchangeable in their dogged willingness to honor their

---

[14]   Robert M. Philmus attributes the review "The Method of Mr. George Meredith" to H.G. Wells in his article "H.G. Wells as Literary Critic for the *Saturday Review*" (1977).

father's literary remains, but the novel expresses ambivalence when the sister ventures too far into the father's library. Such ambivalence appears in an early conversation during a brother-sister excursion to "call the morning," one of their father's traditions. Carinthia jumps out of a window (one of "many other practical things" taught by her father), and then "quoted her father: '*Mean it when you're doing it.*'" Chillon immediately completes the quotation, "'*For no enemy's shot is equal to a weak heart in the act*'" and then "lay[s] his hand on her shoulder for a sign of approval" (36). The daughter and son reinforce the father's prominence by mechanically following his instructions and reconstructing his sayings.

Some maxims are described as universally applicable, "as sharply bracing for women as for men" (310). However, others remind us that Carinthia is reading a book not meant for her. When Carinthia says, "Father says, '*The Habit of the defensive paralyzes will,*'" Chillon corrects her, "'*Womanizes,*' he says, Carin. You quote him falsely, to shield the sex" (379). Still other maxims go, says Carinthia, against her training as a woman. When Carinthia and Fleetwood discuss her father's advice about not forgiving an injury, Carinthia must admit: "Women do, and are disgraced, they are thought slavish. My brother is much stronger than I am. He is my father alive in that" (437–8).

Despite its superiority to the "Pilgrim's Scrip" (in that this text is *chosen by* rather than *imposed on* the child), the Old Buccaneer's text, as with Sir Austin's, loses authority when it comes to sex. In chapter 32, titled "In which we see Carinthia Put into Practice one of her father's lessons," Carinthia saves a child from a wild dog while Fleetwood watches helplessly. She explains afterwards: "Father told me women have a better chance than men with a biting dog. He put me before him and drilled me. He thought of everything" (337). Yet, Chillon's new wife, Henrietta, exclaims: "Oh! she is wild! She knows absolutely nothing of the world. She can do everything we can't—or don't dare to try. Men would like her" (115). The Old Buccaneer's drills left out "the world" of men, leaving his daughter at risk in that world. The critique levied against this father's text of education recalls Wollstonecraft's criticism of conduct books such as Gregory's *A Father's Legacy to his Daughters* or Fordyce's *Sermons for Young Women*. Wollstonecraft laments that they create woman who know the arts of pleasing men, but who lack the wisdom to become their equals.[15] Eventually, Fleetwood himself proves that Carinthia's education by her author-father is incomplete. Fleetwood's betrayal and abandonment of Carinthia reminds us that her father had not "thought of everything."

The Amazing Marriage ends with Meredith's Philosopher narrator, who claims to be writing "fact," expressing a lament similar to Elizabeth Gaskell's refusal to turn Patrick Bronte into a "consistent and intelligible whole" in her biography *The Life of Charlotte Brontë* (43):

> So much I can say: the facts related, with some regretted omissions, by which my story has so skeleton a look, are those that led to this lamentable

---

[15] Jenny Davidson's *Hypocrisy and the Politics of Politeness: Manners and Morals from Locke to Austen* (2004) studies Wollstonecraft's argument in light of her conflict with male authors in her views on education, sexuality, and dissimulation.

conclusion ... Character must ever be a mystery, only to be explained in some degree by conduct; and that is very dependent upon accident: and unless we have a perpetual whipping of the tender part of the reader's mind, interest in invisible persons must needs flag. For it is an infant we address, and the story-teller whose art excites an infant to serious attention succeeds best. (*Amazing* 510–11)

In classifying the average reader as an "infant," Meredith's narrator turns himself into a father, his book into an educational text, and his reader into a malleable child. Yet the lesson imparted by the educational text is one of skeletal incompleteness. For the narrator, character is not easily or consistently revealed in the record of "conduct," nor can it be found in the details of an incomplete life. As with the infant reader described at the end of the novel, Carinthia in *The Amazing Marriage* is a blank page waiting to be imprinted, as Lord Fleetwood realizes when he looks back on their wedding day: "here, on the box of this coach, the bride just bursting her sheath sat, and was like warm wax to take impressions. She was like hard stone to retain them, pretty evidently" (389). Several printing processes in the nineteenth century involved molds, so the description of Carinthia mirrors what Meredith would have experienced as an author and reader for Chapman and Hall. Stereotyping, involving a mold from plaster (and, later, paper [Dooley 64–8]) "fixed a text for future impressions" but preserved errors (56). Electrotyping, which used a "large sheet of wax, molded into a shallow tray and coated with graphite" (68), was far less popular when printing text but was more often "used for illustrations" (69).

Carinthia, warm wax, retains all impressions of her father's words and advice, as well as all negative impressions of Fleetwood's treatment of her. It turns out that Carinthia's imprinting with her father's words (even though they were words addressed to men) becomes crucial to understanding her as a character. Fleetwood runs through a litany of literary possibilities as he attempts to define his new wife: "beautiful Gorgon, haggard Venus ... doughtiest of Amazons. A mate for the caress, an electrical heroine ... —a demoiselle Moll Flanders,—the world's Whitechapel Countess out for an airing, madly ludicrous; the schemer to catch his word, the petticoated Shylock to bind him to the letter of it" (274). Yet he returns twice to a simpler formulation, that Carinthia "is the daughter of the rascal Old Buccaneer" (225, 364).

Despite Meredith's celebrated feminism, his final novel is conservative about the relation between conduct books and female education.[16] This is not to say that

---

[16]   See Elizabeth Grosz in *Volatile Bodies* (1994), speaking in general terms about the metaphors used to discuss women in/as text: "in feminist terms at least, it is problematic to see the body as a blank, passive page, a neutral 'medium' or signifier for the inscription of a text. If the writing or inscription metaphor is to be of any use to feminism—and I believe that it can be extremely useful—the specific modes of materiality of the 'page'/body must be taken into account: one and the same message, inscribed on a male or female body, does not always or even usually mean the same thing or result in the same text" (156). Meredith's final woman-as-text falls short; Carinthia becomes legible only in the context of the "man's book."

the philosophies underlying conduct books are necessarily conservative. Vivien Jones, in her writing about Mary Wollstonecraft's feminist renovations of conduct literature in the eighteenth century, denies an inevitable connection between conduct literature and conservative impulses (V. Jones, "Mary" 120). Wollstonecraft and others, Jones argues, used the conduct book form to advocate for a woman's freedom rather than her restriction (V. Jones, "Mary" 121, 138; "Seductions" 125). In addition, conduct books become even more open to "play" when the unpredictable nature of reader response becomes a factor (V. Jones, "Seductions" 112). Conduct books, like novels, have their own "seduction plot[s]," laying out for young female readers the multiple alternatives to a virtuous life path. In being asked to avoid these alternatives, they are invited to imagine them (117).

In Meredith's reimagining of the literature of conduct, however, he seems to believe that patriarchal texts have more to say to sons than to daughters, even as he increasingly allows for an androgynous or even feminized narrator and narrative. Carinthia's mother was an author, writing "a "little volume of *Meditations in Prospect for Approaching Motherhood*," but it is an out-of-print pamphlet that Dame Gossip has "never been able to procure" (29). Carinthia does not have access to, and has not inherited, any texts directed specifically to women, and when she reads "men's books," she does so to aid men. She becomes the walking representative of her father's "scrip," the child Sir Austin failed to create. Carinthia, whom Gower Woodseer calls a "perpetual student," eventually begins to imitate Gower Woodseer's father in the absence of her own: "She made use of some of his father's words, and had assimilated them mentally besides appropriating them: the verbalizing of 'purpose,' then peculiar to his father, for example … Gower was touched to the quick through the use of the word" (257). As she prepares for her brother's departure to Spain, she "pleased her brother by talking like a girl" (498) meaning that she was helpful in a gentle and feminine way, organizing the domestic details but not pressing to join him. She is not trying to become another Diana. Carinthia reads what is considered to be masculine literature,[17] but for her brother's edification. She "had learned to read medical prescriptions for the composition of drugs. She was at her Spanish still, not behind him in the ordinary dialogue, and able to correct him on points of Spanish history relating to fortresses, especially the Basque. A French bookseller had supplied her with the Vicomte d'Eschargue's recently published volume of a *Travels in Catalonia*. Chillon saw paragraphs marked, pages dog-eared, for reference" (498–9).

The English contingent leaving for Spain at the end of the novel is described as "sample print of a book's first page, blank sheets for the rest of the volume" (502). This description foreshadows Carinthia's inability to leave her domestic role as caretaker of her brother's wife. Unlike the travelers, Carinthia is a thing already printed, full of multiple sources, dog-eared for reference, none as lasting as her father's words. Meredith's final heroine becomes little more than her father's creation and her brother's most important reference work.

---

[17]   See E. Lynn Linton, "Candour in English Fiction," in which she charges culture with gendering literary modes along the same lines followed by Carinthia, including the gendering of nonfiction as masculine and fiction as feminine.

Fleetwood, Carinthia's ne'er-do-well suitor, is a better audience for the *Maxims for Men*. In Fleetwood's final attempt to win Carinthia, he calls for a copy of her father's Book of Maxims (495). He is finally touched by the book by proxy, as Carinthia becomes a walking representative of it for him:

> he mourned her day and night, knowing her spotless, however wild a follower of her father's MAXIMS FOR MEN. He believed—some have said his belief was not in error—that the woman to aid and make him man and be the star in human form to him, was miraculously revealed on the day of his walk through the foreign pine forest. (508)

The conduct book does not save Carinthia from abandonment, although it does give her limited assistance in raising her own son without his father. She weans her son on schedule "because her father had said: 'Not a quarter of a month more than nine for the milk of the mother'" (300). She does so despite her real fear that Fleetwood will claim her son, because "the dead father wanting to build a great race of men and women ruled" (300). One wonders, however, what Carinthia would have done differently, if she had been holding her mother's lost volume of *Meditations*, instead.

As I close a pair of chapters dedicated to contesting the father's traditional authority, and turn to tests of his charismatic authority, I pause to discuss the implications of Meredith's trajectory for relating literary and extraliterary displays of paternal authority. George Meredith's uneasy relationship with his own time has likely affected recent critical assessments of his work. Though his canonical status exceeded George Eliot's in the 1940s, and although there was a mini-explosion of Meredith scholarship in the 1970s,[18] most recent work on George Meredith has been limited to his sonnet sequence *Modern Love* (1862) and his psychological novel *The Egoist* (1879). However, with the rise of interest in the history of the book, gender and sexuality studies, and Victorian publishing, Meredith's novels are becoming the subject of renewed attention. His novels can technically be classified as "realist" in that he eschews overly determined plotting. However, Wilde's description of Meredith as a discontented son of realism registers the idealist strain that runs through his writing, a crusading spirit that cannot write without simultaneously reconsidering the act of writing.

George Meredith, who spent seven years as a single father after his first wife eloped with the artist Henry Wallis, was reluctant to be a father figure to the next generation of writers. In an April 1906 letter, Meredith expressed regret for some past specimens of "didactive verse," writing that "the muse shuns the pedagogue" (*Selected Letters* 187). More and more often as he aged, he marked letters to young authors as "Private" so that they would not appear in print as universally applicable advice (189). His anxiety about being imitated and duplicated, or his books seen as instruction manuals, relates to the contrast in his novels between

---

[18]   Prominent works include the 1971 collection *Meredith Now*, edited by Ian Fletcher, and book-length studies by Judith Wilt (1975) and Gillian Beer (1970).

personal and impersonal approaches to writing. His frustration with his own literary forebears prevented him from voluntarily standing in that symbolic role for future authors. Looking back to *Feverel* in a letter to Edmund Gosse, about a year and a half after reading a manuscript of his autobiography *Father and Son*,[19] he writes in November of 1889:

> My first novel dealt with your question. It was, I heard, denounced over the country by clergymen, at book-club, and it fell dead. They have since had their drenching of the abominable—as all do, who stand against the plea for the painting of what is natural to us. It may be shown recurring through literary history. (*Letters* 110)

Meredith reframes the trajectory of writers in terms of parents and children. He is deeply aware of the cycles of imitation, rejection, and Darwinian descent with modification that link texts across generations.

Meredith's *The Egoist* (1879) compares father/son dynamics with the workings of the individual psyche: "The two rub together in sympathy ... the younger has offered a dainty morsel to the elder, or the elder to the younger. Absorbed in their great example of devotion, they do not think of you. They are beautiful" (324). The sinister dynamic refers to the novel's potential son-in-law, Willoughby Patterne, who courts the father to win the daughter against her will. It also has broader philosophical implications. Later in the passage, the incestuous soul of the Egoist is made both universal and deeply personal: "The Egoist is our fountain-head, primeval man: the primitive is born again, the elemental reconstituted ... He is not only his own father, he is ours: and he is also our son. We have produced him, he us" (324). Meredith was writing *The Egoist* while revising *Feverel* for the 1870s edition (Beer 29), and that first father–son pairing was fresh in his mind as he wrote these lines. The two texts circle back on each other, in an act of revision reminiscent of Gaskell's work across biography and novel. Just as Gaskell's engagement with biography led her to reconsider the form and function of her novels, Meredith's insertion of conduct literature within his first and final novel allows him to end where he started. The sentiment behind the passage from *The Egoist*, related to the inescapable structure of father and son, reminds us why the child cannot completely free himself from the father's mold. Richard thinks he is writing his way out of a preset pattern, but is instead just writing his way into a different system. Carinthia thinks that she is learning independence through her devoted absorption of her father's words, but is instead writing her way into her *brother's* system.

A possibility of reversal, of the child becoming the father of the man, appears in the subplot of Woodseer, who collects aphorisms for his father rather than the other way around. Fleetwood notices that Woodseer writes beside one of his own

---

[19]   See Meredith's note to Gosse in *Selected Letters*, February 15, 1888, in reference to what would become *Father and Son*: "I return the enclosed, with my thanks to you for the privilege of reading it" (111n2). I expand upon this connection in the book's conclusion, in which I discuss *Father and Son* at length.

sayings in his notebook, "*A text for Dada.*" (78). Of his relationship with his father, a former shoe mender turned Dissenting preacher, Woodseer says, "When I strike a truism, I've a habit of scoring it to give him a peg or tuning fork for one of his discourses ... He and I are hunters of Wisdom on different tracks; and he, as he says, 'waits for me'" (78). Finally, though Carinthia is in everything her father's daughter, there are hints that *some* sons of daughters can be authors of themselves. Fleetwood looks into the eyes of his son with Carinthia and sees "a thing made already, and active on his own account" (386).

As evidence of Meredith's deep interest in patriarchal texts, but his deep ambivalence about "fathering" them himself, one need only to look to the first reviews of his first novel, *The Ordeal of Richard Feverel*. For example, consider this assessment from the *Saturday Review* of Meredith's "thesis" that "nature will best a system" (49):

> The doctrine is unquestionably true, but we confess it seems also to us to be a truism. We do not see that this moral has any bearing on human life which it can have been worth so much trouble and thought to illustrate. For, if we accept the tale literally, we know at once that the whole thing is entirely imaginary. No real fathers try to bring up their sons on a rigid system that aims at producing virtue by wholly excluding temptation. If there are any who make this attempt, they must be very few, and far too exceptional for the teaching of the book to have any general value. And if we set down the extremity to which the system of the elder Feverel is carried as an artistic exaggeration designed merely to produce a strong impression, and suppose that the meaning of the author is merely that systems of education should not be too rigid, this novel fails to throw any light on the question what is meant by a system being too rigid. What ought a father to do?—that is the problem. (49)[20]

Astonishingly, Meredith's novel fails to move this reader because he hoped to find a guide for conduct within it. The reviewer comes to a novel that critiques didactic books looking for "teaching" and "general value." The reviewer comes to a novel that reveals conduct book systems as fiction, by asking for a clear connection between novels and "real fathers." The novel's flaw, it seems, is that it presents a problem that seems detached from the struggles of real fathers in the real world, and then declines to offer a solution. This reader misses Meredith's insistence, in line with the Victorian turn away from conduct books by and for men, that reading cannot always provide a sufficient guide to "real life." Meredith's engagement

---

[20] A review in the *Critic* echoes the assessment in the *Saturday Review*, in again looking for a "lesson" and "purpose":

> It is impossible to deny that this work has a great deal of vigour about it; but whether that vigour be applied to a proper purpose is another question ... Mr. Meredith is a man who has evidently thought much and deeply; but there are many passages in his book which lead us to believe that his mind is none of the purest. To some extent, therefore, he disproves his own lesson, that much knowledge of the world is good for the purity of the soul. (7)

with *literary* fatherhood turns all visions of fatherhood into fictions, which may be why an aphorism extracted from Meredith's novel leads Joyce's Stephen Dedalus to declare "Fatherhood, in the sense of conscious begetting, is unknown to man" (207). Meredith incorporates conduct books—texts that (as with Patrick Brontë's didactic poems) purport to "sing of real life." If conduct books begin to resemble novels, or vice versa, readers may wonder what power exists within either form to offer a lasting shape to a life. The conflation of conduct book and novel calls into question the stability of any sort of "authoritative" narrative voice. As Virginia Woolf suggested, Meredith has "destroyed all the usual staircases by which we have learnt to climb. And what is done so deliberately is done with a purpose" (*Collected Essays* 1.226). Meredith's purpose lies in that very act of thwarting the search for order and system.[21] The claustrophobia described in Meredith's novels transforms the father's library into a set of closed, noncirculating stacks. The only way out is to create open, incomplete narrative systems that declare their own insufficiency. The only way out of a machine is to take it apart.

---

[21] See Vanessa Ryan's chapter on Meredith's *One of Our Conquerors* in *Thinking without Thinking in the Victorian Novel* (2012), as well as Allon White's discussion of Meredith in *The Uses of Obscurity* (1981), for an analysis of the high expectations for readers inherent in what Ryan describes as Meredith's "effortful style" (126).

PART II
Charismatic Authority

"the power of addressing mankind in the name of religion …"

PART II

Chapter 3
"An Attitude of Decent Reverence": Thackeray and the Father at Prayer

Early in William Makepeace Thackeray's novel *The History of Pendennis* (1848–1850), the young Pen, who would grow up to narrate Thackeray's late novels, toddles tipsily into a half-empty theater. He finds Bingley, the manager and actor,

> reading out of the stage-book—that wonderful stage-book—which is not bound like any other book in the world, but is rouged and tawdry like the hero or heroine who holds it; and who holds it as people never do hold books: and points with his finger to a passage, and wags his head ominously at the audience, and then lifts up eyes and finger to the ceiling, professing to derive some intense consolation from the work between which and heaven there is a strong affinity. (40)

This is a farcical image of the didact. Bingley holds a false book—a stage prop—falsely, "as people never do hold books," yet the book is "held up" as if it is sanctioned by "heaven." Bingley "wags his head ominously" as if the words he draws from the book will offer an important warning to the audience he has, up to that point, failed to attract. When Bingley sees the young Pen and his young friend, he renews his attempt to gain influence over their hearts and their pocketbooks. The narrator writes: "As soon as the Stranger saw the young men, he acted at them; eyeing them solemnly over his gilt volume. He was determined to fascinate them, for he knew they had paid their money; and he saw their families coming in from the country and filling the cane chairs in his boxes" (40). In the figures of the boys, Bingley sees the figures of their families. He hopes that gaining their business will turn theatergoing into a family affair. Bingley becomes one of many mock-patriarchal figures in Thackeray's novels—men without a biological claim on a young man, who nevertheless perform as they would "*if* [they] had a son" (Thackeray, *Barry* 154; see also *Vanity Fair* 428).

In the first two chapters of this book, I discussed Weber's category of traditional authority, as paired with J.S. Mill's category of "eminent wisdom and virtue, real or supposed" (Mill, *Spirit* 27). I discussed Elizabeth Gaskell and George Meredith's father-authors as drawing authority from their libraries, both in looking to eighteenth-century model lives and creating new works that they hoped would become models for their children's lives. Gaskell and Meredith, in assessing the real and fictional fathers they encountered, assessed biography and conduct books as potential sources for a father's didactic power. In both cases, authority was located outside of the father's body, in tradition and history. Mill, for example, locates "eminent wisdom and virtue" within "ancestors: their old laws, their old maxims, the opinions of their ancient statesmen" (29). Now I turn to charismatic authority, a form that depends much more on the father's body, even as the father continues to depend on books. In Part II, the father is the "character" and the child is the writer who must interpret him.

This chapter, the first of two that discuss a father's charismatic authority as defined by Weber alongside "the power of addressing mankind in the name of religion," in J.S. Mill's formulation, triangulates "fathers" (religious and secular), actors, and books. I discuss Thackeray's recurring descriptions of the father preaching, and the father at prayer, showing how they intersect with both theatricality and sentimentality. I connect "gilt volumes" such as Bingley's with the volumes of the Peerage, the Bibles, and the Prayer Books that compete for space in the reading rooms occupied by Thackeray's patriarchs. In littering his novels with Prayer Books, Bibles, and religious tracts—the *things* "between which and heaven there is," supposedly, "a strong affinity"—Thackeray tests a trove of extraliterary sources of authority.

Max Weber defines charisma as a quality "not accessible to the ordinary person," but rather "regarded as of divine origin or as exemplary" (1.241). It seems to transcend, or even reject, the other two forms: "charismatic authority is sharply opposed to rational, and particularly bureaucratic, authority, and to traditional authority, whether in its patriarchal, patrimonial, or estate variants, all of which are everyday forms of domination ... charismatic authority repudiates the past, and is in this sense a specifically revolutionary force" (1.244). Though charismatic authority seems to break with the past, it transforms when inevitable questions of "succession" arise. Weber argues that, in order to transcend the limitations of an individual body and life, charismatic authority must give way to either traditional or legal-rational justifications (1.248). This "revolutionary force" is tamed into "hereditary charisma" or "the charisma of office" (1.248).

J.S. Mill's related category is "the power of addressing mankind in the name of religion," and Mill is as practical as Weber in discussing the limitations of this power across generations. Mill distinguishes between Catholic and Protestant traditions, attributing more agency to the priest in the former case and to the institution in the latter case (36). All denominations depend on the personal attractions of their leaders, he argues, but High Church Anglicanism and Catholic churches heighten that dependence.[1] In Dissenting or Protestant denominations, what Weber calls

---

[1]   See Lori M. Miller's "The (Re)Gendering of High Anglicanism" (2000) for an extended argument about the performance of masculinity across the Low Church/High Church spectrum. Miller argues that "Anglo-Catholic masculinity was not altogether different from muscular Christianity, or indeed from Evangelical masculinity," as in both cases the "enactments of masculinity were dependent on the audiences they were addressing" (28). Miller's assessment contrasts John Reed's *Glorious Battle* (1996) and James Eli Adams' *Dandies and Desert Saints* (1995) on the spectrum of hypermasculine or effeminate presentations of Anglo-Catholicism by critics (28). She says that "the notion of spiritual 'fatherhood' was welcomed by Roman Catholicism and High Anglican leaders such as E.B. Pusey," but "would have been viewed with suspicion by both Low and Broad Churchmen" (31).

"the charisma of office" has already taken hold, in that worshippers can bypass the man holding the book and consult the book directly. Thackeray and George Eliot tackle this conundrum, Thackeray in the context of religion, and Eliot, as I will discuss in Chapter 4, in the context of politics and education. Thackeray's fathers consult religious books in hopes of learning how to be charismatic. Eliot's fathers try to turn themselves and their children into ideal texts, depending on the power of curses, oaths, sermons, and speeches.

Despite his own transition to unbelief, J.S. Mill saw the prophet's brand of power from a utilitarian standpoint. In the essay "Utility of Religion," Mill warns readers not to underestimate "any doctrine received with tolerable unanimity as true, and impressed on the mind from the earliest childhood as duty" (Mill, *Nature* 78). "Authority," he writes, "is the evidence on which the mass of mankind believe everything which they are said to know, except facts of which their own senses have taken cognizance" (78). As with poetry, which serves a similar purpose as religion and can even replace it, religion has political but also aesthetic power. Mill writes, "Belief in a God or Gods, and in a life after death, becomes the canvas which every mind, according to its capacity, covers with such ideal pictures as it can either invent or copy" (104). This shift—from believing in a created God to creating belief in others through "ideal pictures"—will be especially important in George Eliot's examination of a father's moral influence. The fathers I consider here and in the next chapter are speakers rather than writers. Eliot's male author-characters (Casaubon, Theophrastus) are bachelors or childless. By contrast, "old-fashioned" fathers such as Mr. Tulliver struggle to make the transition from orality to literacy. Similarly, the men in Thackeray's novels that hope to hold influence do so by consulting books rather than writing them.

This chapter puts Thackeray's novels into conversation with manuals from the 1830s through the 1850s, marketed to father figures charged with engaging mixed households during daily family prayer. I will also discuss intersections between religious and sentimental writing within the Victorian literary marketplace. The theatrical impulses found in both prayer manuals and sentimental texts, I will argue, reappear in Thackeray's scenes of fathers presenting themselves as religious or sentimental authorities. Thackeray employs a particular paternal narrator, Pendennis, to embody his evolving ideas about the author as preacher.

"We Must Really Feel Interested Ourselves": The Policing of Affect

Mary Wilson Carpenter documents the rise of the "serialized 'Family Bible with Notes,'" during the Victorian period, calling its advent "the first large-scale inauguration of Consumer Christianity" (Carpenter 5). The family Bible became symbolic as "both advertisement and cultural icon for what the British family wanted to be" (5). In Anglican traditions, the Book of Common Prayer accompanies the Bible as a guide to worship. In the nineteenth century, both texts were offered in new forms that sought a specific segment of the audience—the Christian family. The Bible and Prayer book were part of the hour of family prayer, an hour that gave "the family's daily time ... order and value" (65). The serialized Bible yoked the experience of reading the Bible together, over time, to the market for fiction (66). Other options joined the Bible and Prayer book for domestic readers who wanted to supplement a family's religious experience. These documents included published sermons, religious books and periodicals aimed at children, and religious advice manuals.

The divide between religious and secular ways of narrating lives was further narrowed by the experience of reading serial fiction. As Linda K. Hughes and Michael Lund note in *The Victorian Serial:*

> many still considered an underlying pattern in life of the Christian's journey from this world to the next, powerfully represented in *Pilgrim's Progress,* a work read by more people in England than any book except the Bible, and in the calendar for the church year, which retraced Christ's life from Advent to Pentecost. (5)

Similarly, serialization of secular texts, they argue, seemed to overlap with expectations for domesticity as "a continuing sequence of nonreversible stages, whether applied to courtship leading to marriage, marriage itself, or child-rearing" (Hughes and Lund, *Victorian Serial* 17). In the reading of fiction, the long period of serialization "created a 'family' of author, characters, and readers" (43), in which readers had to hope that their expectations for the upholding of social mores would not be overthrown by an unpredictable turn of events in the final number (43, 45). Readers would entertain threats to the comforts of pattern during the early numbers, but a writer risked censure and outrage if he or she did not offer resolution. The cleverest Victorian authors inscribed the tension between invention and reader expectation into the fabric of their texts.

The manuals I discuss in this chapter are prominent representatives of a mode that has been overlooked by critics. WorldCat, a database covering most of the academic libraries in the United States and United Kingdom, but excluding private collections, lists, between 1830 and 1860, over 450 works with the words "family" and "prayer" in the titles, 40 of which include the word "daily." Another 17 of these titles include the word "guide" and 38 call themselves a "manual." Most of the titles are published by and for specific religious denominations that draw from the Book of Common Prayer; the books seem to have circulated most widely in America, though the most prominent titles were printed in multiple editions in both Britain and America.

Such guides to family religion offer texts for patriarchs to use during domestic services, but also suggestions about how to make those services effective and affecting. Three of the texts I will discuss are offered by prominent Anglican ministers: *Essay on Family Prayer* (1847) by Suffolk and Dorset vicar Charles Bridges (1794–1869); *Daily Family Prayer for Churchmen* (1852) by William Walsham How (1823–1897);[2] and *The Householder's Manual of Family Prayer*

---

2   How is now famous for publicly burning a copy of Thomas Hardy's *Jude the Obscure* (1895) to protest its moral stances.

(1853) by William Thornton, Vicar of Dodford. Another, *The Fire-Side; or, The Duties and Enjoyments of Family Religion* (1836) was written by the prolific American writer and minister Jacob Abbott (1803–1879), and published widely in the United States and the United Kingdom. I therefore sample texts written by a variety of writers with varied affiliations; they have in common advice to the average householder, that warns him about the relation between the stimulation of the senses and the salvation of souls. The manuals introduced the importance of theatricality in the successful spread of family religion. What is presented earnestly in these volumes will be investigated by Thackeray in a different light.

Many of these manuals are now hard to find, but reviews of the books are plentiful, indicating market saturation and critical interest. Reviews discuss the hybrid status of the texts, as mixtures of old and new material. Guides to family prayer repackage material from the Bible and Book of Common Prayer, but also include original prayers and generalized advice for the users of the books. A review of William Walsham How's *Daily Family Prayer for Churchmen* in *The English Review* (1852) stated, "We are glad to see these prayers are not *wholly* compiled ... from the Book of Common Prayer, because family worship may need some additional matter" ("Daily Family Prayer" 456). The review posits that How has achieved the correct balance between old and new, adding "that those [prayers] of his own composition are about the best" in this "very good and useful book" (456). A review of *Form of Family Prayer for Sunday and Daily Use*, from the September 1839 *Christian Remembrancer*, offers an additional rationale behind the volumes. In calling *Form of Family Prayer* "a very valuable compilation," the reviewer opines, "Those who are not always at church on the Sunday, but who state that they always 'read *good books* on that day,' would do well to possess themselves of this really *good* book" ("Form of Family Prayer" 535). In the best circumstances, daily family prayer supplemented community religious gatherings. Practically speaking, family prayer, and family prayer books, might do work that would otherwise be neglected.

Commercial collections of family prayers included instructions meant to help the patriarch who was suffering from stage fright. William Thornton's *Householder's Manual of Family Prayer* (1853) suggests that heads of families recite aloud from the manual in the privacy of their own chambers, for two or three Sundays in a row, before doing so before a domestic audience. Thornton writes, "With most persons, it requires some courage, to begin doing any unaccustomed thing before many witnesses" (5). The Rev. Charles Bridges argues, in his *Essay on Family Prayer* (1847), that "Secret prayer is the best preparation for family prayer. Without this preparation, all will be routine, formality, deadness, death" (29). Freedom of form is a particular concern in these manuals because they are designed to be read aloud, but with energy and vigor. The householder must find a way to read from the book as if he were not merely reciting. "In the use of a form, no less than in extemporaneous supplication," writes Bridges, "it will be evident, whether his own affections are quickened in spiritual liveliness ... any lack of liveliness—how speedily, as in the congregation, does it communicate deadness and formality! Is it not offering the blind and the lame for sacrifice? Is it not evil?" (28). The domestic audience waits for proof that the householder is both skilled and sincere. If he lacks the ability to hold his family's attention, the audience may turn its attention elsewhere. "After all," writes Jacob Abbott in *The Fire-Side; or, the Duties and Enjoyments of Family Religion* (1836), "we must remember that we must feel really interested ourselves, and really make an effort to interest our children, or we cannot expect to succeed" (12). This advice echoes what appears in prominent Victorian acting manuals. G.H. Lewes's essay "On Natural Acting," reprinted in *On Actors and the Art of Acting* (1875), connects the work of actors with the work of writers. He argues: "we call the actor tame if he cannot present the character so as to interest us. The most general error of authors, and of actors, is turgidity rather than flatness ... Exaggeration is a fault because it is an untruth; but in art it is as easy to be untrue by falling below as by rising above naturalness" (113). Lewes, as with the authors of the prayer manuals, has no trouble discussing "naturalness" as an acquired skill, or with connecting good *acting* with "truth."[3]

The authors of the prayer manuals hoped that the works themselves, when designed thoughtfully, would make it even easier for the patriarch to succeed. How's *Daily Family Prayer for Churchmen* (1852) offers its prayers in small segments, for ease of reference and with attention to the audience's limited attention span. "Besides the *authority* which these prayers possess," How writes,

> two important advantages appear to arise from the disjointed form in which they are composed. First, the attention is better kept alive, or recalled, if wandering, by the assent required to be given in the "Amen," at the end of each Prayer. And secondly, the different acts of worship (such as Confession, Intercession, Thanksgiving,) are better marked, and therefore more intelligible, when separated by a definite break, than they can be when the whole service consists, (as is the case in most Books of Family Prayer,) of one long undivided Prayer. (v)

The pitch for this book of Family Prayer, as opposed to others, stakes a claim to both traditional and charismatic authority. Traditional authority is made available through the prayers themselves, and charismatic authority through the clever design of the book. As Weber claimed, charismatic authority is revolutionary, but unstable, on its own, and generally gives way to one of the other two forms. The patriarch who uses this work, How argues, will benefit from the hints it offers about maintaining the audience's interest, and that benefit is transferrable from one patriarch to another, as long as the book can be read and reread.

---

[3]   See Lynn Voskuil's *Acting Naturally: Victorian Theatricality and Authenticity* (2004) for an extended argument about comfort with this paradox among Victorians, their "sophisticated capacity to suspend their disbelief, to act authentically and be theatrical at the same time" (3). Lewes's *On Actors and the Art of Acting* plays an important role in her account. Her third chapter, "Daniel Deronda and the Theatricality of Nationhood" (95–139), argues for George Eliot's interest in the political stakes of theatricality in that late novel, which relates to the claims I make in the next chapter, about *Felix Holt*.

Pleasure and instruction only emerge from these prayer books if the person reading aloud from them has some innate or learned talent to offer. Prefaces of these volumes tend to argue for a mixture of extemporaneous and structured prayer. Fathers must practice privately, convey and therefore cultivate enthusiasm, and selectively draw from and diverge from the provided form. This paradox parallel's Thackeray's arguments about writers, whom he thought of as secular preachers, and his thoughts about novels of sentiment.

In the 1840s and 1850s, Thackeray was part of a backlash against "Condition of England" novels that sought, he believed, to do overly specific social work. In his review of Disraeli's *Sybil,* published in the *Morning Chronicle* on May 13, 1845, he argues that "morals and manners" are "the novelist's best themes," as opposed to those which aspire to "algebra, religion, political economy, or other abstract science" (qtd. in Keen 152). His inclusion of "morals and manners" but exclusion of "religion" underscores his aversion to the letter as opposed to the spirit. In *The Yellowplush Papers* (1838), Thackeray parodies John Henry Skelton's *My Book, or the Anatomy of Conduct* (1837) on similar lines, related to the distinction between ideals and specific road maps for individual behavior. In *Victorian Will,* John Reed writes that Thackeray's "narrative manipulations constantly elude the certainty of philosophical assertion" (277). Reed turns to *The Newcomes'* many allusions to fairy tale as key to how Thackeray cultivates "an ironic flavor" as regards heroism, both in terms of his story and the fables on which he draws (200).

Thackeray's understanding that good parenting was traditionally coupled with the rhetoric of religion, and the practice of religion in the home, is presented in his letters to his mother. He writes, for example:

> In the summer P.G. I shall send over the little ones to see their Granny, if she has room for them. They both yearn after you … But I know it is best they should remain with their father. God mend his sins, and make him do his duty. Last Sunday was March 14—my dear little Jane died on that day—Anny & I went to Church in the morning: and I'm thinking of having a home-church every morning. All this writing is very virtuous isn't it? O God purify us and make clean our hearts. (*Letters* 2.286)

If only the modern critic could regard Thackeray's face as he composed these lines. Is he smiling at the ease with which his disingenuous words placate his evangelical mother? Is he moved by thoughts of the death of his daughter and sincere about the new incorporation of daily family prayers into his life? There is no way to know for sure. What we do uncover in passages like this one is Thackeray's knowledge of what "virtuous" writing looks like, and the powerful emotional effect it can have when it is performed well. In another letter to his mother later in the year, he swings from Shakespeare to the psalms to daily family prayer over the course of four sentences. He admits to the "blasphemy" of feeling bored while watching *King Lear* with his daughters, and offers the analogous experience of reading "the savage curses and cut-throat imprecations in the Psalms … [which] come alongside of passages of the utmost beauty & piety" (*Letters* 2.292). Thoughts of King Lear "cursing his children" and the "savage curses" of the Psalms take him directly to the question of this chapter, "The prayer-saying of a morning is a very good thing though I trust. &c &c Amen that it may prove so—" (2.292).

   Despite having once said of Charles Dickens, "He knows that my books are a protest against his—that if one set are true, the other must be false" ("Reminiscences" 572), one aspect of Dickens' writing gained more than his grudging admiration. Upon reading the installment of *Dombey and Son* in which little Paul dies, Thackeray carried the number to the *Punch* office, banged it on the table, and shouted, "There's no writing against such power as this; one has no chance!" (572). Thackeray's response to what he deemed as Dickens' "unsurpassed" and "stupendous" (572) death scene was less about the effect of the scene on him as a reader than about the effect he imagined the scene to have on other readers—the very readers that Dickens may draw away from Thackeray's own novels. How, he wonders, can he "writ[e] against such power?" And what are the implications for a writer's sense of himself when his power relates to making others cry?

   Dickens and Thackeray both used their novels to reconceive manliness; in Thackeray's *History of Pendennis* (1848–1850) and Dickens' *David Copperfield* (1849–1850), this reconception focuses on the male author (Dowling 80). Andrew Dowling claims that Thackeray "defines the male novelist against immaturity and effeminacy," whereas "Dickens defines this figure against cruelty and ignoble ambition" (80). In other words, Thackeray wanted the male novelist to be steady, and Dickens wanted him to strive for softness. In both cases, the novelists respond to the "man of feeling" who dominated sentimental writing of the eighteenth century, and to a contemporary context in which "weeping openly and emotionally" was reserved for "girls and women" (Warhol, *Having* 29). Thus, the spectrum that defines the male against weeping is complicated by the addition of authorship as that man's profession. Men do not cry, but what about the male novelist? G.H. Lewes writes of this distinction in his 1852 essay "The Lady Novelists," published in the *Westminster Review.* First, he presents the expected generalization: "in most men the intellect does not move in such inseparable alliance with the emotions as in most women ... the intellect is more commonly dominant" (48). When he turns to "poets, artists, and men of letters *par excellence*" (48), however, he sees "this feminine trait, that their intellect habitually moves in alliance with their emotions" (48). Thus, a man is masculine, a woman is feminine, and a male writer lies in between. Postmodern theorists in the field of sexuality studies have taken Lewes's lead, adding "effeminacy" as a new "performative" category that figures "the body not as the location where gender and affect are expressed, but rather as the medium through which they come into being" (Warhol, *Having* 10). The sentimental novelist, intuiting the relationship between physical performance and feeling, "us[es] technologies of affect to get the body of the reader into the pose that would generate real compassion or real joy, the pose of weeping" (20). The sentimental novelist and the *religious* "man of feeling" both take on potentially "effeminate" stances. As Mary Lenard notes in *Preaching Pity* (1999), in regard to Elizabeth Gaskell's use of religious rhetoric, the "use of biblical authority is a key part of sentimentalist discourse, which influences the reader not only through pathos but through the whole 'feminine' system of moral and religious values that the pathos epitomizes" (119).

An essay from the *Theatrical Journal* (June 1851), titled "The Morality of the Church and the Drama," defends secular drama from the condemnation of the church by claiming that drama and the church can offer parallel types of moral instruction. Within the argument, its writer refuses to let Shakespeare's moral authority fall victim to the dictates of the church. The writer uses Thackeray's philosophy to bolster his claim:

> Thackeray, in his lecture on Addison and Congreve, said "the wits and humouri[sts] are our week-day preachers," and there are finer sermons in the works of great poets and thinkers than we could find in all the writings of the bench of bishops. But the Church, jealous of its authority, has disparaged the philosophy of lay authors, and there is a feeling of animosity between the drama and the pulpit, which does not seem likely to abate. We doubt not, however, that they will be reconciled—all things will be reconciled in the progress of the world, and men will see the reason eventually for the antagonism between these elements, of which the one is the corrective of the other. (206)

The editorial writer opines, as Mill does in "The Utility of Religion," that the reconciliation will occur when the secular preachers realize that their writing can have as much power as the "bench of bishops." Thackeray is particularly interested in how the spaces of the drama and the pulpit already have innate similarities. He is particularly interested in how "wits and humourists" could offer real moral edification along with their imperatives to entertain.

Thackeray's rare bouts of public weeping, as documented in letters and by his biographers, evidenced his soft spot for children. Joseph Foster claimed, in his 1888 retrospective, "Thackeray loved children with all his great heart. He loved their laugh; he loved their play, and for a very simple reason: like a real man of genius he was a child at heart to the last day" (144). Thackeray wrote to his mother in 1844, "I never could bear to think of children parted from their parents somehow without a tendency to blubbering; and am as weak to this day upon the point, as I used to be at school" (*Some* 28). Importantly, though, he reassures her that his blubbering is a temporary condition: "it's only the abstract pathos of the thing that moves me" (28). When he was in Ireland researching the *Irish Sketchbook* (1843), he experienced "such a turn of the stomach as never was" when a child's cry of "Papa, Papa" recalled his distant daughters (Taylor 185). He also cried when visiting his elderly cousin's nursing school, when he regarded "its fresh-faced children singing hymns" (188).

Thackeray's feelings of displacement come in part from the eighteenth-century models that were such an important part of his literary imagination. As with George Meredith's writing against Richardson and with Sterne, Thackeray's explicit literary allusions and responses drew from the previous century.[4] The

---

[4]   Thackeray's Colonel Newcome enjoys reading *The Spectator*, *Don Quixote*, and *Sir Charles Grandison* because he "liked to be in the company of gentlemen," but "in secret" he reads the racier texts *Tom Jones and Joseph Andrews* (41).

"Age of Sentiment" set the philosophical terms for the discussions of sentiment in his novels. Eighteenth-century texts of sentiment were paternalistic and imperial in aims and approach—in how they, writes Lynn Festa, "polic[e] the division of the self from the world" (3). The sentimental text wore a veneer of realism, but omitted details "deemed unfit for the sentimental education of the reader" (Ahern 30). The texts encouraged the formation of kinship groups, offering a "consoling illusion of a community based on resemblance" (Burnham 68). No wonder, then, that the novels "enjoyed their greatest popularity in the eighteenth century during periods of crisis in national coherence" (68).

George Meredith introduces Thackeray's lecture series, *The Four Georges* (1855), by painting Thackeray as a child of the eighteenth century. "To judge by quotations and allusions," Meredith writes, "his favourite of the classics was Horace, the chosen of the eighteenth century, and generally the voice of its philosophy in a prosperous country" (*Miscellaneous* 65). *Henry Esmond,* despite its troubling of "old-fashioned" morality in its sexual politics, entered the marketplace in full eighteenth-century garb. Charlotte Brontë commented to George Smith in November 1852 that the first edition looked "very antique and distinguished in his Queen Anne's garb," and "the periwig, sword, lace, and ruffles are very well represented by the old *Spectator* type" (qtd. in Hack 14–15). Thackeray appropriates visual cues from *The Spectator* alongside its approach to didactic utterance. Addison and Steele wrote to entertain, primarily through satirizing the manners and tastes of the day, but also to instruct. Elwin Whitewell's assessment of Thackeray in *The Quarterly Review* (September 1855) argued that he "disclaims the assumption of the preacher's office" but still "enforces maxims as serious and as important, as any that are contained in the didactic parts of the *Spectator*, and much more impressive and profound" (352). Walter Bagehot wrote in an 1862 review of *Philip*, "His books are not sermons with narrative between them. Mr. Thackeray's favourite art is a sort of annotated picture" (885). To understand the narrative stance in Thackeray's novels, then, one must look for an approach to moralizing that improves upon the work of the minister, by offering both image and commentary, verse and exegesis.

Fred Kaplan's *Sacred Tears: Sentimentality in Victorian Literature* (1987) dedicates two chapters to Thackeray and sentiment. He tracks Thackeray's extensive knowledge of eighteenth century philosophies of sentiment, and concludes that "despite his 'irony,' his 'realism,' and his alleged 'cynicism,' Thackeray was as much a sentimentalist in his view of human nature and its moral instincts as was Dickens" (8). Kaplan also untangles the relationship between Victorian sentimentality and Victorian religious feeling. He argues that Victorian sentimentality was "anti-sectarian" and "anti-Puritanical," but "not anti-Christian"; it battled "Protestant fundamentalism" and "the gloomy strait-jacket of religious literalism," promoting among dissenters "religion as an experience of the feelings rather than of the intellect" (36). In his readings of Thackeray, Kaplan decides that Thackeray's sentimentality is, indeed, if not "anti-Christian" (36), at least "persistently anti-theological" (81). Kaplan rejects spiritualized readings of

Thackeray's death scenes ("usually in Thackeray's fiction death provides only an ironic coda … it facilitates plots, not themes" [81]), and claims that Thackeray wanted his books to *replace* religious texts, not draw from them (95, 96, 101). This is where my reading of the religious content in *The Newcomes* diverges from Kaplan. I argue that Thackeray did want his readers to feel, not just to think about feeling, in an attempt to appropriate Dickensian "power" ("Reminiscences" 572) over the reader. Thackeray's books may not *be* sermons, but they perform sermons in an attempt to have a similar effect. The performance is all that is required for the full employment of charismatic authority.

In an 1848 letter to W.S. Williams, Charlotte Brontë argued that Thackeray "is never borne away by his own ardour—he has it under control" (Tilloston and Hawess 51). George Meredith described the "attitude in his great novels" as "that of the composedly urbane lecturer" (*Miscellaneous* 66). Rather than engage in hero-worship, the level-headed Thackeray found "here and there a plain good soul to whom he was affectionate in the unhysterical way of an English father patting a son on the head" (*Miscellaneous* 66). These readers find Thackeray unruffled by the storms of satire in his books. Even his most Swiftian satires seem to have a low emotional temperature, to modern critics as well as to Victorian ones.[5] Anthony Trollope, who regarded Thackeray's bust with every visit to his writing desk (Taylor 2), wanted his biography to soften the image of Thackeray as cynic. Trollope writes of Thackeray:

> If he wrote as a cynic—a point which I will not discuss here—it may be fair that he who is to be known as a writer should be so called. But, as a man, I protest that it would be hard to find an individual farther removed from the character. (59–60)

Trollope was anxious for his readers to distinguish between the coolness of Thackeray's narrators and the warmth of the author, especially given what he knew about Thackeray's aversion to evangelicalism, and the possible blots on his character that may emerge as a result from religious readers.[6] Thackeray's "character," and characters, linked writing to the performance of emotions that

---

[5]   Due in part to a modern critical focus on *Vanity Fair* (1848) and neglect of later novels narrated by Pendennis, his narrators are most often figured as dispassionate observers or wily jokesters. U.C. Knoepflmacher wrote in *Laughter and Despair* (1971), "Unlike the Brontës, Meredith, George Eliot, or Dickens, Thackeray refuses to impose a moral order on the erratic universe he portrays" (83). In *Gendered Interventions* (1988), Robyn Warhol contrasts Thackeray's cynical narrators with Gaskell's earnest ones. Judith L Fisher offers two studies—"Ethical Narrative in Dickens and Thackeray" (1997) and *Thackeray's Skeptical Narrative and the 'Perilous Trade' of Authorship* (2002)—to detach Thackeray from Dickensian sentimentality.

[6]   Trollope, writing of the large number of clergymen in Thackeray's family, asserted that "such was not at any period of his life the bias of our novelist's mind" (3). Thackeray's "disagreement" with his evangelical mother caused, opines Trollope, "possibly unhappiness at intervals, but never, I think, quarrelling" (4). Thackeray was especially uncomfortable with his mother's belief in hell as everlasting (Taylor 228).

might, as with the most skilled performance on stage, lead to a genuine response from readers. In a review entitled "W.M. Thackeray, Artist and Moralist," (1856), William Caldwell Roscoe calls him, "[n]ot a skeptic in religious conviction, or one who ignores devotional feeling—far from it; but a skeptic of principles, of human will, of the power in man to ascertain his duties or direct his aims. He believes in God *out of the world*" (194). According to Roscoe, then, who may have the same motivations in his defense as Trollope, Thackeray does not deny the power of "devotional feeling," but doubts that the vehicles of such feeling have been effective in changing behavior. His novels depend, more than has been noted by most critics, on biblical stories that may hold that kind of power.[7] "Devotional feeling" is key to how he theorizes—and hopes to reinforce—paternal authority.

The Newly Respectable Family

Until *The Newcomes*, Thackeray's readers were not inclined to shed tears over his fathers or children. The portrait of the father in *The Newcomes* differs from the satires that made Thackeray famous.[8] This is in part because Arthur Pendennis, a proud father, takes over as narrator of his final novels.[9] Previous narrators are unapologetically childless. In the *Punch* series *Sketches and Travels in London* (1847–1850) the narrator is an uncle with nothing but dubious advice for his "dear nephew" Bob Brown. The Chesterfieldian narrator's supposed words of wisdom—on everything from bathing to courtship to fashion—seem especially misplaced because of his weaker familial relationship with Bob. The orphaned Redmond Barry tells his own story in *The Luck of Barry Lyndon: A Romance of the Last Century* (1844). Redmond is left to make a new name for himself through trickery and his wits. Redmond, whose only son died shortly after his birth, writes retrospectively, "I, who have seen more of life than most men, if I had a son, would go on my knees and beg him to avoid women" (154). The narrator of *Vanity Fair* is similarly playful, writing, "My son, I would say, were I blessed with a child, you may, by deep inquiry and constant intercourse with [a conduct book

---

[7]   See Marion Helfer Wajnot's *The Birthright and the Blessing* (2000) for a book-length overview of Thackeray's use of biblical allusions. In some cases, the allusions were crucial to the structure of the whole, as with the parable of the Good Samaritan that gives *The Adventures of Philip* (1862) its subtitle.

[8]   In "Cruikshank, Thackeray, and the Victorian Eclipse of Satire" (2004), Frank Palmeri registers *The Newcomes* as evidence of a kinder, gentler Thackeray (770). In *Thackeray and Women* (1995), Micael Clarke offers a comprehensive list of Thackeray's villainous fathers, a list that includes seven heavy drinkers (64).

[9]   Even Pendennis seems to back away from the affection he shows for patriarchs in *The Newcomes*. When he returns as narrator of *Philip* (1862), Thackeray uses him to revisit, writes Walter Bagehot in a review of the novel, his customary "eager impetuous hero," "nice little heroine," "bad father," and "bad mother" (885). The novel offers glimpses of a more bitter Pendennis. He pauses the story in one moment to ask, "Why am I, Philip's biographer, going out of my way to abuse Philip's Papa?" (Thackeray, *Philip*, 306).

writer] learn how a man lives comfortably on nothing a year" (428). The narrator immediately retreats from his brief experiment with paternal authority, however, instead offering advice against accepting advice: "it is best not to be intimate with gentlemen of this profession, and to take calculations at second hand" (428).

Scenes of prayer in Thackeray's earlier works focus on the father's hypocrisy and shortcomings. The penultimate number of *The Book of Snobs* (1846–1847), on Club Snobs, mocks a father who leaves his "poor Laura" alone with the children. "While yonder good-for-nothing is swilling his wine," the narrator recalls, "the little ones are at Laura's knees lisping their prayers, and she is teaching them to say—'Pray God Bless Papa!'" (155). The narrator of *Vanity Fair* explicitly rejects the preacher role:

> Sick-bed homilies and pious reflections are, to be sure, out of place in mere story-books, and we are not going (after the fashion of some novelists of the present day) to cajole the public into a sermon, when it is only a comedy that the reader pays his money to witness. (229)

A reader can choose to take the narrator at his word, or, as with the jurist who has been asked to disregard evidence, to see the statement as a challenge, an invitation to look for what the narrator supposedly disavows. When the narrator decides to "adroitly shut the door" on the reconciliation between Jos and his elderly father, because "[i]n that long absence of ten years, the most selfish will think about home and early ties" (686), the reader is invited to imagine the scene for herself. When he refuses to narrate Amelia caring for her ailing father because "it would be too dreary and stupid. I can see Vanity Fair yawning over it" (660), the reader is challenged to create the scene herself. Writing again to his mother about the "odious" individuals in his novel, he writes that he wants to "make a set of people living without God in the world" (2.309), which quotes Ephesians 2:12 and Newman's *Apologia* (2.309n80), and is, Thackeray admits, a "cant phrase" (2.309). In the narrator's impatience with his readers, who seem to be missing his point, one is reminded that *Vanity Fair*'s title and premise are lifted from Bunyan's *Pilgrim's Progress*. Again, this is not to say that Thackeray is in the business of conversion, only that he is exceedingly interested in the power of conversion narratives, and in finding ways to perform that power.

Vanity Fair asks readers to compare two patriarch's libraries, libraries in which religious and secular texts are juxtaposed. In the first, chapter 24, "In Which Mr. Osborne takes down the family Bible," Thackeray's narrator channels the same anxieties that fueled the authors of family prayer manuals:

> Behind Mr. Osborne's dining-room was the usual apartment which went in his house by the name of the study; and was sacred to the master of the house. Hither Mr Osborne would retire of a Sunday forenoon when not minded to go to church; and here pass the morning in his crimson leather chair, reading the paper. A couple of glazed book-cases were here, containing standard works in stout gilt bindings. The "Annual Register," the "Gentleman's Magazine,"

"Blair's Sermons," and "Hume and Smollett." From year's end to year's end he never took one of these volumes from the shelf; but there was no member of the family that would dare for his life to touch one of the books, except upon those rare Sunday evenings when there was no dinner-party, and when the great scarlet Bible and Prayer-book were taken out from the corner where they stood beside his copy of the Peerage, and the servants being rung up to the dining-parlour, Osborne read the evening service to his family in a loud grating pompous voice. No member of the household, child or domestic, ever entered that room without a certain terror. (278)

Osborne is in full control over the volumes in his library, but shows little sign that he is aware of the contents of these volumes. These are display books, as much stage books as the work held by Bingley in *Pendennis*. The Bible and the Prayer Book sit unused, adjacent to the Peerage; the Peerage replaces the Bible as the ultimate parental text, laying claim to ownership of a particular family line. In fact, Osborne lifts the family Bible to *erase* his son's name from its opening pages, foreshadowing—perhaps even orchestrating—George's death on the battlefield and the orphaning of Osborne's grandson (386). Osborne's study is an alternative to church services, and the newspaper the preferred alternative to religious texts. When the evening service is called for (in the absence of preferable entertainments), it fails to entertain because of Osborne's failure as a performer. His "loud, grating pompous voice" reveals the human rather than the divine.

The next study dissected by Thackeray's narrator is Sir Pitt Crawley's, described in chapter 54 of the novel, "Sunday after the Battle":

Rawdon sat down in the study before the Baronet's table, set out with the orderly blue books and the letters, the neatly docketed bills and symmetrical pamphlets; the locked account-books, desks, and dispatch boxes, the Bible, the *Quarterly Review*, and the *Court Guide*, which all stood as if on parade awaiting the inspection of their chief.

A book of family sermons, one of which Sir Pitt was in the habit of administering to his family on Sunday mornings, lay ready at the study table, and awaiting his judicious selection. And by the sermon-book was the *Observer* newspaper, damp and neatly folded, and for Sir Pitt's own private use. His gentleman alone took the opportunity of perusing the newspaper before he laid it by his master's desk. (623)

Rawdon, who joins Colonel Newcome in the elite ranks of Thackeray's sympathetic father figures,[10] stands with the narrator in his brother's study, while Lady Jane "was up and above the stairs in the nursery … listening to the morning prayers which the little creatures performed at her knee" (622–3). The prayers of "the little creatures" are surely more moving than the "public ceremonial at which

---

[10]   Claudia Nelson argues that Rawdon Crawley's "heartfelt love" for his son is "the narrative's signal that Rawdon deserves the reader's sympathy and perhaps even admiration" (*Family* 64). She writes, "As a military man Rawdon is negligible, as a husband he is a dupe, but as a father he comes into his own" (64).

Sir Pitt presided, and at which all the people of the household were expected to assemble" (62). Unlike Osborne, who reads directly from the Bible and Book of Common Prayer, Sir Pitt presides over family prayers regularly, with the help of "a book of family sermons" marketed and sold for the occasion. In other ways, his study becomes the mirror image of Osborne's, again part of a performance. The juxtaposition of disparate works—economic, legal, and religious texts—implies equivalence. Perhaps the study aid helps Sir Pitt add more regularity to the religion he "administers" to his family. Again, the text that promises charismatic authority is folded into a library that is dominated by texts emphasizing traditional and legal-rational authority.

The Newcomes offers a third space in which the patriarch presides over family prayer, but Pendennis, unlike the narrator of *Vanity Fair*, who highlights the absence of narrated sentimental scenes, feels comfortable presenting and annotating the pictures. Pendennis stages a general scene of family prayer in order to clarify the exact nature of his cynicism:

> I do not sneer at the purpose for which, at that chiming eight o'clock bell, the household is called together. The urns are hissing, the plate is shining; the father of the house, standing up, reads from a gilt book for three or four minutes in a measured cadence. The members of the family are around the table in an attitude of decent reverence; the younger children whisper responses at their mother's knees; the governess whispers a little apart; the maids and the large footmen are in a cluster before their chairs, the upper servants performing their devotion on the other side of the side-board; the nurse whisks about the unconscious last-born, and tosses it up and down during the ceremony. (144)

The passage speaks directly to the differences between *Vanity Fair* and *The Newcomes*. The remark "I do not sneer at the purpose…" is certainly a response to criticism of *Vanity Fair* by John Forster, especially given other echoes of the critique in Pendennis' later defenses of his narrative approach. Forster wrote that a reader can never appreciate "gentle and kind things" in Thackeray's works "without some neighbouring quip or sneer that would seem to show the author ashamed of what he yet cannot help giving way to" (Tilloston and Hawess 54, 54n1). Of course, Pendennis is slightly disingenuous when he claims not to "sneer." The passage is not "gentle and kind," but its criticism is geared toward improvement rather than dismissal. Pendennis uncovers the performative nature of the opening of this additional "gilt book." The audience assumes an "attitude of decent reverence," the servants are "performing their devotion," and the nurse distracts the baby during the "ceremony." The other details of the scene—the rhythmic tossing of the baby, the "urns hissing" and the "plate shining"—evoke mechanism, as if family religion runs like a steam engine. Yet Pendennis reveals nothing that family prayer books did not openly share with their audiences. In *The Fire-Side*, Jacob Abbott suggests that family prayer "is the oil which removes friction, and causes all the complicated wheels of the family to move smoothly and noiselessly" (12). And, the regular starting of the "machine" at eight can occasionally be reason to celebrate, as it works, as in sentimental fiction, to offer the "consoling illusion of a community based on resemblance" (Burnham 68). The author of *A Street I've Lived In: A Sabbath Morning's Scene* (1858), another dramatic piece set on Sunday morning, writes, "The clock had just struck eight, and the bell of the parish church was ... calling upon all to prepare for the sacred hour of worship. Welcome, thrice welcome, was the sound!" (5).[11]

Unlike *Vanity Fair's* critique of the "yawning" audience for sentimental scenes, Pendennis charges the audience for part of the failed performance of family prayer:

> I do not sneer at ... the act at which all these people are assembled—it is at the rest of the day I marvel; all the rest of the day, and what it brings. At the very instant when the voice has ceased speaking ... the world begins again, and the next twenty-three hours and fifty-seven minutes all that household is given up to it (144).

He questions whether family prayer, as practiced, holds the utility that is promised. Unless the reader is uncharacteristically powerful, the weak spell cast by his brief reading is quickly broken. Pendennis's critique echoes that of the writers of the "books of family sermons" "administer[ed]" by Sir Pitt Crawley (*Vanity Fair* 623). Charles Bridges writes, in *An Essay on Family Prayer* (1847), "Christian watchfulness is essential to preserve the fragrance of this holy service. The instant transition, too often made, to levity and frivolous conversation, tends greatly to dampen its unction and abiding impression" (48).

An iconic scene in *The Newcomes* depicts grandfather, father, and son, in the grandson's room as he kneels to pray the "Our Father." Arthur Pendennis narrates Colonel Newcome's account of the event, and then offers reflections that are meant to amplify the Colonel's more straightforward account:

> Boy presently fell a-crying: in spite of all the battle and fury, there was sleep in his eyes.
> "Maria is too busy, I suppose, to put him to bed," said Clive, with a sad smile, "shall we do it, father? Come, Tommy my son!" And he folded his arms round the child, and walked with him to the upper regions. The old man's eyes lighted up; his scared thoughts returned to him; he followed his two children up the stairs, and saw his grandson in the little bed; and, as we walked home with him, he told me how sweetly Boy said, "Our Father," and prayed God bless all those who loved him, as they laid him to rest.

---

[11] *A Street I've Lived in: A Sabbath Morning's Scene* by "T.H.W." (1858), was published by the Wesleyan Conference Office. The Wesleyan Methodists in Britain, as discussed in several early works by George Eliot, distinguished themselves in issues related to affect. Writes Mary Lenard, "much of the Methodist movements' success was due to its attention to enthusiasm and sentimental emotional drama" (14). The importance of bells for missionary work has been studied by Giordano Nanni. Supporters of missionary work would donate Bibles, but also donate bells to toll the hours of work and worship, in hopes that this spreads to a larger system of law and order in the colony (Nanni 16).

So these three generations had joined in that supplication: the strong man, humbled by trial and grief, whose loyal heard was yet full of love;—the child, of the sweet age of those little ones whom the Blessed Speaker of the prayer first bade come unto Him:—and the old man, whose heart was well nigh as tender and as innocent; and whose day was approaching, when he should be drawn to the bosom of the Eternal Pity. (764)

The affecting scene is presented to readers twice. Pendennis first offers a paraphrase of Colonel Newcomes's account, which gives the specific actions of "Clive," "Tommy," "Maria," and "Boy." The only tears shed are those of the immature grandson, who has not even evolved into his proper name. The union of father, son, and grandson occurs because "Maria is too busy." "Boy" prays, with the glorious selfishness of children, only for "all those who loved him." The phrasing "as they laid him to rest" cast the shadow of death over the otherwise sweet scene, and Pendennis capitalizes on the pathos as he turns to add a caption to the image. Pendennis' immediate retelling—or, rather, allegorizing—of the scene turns it into a *Pilgrim's Progress* narrative in which the three figures represent the stages of one life. Specific characters—all named except for "Boy—become "the strong man," "the child," and "the old man," and the tableau in which they play a part becomes a memento mori for the reader. "Usually," argues Fred Kaplan, "death provides only an ironic coda" for Thackeray; "it facilitates plots, not themes" (81). In Colonel Newcomes's narration of the scene, this is true. Soon after this moment, the action of the novel quickens in response to the foreshadowing provided in the scene. Colonel Newcomes's second grandchild is stillborn, his daughter-in-law dies, and Colonel Newcome dies broken and disgraced. Pendennis's narration offers an alternative reading, in which the fates of the individuals within the plot give way to theme, a moment that offers, as did sentimental fiction of the previous century, the "consoling illusion of a community based on resemblance" (Burnham 68).

To understand how these scenes of family prayer, against all outward appearances, transcend "sneering" and instead perform preaching, we must remember Thackeray's abiding interest in the world-changing potential of sentimental narratives. Thackeray's biographer, D.J. Taylor, notes the "obvious irony in the process by which the cutting young satirist of *Fraser's* and *Punch* transformed himself into the sedate and sentimental fogey of *The Newcomes*," seeing this as an unconscious lapse on Thackeray's part, a sign of his "inability to prevent himself falling victim to the attitudes he had burlesqued in his early work" (276). I argue that Thackeray was supremely aware of the "obvious irony," but wanted to use *The Newcomes* to experiment with the kinds of power the pure ironist cannot wield. Some of the many narrative modes sampled in the novel are family chronicle, sketch, historical novel, drawing room drama, neo-picaresque novel, and fable (Knezevic 114–16). Religious writing, and its companion, secular sentimental writing, are the easiest modes to overlook within this novel's reassessment of paternal authority.

Philip Davis offers a moving defense of Victorian sentimentality. At first, he writes, it "seems to exist defensively and protectively, putting women and children first, and if men thereafter, only little, weak, foolish, childish, or underprivileged men from the lower order" (23). Yet, in a "harsher and faster world," he asks, might sentimentality become "a defensive part of urban social history, democratizing inarticulate good feeling, offering family feeling a place in the new world?" (23). Davis returns his readers to Wordsworth's model of "thinking in the spirit of human passions" within his preface to *Lyrical Ballads*, "a founding text for Victorian fictional prose rather than Victorian poetry" (27). Pendennis, and his author, present *The Newcomes* as a hymn to all of the debts Victorian prose owes to Wordsworth's idealism about literature's role in developing a reader's moral sense.

By the 1850s, having fielded harsh criticism of *Henry Esmond* (1852) by conservative readers, Thackeray was perhaps ready for a change. *Henry Esmond* was published in three volumes rather than being serialized, which may have made the backlash against it even more surprising, or perhaps offered the latitude necessary to write more radically. The novel diverged far from traditional models of family. Children are born out of wedlock, and Henry marries the mother of one of his paramours. The book's effusive preface has led some readers to uncomfortable conclusions about Henry Esmond's relationship with his daughter (Scarry 133–5). In a letter to Sarah Baxter, written July 4, 1853, he called his new novel, *The Newcomes: Memoirs of a Most Respectable Family*, "not a step forwards as some ambitious young American folks would have it, but a retreat rather" (*Letters* 3.283). Thackeray was unsure about the compromises he would have to make to appease his audience, and unsure if a novel of his would ever meet the expectations of the moralists. In August of that year he wrote:

> I'm in low spirits about The Newcomes. It's not good. It's stupid. It haunts me like a great stupid ghost. I think it says why do you go on writing this rubbish? You are old, you have no more invention &c. Write sober books, books of history, leave novels to the younger folks. You see half my life is grumbling; and lecturing or novel-writing or sentimentalizing[.] I am never content... (Letters 3.299)

Thackeray draws a generational line, wondering if he has outgrown his usefulness as a writer of novels, or if he would be more useful writing something else. He begins to doubt his own charismatic authority; if charismatic authority is by its nature a revolutionary force, perhaps he is too traditional to wield it. One senses echoes of his distressed response to *Dombey and Son*—"there's no writing against such power as this; one has no chance!" ("Reminiscences" 572). One also senses dissatisfaction with what one author can accomplish within a work of fiction.

The Newcomes begins with a child's fable, cobbled together by the author—who has not yet ceded the novel to his narrator, Pendennis—from seven fables by Aesop (McMaster 8; *Newcomes* 3). Thackeray anticipates the rejection of his "old fables" in "old clothes," as the critic is "Solomon that sits in judgment over us authors and chops up our children" (5). Thackeray's Colonel, in *The Newcomes*, expresses a similar anxiety. The Colonel was afraid that he was going out of style. In a scene that Nicholas Dames calls a "representative picture of changing tastes" (41), the Colonel exclaims, "Doctor Johnson not write English! Lord Byron not one of the greatest poets in the world! Sir Walter a poet of the second order! Mr Pope attacked for inferiority and want of imagination!" (200). Thackeray knew that his Colonel contributed to the old-fashioned feel of the book. When the Colonel takes his leave for several numbers of the serial, he says, "You young fellows are too clever for me. I haven't learned your ideas or read your books. I feel myself often an old damper on your company" (255). Thackeray foreshadowed his Colonel's utterance in a letter to Mrs. Proctor in January of 1854, writing, "The Colonel is going to India the day after to-morrow. You'll be glad to hear that, I know. He is a dear old boy, but confess you think he is rather a twaddler?" (3.341).

Colonel Newcome is far from perfect; indeed, his "ambitions for his son" lead to "most of the major disasters in the book" (Taylor 352). In other ways, he is Thackeray's über-father. He is Clive's father, Pendennis's substitute father (255) and, for "a score, at least, of adopted children," the offspring of dead or absent military officers, "he chose to stand in the light of a father" (55). Pendennis decides to focus his narrative on the father and the son, since this is the pairing that stirs his feelings: "my intimacy with the father and son grew to be considerable, and a great deal more to my liking than my relations with Clive's city uncles ... which were, in truth, exceedingly distant and awful" (44). Colonel Newcome also stirred Thackeray's feelings. Although his daughter Annie served as amanuensis for much of the novel's composition, the manuscript's handwriting shifts back to Thackeray when the text reaches Colonel Newcome's death (Taylor 355, 368). One can imagine Thackeray thinking back to his response to the death of little Paul Dombey in Dickens's *Dombey and Son*—"There's no writing against such power as this; one has no chance!" ("Reminiscences" 572)—and deciding that he was going to give it a try.

As he embarked on *The Newcomes* (1855), Thackeray described a new sense of moral obligation towards his readers, coupled with a sense that his old-fashioned book would not attract new readers. In another letter to Sarah Baxter (July 26, 1853) he enters into a diatribe about heartless parents breeding heartless children, and stops himself: "Hullo!—I say—Stop!—where is this tirade a-going to and apropos of what?" (3.296). The "Immense Moralist!" (3.297) then decides to "call in Anny ... and give her a turn at the new novel," since he "see[s] a chapter out of the above sermon" (3.297). He then explains the conceit of having Pendennis, rather than himself, as the "author" of *The Newcomes*: "by the help of this little mask ... I shall be able to talk more at ease than in my own person. I only thought of the plan last night and am immensely relieved by adopting it" (3.298). He has new goals and strategies in this new novel, and knows that he needs a different kind of narrator in order to execute it.

Crucially, however, Thackeray discards the "mask" (3.298) of Pendennis at the end of the novel. A line across the page separates the end of Pendennis's narration from the beginning of Thackeray's. Thackeray reminds readers of the real date and his true location ("Paris, 28 June, 1855"), and recovers the true chronology, telling readers that his tale has unfolded over the course of 23 months (772). Thackeray reclaims possession of his novel to speculate about how Clive—who may or may not become a father himself—would fit into the sentimental story that Pendennis spun for him. Thackeray alludes to the fractured fables with which he began by writing, "But have they any children? I, for my part, should like her best without, and entirely devoted to little Tommy. But for you, dear friend, it is as you like ... Anything you like happens in Fairyland" (774). Fred Kaplan calls this ending a forced exit from Eden and an entry into the "'fable-land' of literature" (114). I instead see it as an invitation for the reader to remain in Eden if she wishes to, perhaps even finding a way to transport Eden with her into the "real world." Importantly, when Thackeray emerges as himself in the novel's final number, he "appears as the head of a family, the father of real as well as fictional children" (Hughes and Lund, *Victorian Serial* 57). He writes from Paris, and away from his own daughters, but alludes to the "safe haven" to which he hopes all of his characters return (57).

When Thomas Carlyle dismissed Thackeray's lectures on *The English Humourists of the Eighteenth Century*, the lectures he delivered in America in 1851 and subsequently published as a volume, he did so in the style of the lectures themselves (Carlyle, *New* 2.122). Thackeray's essays on the great and good writers of the previous century focused extensively on the relationship between men and their works. Where Thackeray saw an immoral life, it inflected his assessment of the writing. He writes of Sterne's inconstancy, for example:

> the charming Sterne was at the Mount Coffee-house, with a sheet of gilt-edged paper before him, offering that precious treasure his heart to Lady P— ... quoting the Lord's Prayer, with a horrible baseness of blasphemy, as a proof that he had desired not to be led into temptation, and swearing himself the most tender and sincere fool in the world. (Thackeray, *English* 158)[12]

He then pictures Sterne "with his 'Sentimental Journey' to launch upon the town, eager as ever for praise and pleasure" (158–9). These kinds of gestures were off-putting to Carlyle. Writing to his brother in January 1852, Carlyle assesses Thackeray's character, as it emerges, he thinks, from the lectures and the sight of him with his daughters:

> I had never seen him so well before. There is a great deal of talent in him, a great deal of sensibility,—irritability, sensuality, vanity without limit;—and nothing or little but sentimentalism and playactorism to guide it all with: not a good or well-found ship in such waters on such a voyage. (Carlyle, *New* 2.122)

What Carlyle may not have realized is that, in considering these great writers of the past, Thackeray was also thinking about himself, and not seeing "sentimentalism"

---

[12] Virginia Woolf defends Sterne from Thackeray's charges, in a way that resonates with the turn Thackeray would take later in his lecture in connecting Sterne with all writers of satire, including himself. She writes:

> Was not Thackeray's coward—the man who trifled so immorally with so many women and wrote love-letters on gilt-edged paper when he should have been lying on a sick-bed or writing sermons—was he not a stoic in his own way and a moralist, and a teacher? Most great writers are, after all. [*Collected Essays* 1.101]

and "playactorism" as such a bad pair. The differences between Sterne's books and his life led Thackeray to this crucial reflection:

> A perilous trade, indeed, is that of a man who has to bring his tears and laughter, his recollections, his personal griefs and joys, his private thoughts and feelings to market, to write them on paper, and sell them for money ... How much of the paint and emphasis is necessary for the fair business of the stage, and how much of the rant and rouge is put on for the vanity of the actor[?] His audience trusts him: can he trust himself? How much was deliberate calculation and imposture— how much was false sensibility—and how much true feeling? Where did the lie begin, and did he know where? and where did the truth end in the art and scheme of this man of genius, this actor, this quack?" (Thackeray, *English* 159)

Such questions, I argue, prodded Thackeray to draw the line between Pendennis and himself in the final pages of his "Memoir of a Most Respectable Family," as well as to draw as many lines as he could between his new novel and what had come before. He realizes the extent to which all books are "stage books." He asks of Sterne what modern readers ask when reading Thackeray's letters, his sketches, his lectures, and his novels: "How much was deliberate calculation and imposture—how much was false sensibility—and how much true feeling?" (Thackeray, *English* 159). It is impossible to separate "man of genius," "actor," and "quack," but Thackeray and his narrators seem interested in the reader's attempt to do so—as interested in the audience as in the actor.

In *How Novels Think* (2005), Nancy Armstrong describes mainstream Victorian fiction as concerned with "the problem of how to harness the individual's energy for social purposes" (105). She argues that different subgenres and narrative modes emerge when this moral purpose becomes unwieldy within the established forms (22–3). The generic diversity of *The Newcomes* seems to respond to this imperative. Thackeray's thoughts about writing history books after finishing *The Newcomes*— shifting to a mode more appropriate for an old man whose powers as a novelist were waning—was a sign that he, like Gaskell and Meredith, was hoping to strain the limits of the form by harnessing the power of extraliterary alternatives.[13]

Looking back to Thackeray's *The Newcomes* early in the next century, Edith Wharton uses it as her key example when thinking about the aims of fiction and the uses of sentimentality:

> Any subject considered in itself must first of all respond in some way to that mysterious need of a judgment on life of which the most detached human intellect, provided it be a normal one, cannot, apparently, rid itself. Whether the

---

[13] Thackeray wrote to his mother on September 23, 1853, of an invitation he had just received to edit Carlyle's letters:

> [it] is just the sort of work I should like—such as would keep me at home pleasantly employed some evenings and pottering over old volumes—(I'm flying from pen to pen to see [which] will answer best) of old biographies and histories. When the Imaginative work is over, that is the kind of occupation I often propose to myself for my old age. (*Letters* 3.305)

"moral" be present in the guise of a hero rescuing the heroine from the villain at the point of the revolver, or whether it lurk in the quiet irony of such a scene as Pendennis's visit to the Grey Friar's Chapel, and his hearing the choir singing "I have been young, and now am old; yet have I not seen the righteous forsaken, nor his seed begging their bread," at the very moment when he discovers the bent head of Colonel Newcome among the pauper gentlemen—in one form or another there must be some sort of rational response to the reader's unconscious but insistent inner question: "What am I being told this story for? What judgment on life does it contain for me?" (23)

Wharton knows that her statements are as old-fashioned as Thackeray's novel, and she presents them with ironic detachment for that reason ("in some way," "some sort" "that mysterious need," "unconscious but insistent," "cannot, apparently, rid itself"). She knows that art for the soul's sake is a hard sell to the moderns. Yet, she tentatively suggests, armed with Colonel Newcome's effect on readers, even in fiction that "preaches to the nerves," as was famously said of sensation fiction, the reader's "head" and "heart" seek some involvement as well.

Conclusion

Locating charismatic authority within a body requires flexibility. Weber writes about the limitations of an individual body. When the charismatic leader reaches the end of his life, he must find a way to make his power "traditional," heritable, or "legal-rational," institutional (Weber 3.1133). A patriarch may try locating charismatic authority within a body of texts, but this requires generic flexibility. When the Prayer Book or Sermon loses its value, perhaps a repackaged form can renovate both. Similarly, when the sentimental novel, the historical fiction, the fable, or the romance lose affective power, perhaps new forms of writing can take over. In his essay "The Utility of Religion," John Stuart Mill transfers the waning power of religion to poetry. "Religion and poetry address themselves, at least in one of their aspects, to the same part of the human constitution," he writes, "They both supply the same want, that of ideal conceptions grander and more beautiful than we see realized in the prose of human life" (103). In writing *The Newcomes*, Thackeray was not sure if novels were his proper format any longer, but with Pendennis as his "little mask" (*Letters* 3.298), he was willing to try a different approach to the role.

In a retrospective on Thackeray's works from *London Society* (1888), Joseph Foster wrote of Thackeray, "he throughout believed, and acted on the belief, that easy writing is hard reading. He polished his prose more than some poets do their verse: he returned to it again and again" (145). Thackeray called the average Protestant religious tracts "detestable mixtures of truth, lies, false sentiment, false reasoning, bad grammar, correct and genuine philanthropy and piety" (Thackeray, *Paris* 203). In other words, he found in them some decent ideas, presented in unfortunate packaging. The assessment recalls the narrator's judgment of Bingley in Thackeray's *Pendennis,* as he "acted at them; eyeing them solemnly over his gilt volume … determined to fascinate them, for he knew they had paid their money" (40). The narrator knows that his "talk is sham, like the book he reads, and the hair he wears, and the bank he sits on, and the diamond ring he makes play with" (43). However, "in the midst of all the balderdash, there runs that reality of love, children, and forgiveness of wrong" (44). What happens to Thackeray's legacy if we begin to read his books in that light, if we begin to look for "true feeling" within the "scheme" (Thackeray, *English* 159)?

When Thackeray broke off "A Shabby Genteel Story," a serialized tale from *Fraser's Magazine* (July–August, October 1840) that, two decades later, became the basis for *Philip* (1862), he did not think that the story could ever have a happy ending. The story is about a woman, tricked into a sham marriage and abandoned by her seducer. She is on the verge of madness and despair after having given birth to his child. Thackeray discontinued the story when its fictions approached too close to his own experience—when his wife descended into madness after the birth of their third child, and eventually had to be institutionalized (Thackeray, *Adventures* viii). Thackeray, left to raise his daughters with the help of his mother and others, waited many years to return to the tale. When it was first reprinted seventeen years later in his *Miscellanies*, he claimed that since "the colours are long since dry" and "the artist's hand has changed," it was best to "leave the sketch, as it was when first designed seventeen years ago" (vii). Yet he could not resist the opportunity to turn tragedy into comedy. He recruits Pendennis to narrate *Philip*. Philip's father is imported unchanged from his villainous role in "Shabby Genteel Story," but the novel now belongs to the illegitimate son. Philip's story ends with him sitting with Pendennis and Clive Newcome on the lawn, watching their children frolic around them. Thackeray calls the closing scene "rather a lame ending" (*Letters* 4.270), and suggests again that "the novel-writing vein is used up though and you may be sure some kind critics will say as much for me before long" (*Letters* 4.271). Yet, in the same letter, he compares the "lame" ending of *Philip* with the "real world" lessons to be gained from his own writing life:

> Think of the beginning of the story of the little Sister in the Shabby Genteel Story twenty years ago and the wife crazy and the Publisher refusing me 15£ who owes me £13.10 and the Times to which I apply for a little more than 5 guineas for a week's work, refusing to give me more and all that money difficulty ended, God be praised, and an old gentleman sitting in a fine house like the hero at the end of a story! (*Letters* 4.271)

Thackeray's criticism of Sterne could also be applied, he knew, to himself, another who spent a career bringing "his personal griefs and joys, his private thoughts and feelings to market, to write them on paper, and sell them for money" (Thackeray *English* 159). In this instance, Thackeray feels gratitude that he has been allowed to present the public with one more gilt volume, and wonders whether the "kind critics" will ask him to take his bow "before long" (*Letters* 4.271).

I'll end this chapter where I began, with *Pendennis* and yet another gilt volume. This time, rather than a "stage book" held by an actor performing for a meager audience, Pendennis considers a prayer book, held by a preacher performing for a meager audience. The young Pen regards "the learned Doctor Donne" who "sate magnificent, with his great prayer-book before him, an image of statuesque piety and rigid devotion," while freshmen "in the gentlemen-pensioners' seats" were "giggling and talking as if they had been in so many stalls at the Opera" (189). When he is an adult, Pendennis, Thackeray's "mask," alternates between rejecting and embracing an evangelical mission. He writes:

> Our history ... is of the world, and things pertaining to it. Things beyond it, as the writer imagines, scarcely belong to the novelist's province. Who is he, that he should assume the divine's office, or turn his desk into a preacher's pulpit? (*Newcomes* 371–2)

However, he cannot narrate much more of the story without rethinking his stance:

> I have said this book is all about the world, and a respectable family dwelling in it. It is not a sermon, except where it cannot help itself, and the speaker pursuing the destiny of his narrative finds such a homily before him. O friend, in your life and mine, don't we light upon such sermons daily—don't we see at home as well as amongst our neighbours that battle betwixt Evil and Good? Here on one side is Self and Ambition and Advancement; and Right and Love on the other. Which shall we let to triumph for ourselves—which for our children? (384–5)

Pendennis, presenting himself as a protector of his children and those of the reader, bristles again, on Thackeray's behalf, against Forster's critique of *Vanity Fair*. Here, a Thackeray narrator "cannot help giving way" to the "gentle and kind" rather than to the "quip and sneer" (Tilloston and Hawess 54, 54n1). Pendennis finds the stakes highest of all when "home" is the battlefield in the "battle betwixt Evil and Good" (384). As Pendennis thinks about the "sermon" he is about to administer to his family, he seems to echo "a chapter out of the ... sermon" that led him to call Annie to take down another chapter of *The Newcomes* (*Letters* 3.297). Pendennis finds sermons for "our children" everywhere. When Pendennis thinks about Clive's treatment of his father, he is compelled to allude to another old story, "Did we not say, at our tale's commencement, that all stories were old? Careless prodigals and anxious elders have been from the beginning—and so may love, and repentance, and forgiveness endure even till the end" (186). This narrator "cannot help" giving way to "an attitude of decent reverence," even though he cannot control the nature of his audience's response.

Chapter 4
"Lay Hold of Them by Their Fatherhood": George Eliot, Persuasion, and Abstraction

On the eve of her father's death, Marian (or Mary Ann) Evans wrote to her friends, the Brays, "What shall I be without my Father? It will seem as if part of my moral nature were gone. I had a horrid vision of myself last night becoming earthy sensual and devilish for want of that purifying restraining influence" (George Eliot, *Letters* 1.284). In these lines, Evans expresses both fear and relief. Her years as the caretaker of her widowed father added structure to her life. With his loss, she achieved heady, dizzying, disorienting freedom. When Evans began publishing critical essays anonymously, and then fiction under the pen name "George Eliot," she hoped that her narrative persona would provide a "purifying restraining influence" for her readers. She sought a similar influence over her readers as her father had over her on the eve of his death, if not always during his life. In a December 1857 journal entry entitled, "How I came to Write Fiction," she describes the effect she had on her first readers. She reports that "men at the club seem to have mingled their tears and their tumblers together" after reading "Amos Barton" (Pinion 106). Her first readers assumed that her authority was not only masculine, but paternal: "There was clearly no suspicion that I was a woman ... they were all sure I was a clergyman—a Cambridge man. Agnes [Lewes] thought I was the father of a family—was sure I was a man who had seen a great deal of society etc. etc." (106). The voice within her nonfiction prose, it seems, struck her first readers as worldly, educated, and wise. The opinionated omniscient narrators of her first novels would do the same. Yet, the positive vision of the paternal narrative voice, as presented by her disembodied narrators, would be challenged by the negative visions of paternity that unfold via her embodied characters.

In Eliot's novels, admirable father substitutes include Silas Marner, Bartle Massey, and Mr. Irwine; Mr. Garth and Mr. Lyon are two admirable biological fathers. Yet none of these men are idealized, and Eliot's list of failed fathers is equally hefty. For Eliot's early heroes and heroines—Adam Bede, the son of an alcoholic, Tom and Maggie, subject to the disgraced father's curse in *The Mill on the Floss* (1860), and Eppie, Godfrey Cass's abandoned golden child in *Silas Marner* (1861)—the biological father seems to be the last person who can offer a "purifying restraining influence." Adam Bede, for example, must do the work his father neglected; he constructs an overdue coffin while, unbeknownst to him, his father meets his death. Adam's labor foreshadows his father's end, and cements Adam's replacement of his father in the world of work. Yet Adam's work ethic separates him from his father. His way of life heralds the passing of his father's way of life, as Eve Sedgwick notes in calling "Adam's quiet slippage upward from worker to owner" an announcement by Eliot that "the values of modern industrial society are genetically—and appropriately—individualistic, couched in the mode of private property" (145). Adam educates himself by attending a night school for workers, and thus does not owe his education to his father. Adam Bede physically replaces his father in his workspace, but then emerges from the space via his own efforts rather than from material inheritance. His life makes his father's life "immaterial."

This chapter describes a shift in Eliot's consideration of the father's charismatic power—his ability to stir his children to moral action. A transition from Eliot's early elegiac, pastoral novels such as *Adam Bede* (1859) or *Mill on the Floss* (1860), to historical fictions that draw from contemporary controversies, such as *Felix Holt* (1866) and *Daniel Deronda* (1876), depends on, and invests in, nostalgic disembodiment. Across her career, there is a perceptible shift toward the abstracted "idea" of Fatherhood as crucial to the maintenance of moral feeling and social ties. The father's plan for his children fails dramatically in *Adam Bede* and *Mill on the Floss*; the children instead gain the structuring cues of paternal influence via negative example. Her later works return to Mr. Tulliver's obsession—fathers providing sons with a proper education—but translates it into an ambitious, and ambiguous, project for all English fathers and sons. Her fathers evolve from the wholly embodied and flawed into the disembodied and idealized. What has changed for Eliot? Why does she divest, and then reinvest, her novels with "faith in the father?" It is as if Eliot hopes for transference rather than direct inheritance, for the appropriation of the paternal role by nonpaternal beings, as compensation when embodied fathers falter. In transforming the patriarch from man to metaphor, from performer to performative stance, she reinvests charismatic authority with revolutionary force.

"How Can You Talk So?": *The Mill on the Floss*, Education, and the Failures of the Father as Author(ity)

In his *Reminiscences* (1881), the prominent author and intellectual Thomas Carlyle described himself as "the continuation, and *second volume* of my Father" (52). He was comfortable with his status as sequel, due to the distinction between a second *volume* as a continuation of an unfinished story, and a second *edition* as a twice-told tale. Even more important to his intellectual independence is the differing content of the volumes. Carlyle's father is the author of acts, while Carlyle himself is the author of texts. Although his father was not a writer, Carlyle still turns to text to describe his father's influence. Carlyle writes that he will look on the houses his father built "with a certain proud interest" for they are "little texts, for me, of the Gospel of man's Free-Will" (3) His "Deeds and sayings" are "genuine and fit" (3) because they come not from education or design, but "by the teaching of nature alone" (7). The clarity and brevity of his father's speech is another sign of his father's worth, and another avenue for the son's intervention. "I should say of him, as I did of our Sister whom we lost, that he seldom or never spoke except actually to convey an idea," Carlyle writes, adding that "in few sentences, he would sketch you off an entire Biography, an entire Object or Transaction: keen, clear, rugged, genuine, completely rounded in" (9). Carlyle is enchanted with the "neatness" of his father's utterances, comparing them with short versions of printed texts. Carlyle's labor, in rendering his father, is that of translation from one form to another, which allows for considerable amounts of interpretive freedom. Carlyle calls himself "the humble James Carlyle's work" because "it was he *exclusively* that determined on *educating me*, that from his small hard-earned funds, sent me to School and College; and made me whatever I am or may become" (*Reminiscences* 4, Carlyle's emphasis). Carlyle's praise of his stonemason father presents a key paternal duty, that of ensuring that the child acquires an education. However, the father is no longer expected to provide that education. The father becomes just another "little text," a metaphor through which the child can "authorize" himself.

"In the early ages of the world, before the art of writing was invented," notes the unnamed author of the December 1867 essay "Reading as a Means of Culture," "men had to depend, for the acquisition of knowledge, chiefly upon oral instruction" (316). The author of this essay, printed in *Sharpe's London Magazine*, explains the implications of the explosion of print. Before "the art of writing" took hold, "as the family bond was then a strong one, each child was in a pre-eminent sense the pupil of his parent, and each patriarch was in a pre-eminent sense the teacher of his child" (316). However, "since the art of paper-making was invented, and, as related to this, the art of printing, a mighty change has taken place in respect to the number of books and the number of readers" (316). The essay heralds the beginning of "READING AS THE MEANS OF SELF-CULTURE" (316). Books democratized education by taking knowledge out of the father's mouth and delivering it directly into the son's hands. By mid-century, as Claudia Nelson notes in her extensive study of fatherhood within Victorian periodical culture, the most prominent voices of the Victorian public sphere confirmed that "fathers can't, don't, or shouldn't instruct children on any subject" (*Invisible* 51). Additionally, if the father lacks education, what equips him to make decisions about his son's education? Says the narrator of Eliot's *The Mill on the Floss*, which is set in the 1830s:

> Education was almost entirely a matter of luck—usually of ill luck—in those distant days. The state of mind in which you take a billiard-cue or a dice-box in your hand is one of sober certainty compared with that of old-fashioned fathers, like Mr. Tulliver, when they selected a school or a tutor for their sons. (168)

Critics of *The Mill on the Floss* acknowledge Eliot's focus on Mr. Tulliver as an emotional, rather than intellectual, influence over his children.[1] A review in the *Spectator* (April 7, 1860) called Mr. Tulliver a "man of narrow culture," but one

---

[1]   Although Eliot cautions of *Adam Bede* "there is not a single portrait … only the suggestions of experience wrought up into new combinations" (Pinion 109), the reception history of the novel suggests otherwise. Leslie Stephen is one of many who has called Maggie Tulliver, the heroine of Eliot's second full-length novel, "what George Eliot would have been had she been transplanted in her infancy to some slightly different family in the same district" (*Heroines* 74).

who has a "nature much broader, and which is shown most in his love for 'his little wench'" (Review, *Mill* 441). The characterization of Mr. Tulliver's "narrow culture" paired with a "nature much broader" casts his influence on his children as primal and emotional rather than intellectual, dispassionate, and reasoned. The same reviewer wrote of his relationship with Maggie, "His love for her keeps alive in her a most wholesome and healthy tenderness" (441). Later critics also register the family unit as *the* unit of fellow feeling in the novel. George Levine writes that Eliot's focus "relates directly to the Comtean notion … that the family is the primary means by which man can transcend his egoism and animality" (404). Philip Fisher argues that *The Mill on the Floss* "does not even register the life beyond the family except as a violent, inscrutable, and arbitrary set of events that can make family and personal life unstable" (540). This laser focus on the domestic is only partly because young Maggie, the novel's focalizer, is sheltered within the home during her early life. The limited narrative perspective does not completely explain the focus on the home. Hearkening back to Eliot's thoughts at the eve of her father's death, the novel tests home as the foundation for moral consciousness. Maggie has to decide whether to draw on home's lessons when, as a child, she runs away to a gypsy colony, and, as a young woman, she sets sail with Stephen Guest.

Yet, despite the early emotional hold a father has over his children, the child's exposure to external tutelage increases the rift between the generations. Initially, Tom resists the "eddication" that his father lays out for him, especially the emphasis on proper speaking and writing. He thinks, "He was not going to be a snuffy schoolmaster—he; but a substantial man, like his father, who used to go hunting when he was younger, and rode a capital black mare" (*Mill* 133). These childish thoughts run on trivial signs of identification between father and son, but reflect a more substantial desire for socioeconomic connection and continuity. Tom aspires to become what his father *used* to be, not thinking seriously at that point about becoming what his father had become. He is enchanted by the version of his father that he never met—the young man—and thus turns his father into a mirror rather than a true model.[2]

Tom's thoughts also register an unforeseen consequence of education outside of the home—the threat to traditional masculinity that "book learning" may pose.[3] Young Tom associates masculinity the young version of his father, and with an

---

[2]   In Eliot's *Felix Holt*, Esther Lyon comes to similar conclusions about her father's waning influence, looking for paternal advice in her young lover, Felix, instead. Thus, again, the child is in search for a paternal model, but creates him from the new rather than accepting the old.

[3]   In addition, argues Adam Smith in *The Theory of Moral Sentiments* (1759), written as education away from home became increasingly popular in England and France, sending children away to school damages the authority of the parent over the child: "put them under the necessity of being dutiful children, of being kind and affectionate brothers and sisters: educate them in your own house … Domestic education is the institution of nature; public education, the contrivance of man" (261).

exodus from domestic space—with working with his hands outdoors rather than with his mind indoors. A class divide reinforces the gender divide. Becoming educated may require becoming a "gentle" man. Since Tom Tulliver's father is a mill owner rather than a mill worker, Tom is already poised at the edge of this difference. The young Tom is eager to narrow the distance between himself and the brand of masculinity he most wants to embody. Tom's rift with his father is figured in terms of language, and the novel's sentence-level difficulties, and Maggie's rift with her father is figured in terms of plot, and the novel's structural difficulties. In both cases, the book the father hopes to read is fractured by the children he depends on to write it.

The Mill on the Floss is rife with thematic and formal ruptures, in line with how the old-fashioned father's authority translates poorly into the age of print. Eliot purposefully disrupts her novel of "eddication" with the distorted, tortured language of her characters. Susan Fraiman sees Tom's first words in the novel, "Hallo! Yap—what! are you there" (Eliot, *Mill* 33), spoken "with masculine reticence as to the tender emotions" (33), as a sign of "language estranged from intelligibility" (Fraiman 127). Peter Brooks writes that Eliot falters in attempts to make room for a fully embodied crusading man (111). Paula Cohen writes that Mrs. Tulliver's "literal and domestic" language clashes with the husband's "abstract and publicly political" words (118). Mrs. Tulliver's literalness—her ill-advised exposure of her husband's feeling about his adversary, Wakem—weakens her husband's social standing further. Yet even she is closer to being understood than her husband. The father's aspirations for his son's language contrast starkly with his own vexed relationship with language. Mr. Tulliver "found the relation between spoken and written language, briefly known as spelling, one of the most puzzling things in this puzzling world" (*Mill* 129). Readers meet him as he declares his intent to "give Tom a good eddication" (9). When he exclaims that no one should tell him how to raise his son, his wife asks, "how can you talk so, Mr Tulliver?" (10). In asking how Mr. Tulliver can employ such "sanguinary rhetoric" (10) in declaring his ownership over his son and his fate, she draws attention to the tenuousness of his claim. Mr. Tulliver is not qualified to give his son what he so desperately wants his son to have.

Tulliver's position is weaker than that of Gaskell's or Meredith's patriarchs, who, as I described in Part I, intervene in the stories written about them. Instead, Mr. Tulliver needs his son to be both translator and author, using language to open up otherwise inaccessible territory. Mr. Tulliver wants his son's words to bring things into being, as in the opening passages of the book of Genesis in the Christian Bible. The father hopes that his announcements of what should be will become embodied in the son, present from the beginning as the Word (Genesis 1:1), and helping to give form to the story of creation. The need for the power of writing to replace the power of speech is so powerful for Mr. Tulliver that, in presenting his vow of revenge against Wakem, he asks his son to take the father's idea and put it "i' the right words" (*Mill* 267). He insists, in the face of his son's confused and "gloomy submission" to his request, that his son will instinctively know what to do, given the education purchased for him. "You know how" (267), Mr. Tulliver insists. This relationship of interdependence between aging orator and young amanuensis recalls the metaphors that dominate Elizabeth Gaskell and George Meredith's depiction of a father's traditional authority. Yet with Gaskell and Meredith's patriarchs, the father lays claim to dominant modes of discourse. In George Eliot's formulations, the distinction between orality and literacy changes the power dynamic. Tom is charged with turning incoherence into coherence, blind fury into reasoned argument. The father's charismatic authority has its place—it leads the child to feel. But, how much work must be performed by the child to make a father's feelings "legible" to the outside world?

Mr. Tulliver wants Tom to embody the strength of public, published speech, to "talk pretty nigh as well as if it was all wrote out for him" (11) and to "know figures, and write like print, and see into things quick, and know what folks mean, and how to wrap things up in words as aren't actionable" (22). Says Mr. Tulliver, "It's an uncommon fine thing ... when you can let a man know what you think of him without paying for it" (22–3). George Eliot was influenced by Milton's words in *Areopagitica,* copied into one of her writer's notebooks: "Books are not absolutely dead things, but do contain a potencie of life in them to be as active as that soul whose progeny they are; nay they do preserve as in a viol the purest efficacie & extraction of that living intellect that bred them..." (Eliot, *George Eliot: A Writer's Notebook* 100). Milton, too, thinks about the author/book relation as that between parent and offspring. Yet he registers that the transference from "living intellect" to object is one of "extraction" in which something might be lost; after all, "[b]ooks are not absolutely dead things" (Eliot, *George Eliot: A Writer's Notebook* 100), but nor are they absolutely living. Mr. Tulliver, thus, is hoping for the impossible—that extraction will make his essence more potent rather than less so. Mr. Tulliver's anxious realization about Tom's material inheritance, the mill, is that water is a difficult substance to transfer. He says, frustrated, "water's a very particular thing—you can't pick it up with a pitchfork" (155). So much more so for other, even more slippery extractions, such as the "potencie of life" contained in influential ideas.

The sentence-level difficulties in *Mill on the Floss*, used to figure Tom's conflict with his father, are matched by larger structural ruptures that embody his conflicts with his daughter. In *Adam Bede*, the integration of the father's story with the child's is eased by the father's death at a relatively early point in the narrative. In contrast, numerous critics attribute the formal difficulties of *Mill on the Floss* to Eliot's inability to make the father and child tragedies fit together. U.C. Knoepflmacher writes, for example, that "though treated as a greater character than her father, Maggie seems infinitely punier because she is so irrevocably determined by his genes" (*George Eliot's Early Novels* 213). S.L. Goldberg registers plot points that are "blurred or left out" because of Maggie's ambiguous status as agent (183). Eliot claimed that the novel's abrupt ending is due to a "love of the childhood scenes" that "made [her] linger over them" (183–4). In other words, Eliot's emotional response to Maggie's childhood left her little room for the representation of her young adulthood. In addition, Maggie's story falters once Mr.

Tulliver's narrative-generating lust for revenge is quenched. Without Mr. Tulliver's interactions with his "little wench" (Review, *Mill* 441), she becomes anchorless, and can only be purified by literature's most famous flood since Genesis. Henry James is one of many readers who found the ending of the novel abrupt and unsatisfying. James asked, in his 1866 essay "The Novels of George Eliot," "Did such a *dénouement* lie within the author's intentions from the first, or was it a tardy expedient for the solution of Maggie's difficulties?" (*Views* 32).

Thus, both Tom and Maggie drown under the weight of their inheritance. The narrator of *Mill on the Floss* types "millers and other insignificant people" as part of a "different species," whose tragedies are "of that unwept, hidden sort, that goes on from generation to generation, and leaves no record," just as, in phrasing that foreshadows the novel's ending, "the unexpectant discontent of worn and disappointed parents weighs on the children like a damp, thick air" (197). The lives of millers thus resemble orally-transmitted stories. They are composed of "damp, thick air," and "leav[e] no record" (197). Tom grasped at the dream of becoming his father's younger self, yet he does not live to fulfill his promise. Maggie's lack of agency wrecks her, and the latter portion of the novel that contains her. A different kind of novel would have allowed Tom to abandon the mill for a life as a London intellectual, or Maggie to, say, fall in love with a married man and become a famous author herself. Mr. Tulliver's inheritance, however, even though as slippery as water, is still too substantial. When the patriarch's influence becomes metaphorical, and thus transferable, in later novels, Eliot allows for happier endings.

Felix Holt Persuades: Orality, Authority, and the Political Novel

In "On Art in Fiction" from the *Monthly Chronicle* (April 1838), Edward Bulwer-Lytton expresses a common conception about how individuals listen to speeches as opposed to how they read novels:

> In our closets we should be fatigued with the incessant rush of events that we desire when we make one of a multitude. Oratory and the drama in this resemble each other—that the things best to hear are not always the best to read. In the novel, we address ourselves to the one person—on the stage we address ourselves to a crowd: more rapid effects, broader and more popular sentiments, more condensed grasp of the universal passions are required for the last. The calm advice which persuades our friend would only tire out the patience of the crowd. (31)

The novel relies for its power on an intimate relationship between narrator and reader. It does not depend as much on sonic effects, and demands more of its audience. By contrast, the orator or the actor provides a less personal message for a less patient audience. Since "the calm advice which persuades our friend would only tire out the patience of the crowd," the novel is better at convincing an individual slowly, whereas the speech is better at persuading a group quickly. The novel, presumably, compels through reason, and the speech through emotion. If Bulwer-Lytton is correct, speeches confirm what the listener already believes, whereas novels have the power to change belief. This assessment comes, of course, from an unapologetically popular novelist. Eliot does not draw the same stark distinction, even in her famed suspicion of writing that chases trends, as expressed in "Silly Novels by Lady Novelists." Eliot believes that, if they are written well, novels can move crowds. She adds an interesting complication by inserting speeches *into* novels; in recording the responses of characters to speech acts, she forges an argument about what kinds of speeches are most effective. Then readers are invited to consider the effect of those same speeches on their reading experience. Does the limited power of the novel expand when an author writes the oration of a character? The power dynamic she outlines, finally, privileges utterances in this order, from weakest to strongest: the speeches of embodied fathers, directed to the young; the speeches of young father-substitutes, directed to the young; the speeches of women who have been trained by father-substitutes; speech that is disconnected from specific physical bodies. She argues that speeches are most powerful when they harness patriarchal power that is detached from literal patriarchs.

Walter Benjamin argued that revolution through art requires an art form that can be experienced by many people simultaneously. He writes in "The Work of Art in the Age of Mechanical Reproduction" (1936) that the film and the building are the most powerful modern forms of art, because they know how to speak to the distracted and abstracted modern mind. According to Benjamin, one of the major crises of the Victorian era occurred when the masses put pressure on the painting. This form, meant for the few, was suddenly faced with "the simultaneous contemplation ... by a large public" (*Illuminations* 234). Benjamin describes painting in the same terms that Bulwer-Lytton used for the novel as opposed to the speech:

> Painting simply is in no position to present an object for simultaneous collective experience, as it was possible for architecture at all times, for the epic poem in the past, and for the movie today. Although this circumstance in itself should not lead one to conclusions about the social role of painting, it does constitute a serious threat as soon as painting, under special conditions and, as it were, against its nature, is confronted directly by the masses. (234–5)

Eliot confronts the crisis of "painting" for the masses, venturing to come to "conclusions about the social role of painting" after all. She continually presents us with her particular brand of realism—concretely embodied within the famously metafictional seventeenth chapter of *Adam Bede* as a tarnished mirror (*Adam* 177)—by comparing realist depictions with, for example, Dutch paintings. By the end of her career, she has mastered the building of the kind of edifice that can speak to the modern condition.

Eliot's correspondence imagines her books as public, politically engaged writing. George Henry Lewes wrote with pride to Blackwood that "Adam Bede was quoted in the House of Commons the other night," adding "*that* looks like popularity indeed" (in Eliot, *Letters* 3.39). Eliot hoped that the translation of her historical novel *Romola* (1863) into Italian would improve the relationship between Italian citizens and their own history (*Journal* 146). Publisher John Blackwood, perhaps sensing *Felix Holt*'s special status as a novel engaged with current events, wrote, "it occurs to me that the real plan would be to hire a hundred fellows to go about London with a placard stating 'Felix Holt the Radical is published this day'" (Eliot, *Letters* 4.279). Eliot expressed "deep satisfaction from reading in the *Times* the report of a lecture on *Daniel Deronda* delivered by Dr. Hermann Adler to the Jewish Working Men, a lecture showing much insight and implying an expectation of serious benefit" (*Journal* 146). She reported happily that, according to an American member of the Jewish Theological Seminary at Breslav, *Daniel Deronda* "has even already had an elevating effect on the minds of some among his people—predicting that the effect will spread" (*Journal* 146). The reactions display a strong connection, for Eliot, between artistic and political concerns. She was pleased when her novels found a way to impact the policy makers of the public world. Her insertion of public speech acts into the supposedly "private" spaces of the novel draws out potentialities within the form.[4]

In "Natural History of German Life" (1856) Eliot writes that in a novel "more is done towards linking the higher classes with the lower, towards obliterating the vulgarity of exclusiveness, than by hundreds of sermons and philosophical dissertations" (54). She adds that

> Appeals founded on generalizations and statistics require a sympathy ready-made, a moral sentiment already in activity, but a picture of human life such as a great artist can give, surprises even the trivial and the selfish into that attention to which is apart from themselves, which may be called the raw material of moral sentiment. (54)

Her faith in artistic representations as instigators of moral action, reverses concerns that the feeling evoked by the fiction replaces social action, rather than supplements it.[5] Instead, Eliot presents a Wordsworthian vision of reading as a powerful agent for creating acts of sympathy in the world.[6] Her model also resembles

---

[4]   In *The Affective Life of the Average Man* (2010), Audrey Jaffe argues that "the Victorian novel takes shape in a relation of mutual influence with emerging sociological and mass-cultural representations of the group"; with Catherine Gallagher and Mary Poovey, Jaffe claims that "novels often seem to vivify political economy's more abstract formulations" (Jaffe 6). See, also, Matt Rubery's arguments about intersections between novels and journalism in *The Novelty of Newspapers* (2009).

[5]   This was a common critique of sentimental fiction in the eighteenth century. See Lynn Festa, *Sentimental Figures of Empire in Eighteenth Century Britain and France* (2006), in which she investigates the limits of invoking sympathy across space and culture via the sentimental text. See also Robert C. Solomon's *In Defense of Sentimentality* (2004), in which he tracks the shifting status of feeling from the "'moral sentiment' theorists—David Hume and Adam Smith in particular" (4), to Kant's privileging of reason, to the late twentieth century's return to sentiment as "kitsch."

[6]   In his Preface to *Lyrical Ballads* (1800, 1802), Wordsworth famously argues that good poetry trains readers in "habits of mind" that lead them to respond properly (thoughtfully, sympathetically) to powerful emotions: "the understanding of the being to whom we address ourselves, if he be in a healthful state of association, must necessarily be in some degree enlightened, his taste exalted, and his affections ameliorated" (Wordsworth *Lyrical* 241).

Adam Smith's brief remarks about reading in his *Theory of Moral Sentiments* (1759). In chapter 2, "Of the Pleasure of Mutual Sympathy," Adam Smith argues that when the power of a book has faded for an individual, it regains power when read aloud to a second person, because "we consider all the ideas which it presents rather in the light in which they appear to him, than in that in which they appear to ourselves" (10). The book itself contains no new pleasures until it is shared with a new person. The pleasure of "reading [a book] to a companion" (17) means that reading does not have to be a purely solitary experience. Group reading, and group responses to novels, were more familiar to Victorian readers than to readers today. George Eliot's letters record how readers intervened while waiting for the next installment of a serialized publication, occasionally attempting to change the arc of the story by contacting its author. Such moments could frustrate Eliot, who wanted her novels to direct readers in specific ways of thinking and feeling, occasionally feelings that were more challenging than what they would expect from light or popular reading (Gettleman 25–6). Perhaps the speech-act, an extended monologue by a character that inserts a public moment into an otherwise private reading experience, is one way to reclaim a specific brand of authority from what Leah Price has called her "Over-authoritative fans" (Price, *Anthology* 135; Gettleman 28). The brand of authority Eliot hoped to reclaim is similar to the draw Mr. Tulliver had over his children, her father had over her, or Wordsworth had over the readers of *Lyrical Ballads.* She hopes that she can make them feel, in anticipation of shaping their behavior. To gain this power for herself, she had to detach patriarchal authority from specific patriarchs. It had to become a stance one could present without being a father oneself.

Felix Holt contains Eliot's increased investment in the *idea* of Fatherhood trumping the idiosyncrasies of individual fathers. In this, she seems to intuit much of what John Stuart Mill will suggest in *On Liberty* (1859):

> It is in the case of children that misapplied notions of liberty are a real obstacle to the fulfillment by the State of its duties. One would almost think that a man's children were supposed to be literally, and not metaphorically, a part of himself, so jealous is opinion of the smallest interference of law with his absolute and exclusive control over them ... Consider, for example, the case of education ... Hardly anyone, indeed, will deny that it is one of the most sacred duties of the parents (or, as law and usage now stand, the father), after summoning a human being into the world, to give to that being an education fitting him to perform his part well in life towards others and towards himself. But while this is unanimously declared to be the father's duty, scarcely anybody, in this country, will bear to hear of obliging him to perform it. Instead of his being required to make any exertion or sacrifice for securing education to his child, it is left to his choice to accept it or not when it is provided gratis! ... if the parent does not fulfill this obligation, the state ought to see it fulfilled. (*Spirit of the Age* 123–4)

Mill advises the state to direct fathers in the way that they should go. He advises citizens to reject complete paternal autonomy within systems of education. He holds that some force must exercise the "sacred duty" to educate children, and that "law and usage," the customs that bolster both traditional and legal-rational authority, currently give that role to the father. He bemoans the literalization of the child as part of the father, making it seem to be more of the "slave's share" (Eliot ,*Felix Holt* 289) than anything that the state can impose on the individual. When the role of the father becomes metaphorical, however, anyone, or any group, can step in to play the role when individual fathers falter.[7] As Max Weber states about the familial metaphors that expand more generally to the nation state, "the 'altruistic' concern of the worker for his own family is a typical element of duty contributing to willingness to work generally" (151). Family feeling translates nicely to the smooth functioning of society, as long as it is transmitted outward, with larger duties not being overshadowed by family duties. Instead, family provides the template for national duties. This is Eliot's stance, not only in *Felix Holt*, but also in the increasingly expansive works of her later career. Whereas *Mill on the Floss* "does not even register the life beyond the family except as a violent, inscrutable, and arbitrary set of events" (P. Fisher 540), *Felix Holt* and the novels that follow use family life metaphorically, in hopes of affecting larger life units.

John Stuart Mill ends "Spirit of the Age" at the cusp of the first Reform Bill, announcing its eventual passing as a sign that all the ways in which authority had been figured up to then will change (Mill, *Spirit* 40). *Felix Holt* is set shortly after the passage of the First Reform Act (1832), and was written as interest grew in the Second Reform Act, to be passed in 1867; the novel is steeped in the aims of both acts, and in the strategies employed by proponents and opponents of working class suffrage. The figure of the father comes to symbolize safe reform in that period; the acts added working men to the rolls as voters, in hopes that increased enfranchisement would curb election corruption.[8]. Circulating around both acts was a tendency, in discussions of the working-class man, to focus on the father's obligation to educate his children. Bentham and Mill were among the many Victorian thinkers who called for increased literacy, and Dickens and Trollope were among many who chastised their profligate fathers for failing to provide the proper education for their sons.[9]

As she prepared *Felix Holt*, Eliot studied Henry Fawcett's 1865 *The Economic Position of the English Labourer* and Samuel Bamford's 1842 memoir *Passages from the Life of a Radical* (Eliot, *Letters* 4.208). Fawcett argued that "the labourer's deficits chiefly arose from a want of education (111), and that civil unrest could be avoided through mandatory education for the children of agricultural labourers as well as factory children (112–13). Mandatory education for children would

---

[7]   See Matthew McCormack's *Public Men, Masculinity, and Politics in Modern Britain.*

[8]   See Anna Clark, "Gender, Class, and the Nation: Franchise Reform in England, 1832–1928."

[9]   The Forster Act, or Elementary Education Bill, that made "schooling more widely available for the working classes," appeared in 1870 (Nelson, *Family* 92); it was the culmination of much discourse about the importance of education for disadvantaged classes.

only be possible if the father made a sufficient wage (231). Samuel Bamford was a Middleton weaver whose books, *Early Days* (1849) and *Passages in the Life of a Radical* (1843) are mixtures of autobiography, didactic commentary, and transcripts of speeches. *Early Days* emphasizes Bamford's love of reading and his father's "momentous and ill-advised step" in preventing his pursuit of an academic career (88). *Passages in the Life of a Radical* also foregrounds the crucial role played by the father in the son's education. Bamford argues that "our educators are ... the best reformers" (15), and clarifies that while parents provide the early moral education, it is up to the "schoolmaster" to "finish the intellect" (16). Later, he presents an extended declaration about the working man's duty to family, to emphasize that

> The industrious and poor man best serves his country by doing his duty to family at home;—that he best amends his country by giving it good children, and, if he have not any, by setting a good example himself;—that he best governs by obeying the laws, and by ruling in love and mercy his own little kingdom at home;—that his best reform is that which corrects irregularities on his own hearth. (100).

The following phrase from Wallenstein's lament in Schiller's "The Death of Wallenstein," as translated by Samuel Taylor Coleridge, also found its way from George Eliot's notebooks into the text of *Felix Holt*: "Clothing the palpable & the familiar / With golden exhalations of the dawn" (Schiller 130; Eliot, *Felix* 180). Wallenstein speaks of a trusted friend, now dead, who persuaded by giving touches of the sublime to familiar language. Eliot uses the lines in chapter 16 of *Felix Holt* to draw a distinction between two kinds of reformers: "speakers at reform banquets [who] dwelt on the abolition of all abuses, and millennial blessedness generally" and "others, whose imaginations were less suffused with exhalations of the dawn," and thus "insisted chiefly on the ballot box" (180). The contrast is between a hopelessly idealized use of language and a narrowly pragmatic use of language. They parallel the cynical statements by Johnson, clearly a problematic authority, as he reports Putty's advice about oratory: "there are two ways of speaking an audience will always like: one is, to tell them what they don't understand; and the other is, to tell them what they're used to" (188). Felix, a budding orator, hopes to achieve Putty's end without stooping to Putty's means.

At one of Felix Holt's early speaking engagements, he is preceded by a worker in flannel whose voice was "high and not strong," but with "the fluency and the method of a habitual preacher or lecturer" (288). The worker's speech about the equitable distribution of wealth rejects domestic rhetoric as a threat to real radical change. He says, "[i]t isn't a man's share just to mind your pin-making, or your glass-blowing, and higgle about your own wages, and bring up your family to be ignorant sons of ignorant fathers, and no better prospect; that's a slave's share" (289). This speaker argues that only "slaves" propose a private solution to a public problem. In fact, the man who is content to "mind [his] own pin-making" does his family a disservice, and is indeed failing to assert his masculinity. The speaker calls for a forceful revolution against the "fine gentlemen" who serve as their overseers (289). His vehemence is the kind that could fuel men who are "tired o'jaw" (141) of all sorts. Says one man, Dredge, of talking politics, "It's wriggling work ... I'd as lief hear preaching, on'y there's nought to be got by't" (141). Felix tries a different approach. As foreshadowed by Uncle Lingon's aside early in the novel—"if the mob can't be turned back, a man of family must try and head the mob, and save a few homes and hearths, and keep the country up on its last legs as long as he can" (34) – the quelling of violence hinges on the "man of family." Felix says that the "greatest power under heaven" is "public opinion" (293). He calls it "the steam that is to work the engines" (293). The greatest man, therefore, knows how to act upon the feelings of this powerful public.

Felix thinks, as he plans how he will address the mob, "if he could move the fathers ... if he could move these men to save something from their drink and pay a schoolmaster for their boys, a greater service would be done them than if Mr Garstin and his company were persuaded to establish a school" (130). In hopes of averting the coming crisis and avoiding a working-class revolt, Felix develops the strategy to "lay hold of them by their fatherhood" by "tak[ing] one of their little fellows and set[ting] him in the midst" (130). Felix wants to spur them into conservative action (and, in the short term, to inaction) through reminding them of their status as fathers. "One must begin somewhere" (130), he reflects. Felix doesn't want the children to attend the political rallies unless they are young enough not to "understand what is said" (134). The boys are there for their emotional effect on their fathers, not to gain an uncontrolled, unfiltered education in raw politics. Once the fathers are converted to Felix's way of thinking, it is their job to send their boys to school, telling others to turn the young men into worthy citizens.

As with Eliot's "radical" Felix Holt, Bamford's radicalism looks conservative to a modern eye. Bamford calls for universal suffrage, but seeks to achieve it through the lawful actions of the fathers of families. He adopts as his modus operandi "Hold fast by the laws" (33), the "good and fatherly maxim" (37) of "Major Cartwright, our venerable political father" (33). Bamford dedicates extended passages to the importance of father figures. When he leads a peaceful demonstration, Bamford selects workers who look like the "heads of decent working families" (153). In another chapter, he walks the reader past the threshold of his home. He wants to reader to eavesdrop as his wife and daughter read the Beatitudes together, so that the reader will understand "his heart's treasury," and his authority as a social reformer, through the image of his stable and happy home (68).

Bamford and Fawcett comprised only a small part of Eliot's extensive research for *Felix Holt*. She also consulted *Theatre of the Greeks* by Phillip Wentworth Buckham (d. 1829), and Julius Leopold Klein's *History of Drama* (Eliot, *Journals* 125), perhaps as a guide to staging her scenes in a novel that overflows with dialogue. She also drew on her memory of journalism from the period in which the novel is set, to check facts about the period, but also to gain lessons about style and persuasion:

> My own recollections of [the period] are childish, and of course disjointed, but
> they help illuminate my reading. I went through the Times of 1832–33 at the
> British Museum, to be sure of as many details as I could. It is amazing what
> strong language was used in those days, especially about the church. The Times
> is full of turgid denunciation: "bloated pluralists," "stall-fed dignitaries," etc. are
> the sort of phrases conspicuous in the leaders. There is one passage of prophecy
> which I longed to quote, but I thought it wiser to abstain. (*Letters* 4.248)

George Eliot's forays into *The Times* explore which kinds of language work in which
contexts. Eliot was struck by the lack of artfulness in the paper's "denunciation."

Samuel Bamford had little good to say about the language found in the
Times. He seethed about how the paper turned his involvement with a peaceful
protest into the instigation of a riot. He called their description of him as a play
actor turned patriot "as unfounded as it was absurd" (*Passages* 173–4). In the
debates surrounding the Reform Bill, the *Times* came to be known for its "familiar
contempt for working people," who were often described as little more than a
"mob" (McClelland 76). In *Felix Holt*, Eliot reserves admiration for *The Times* for
her most odious characters. Johnson, who is helping Jermyn, the novel's corrupt
father figure, fix an election in Transome's favor—in other words, engaging in the
very activities that the Reform Act sought to end—praises the language of that
paper. Speaking to Mr. Jermyn about two rival election agents named Makepeace
and Putty, Johnson says:

> as for speaking—it's currently reported in our London circles that Putty writes
> regularly for the "Times." He has that kind of language, and I needn't tell you,
> Mr. Transome, that it's the apex, which I take it, means the tiptop—and nobody
> can get higher than that, I think. (188)

Johnson's lack of fluency and certainty ("I take it ... I think"), as he praises the
supposed fluency and certainty of the paper, transforms the rhetoric of *The Times*,
if not also its conclusions, into negative examples.

In essays such as "Silly Novels by Lady Novelists," Eliot is critical of writers
who give characters artificial dialogue, in a "careful avoidance of the phraseology
as can be heard every day" (449).[10] Eliot entered into a literary environment in
which industrial fiction didn't always aim for perfect verisimilitude in its depiction
of speech across social classes, despite the objective of bridging class divides. As
Joseph Childers points out in *Novel Possibilities*, Elizabeth Gaskell's working-class
characters speak about the middle classes using the language of the middle classes.
Childers cites John Barton's question, "does the rich man share his plenty with me,
as he ought to do, if his religion wasn't a humbug?" (Gaskell, *Mary Barton* 11) as
one key example of how "middle-class Christianity ... has found its way, however
mediated, to the lower classes" (164). Of course, Childers adds, collapsing the

---

[10]   In *Forms of Speech in Victorian Fiction*, Chapman gives several examples of
novelists who signaled rustic language through deviance from standard speech, as in
omitted, aspirate, and misspelled words (2).

linguistic gulf between laborer and professional serves a crucial didactic purpose; these idealistic texts "create the possibility of accessing knowable communities—the communities of the working classes—that were also alien to most of their readers" (130). Eliot also bequeaths her protagonist, Felix Holt, with improbable eloquence, for the same purpose, drawing a middle-class audience into the worker's story. Blackwood wrote of the novel, "it is like looking on at a series of panoramas where human beings speak and act before us. There is hardly a page where there is not some turn of expression, witty or wise or both which one loves to dwell upon" (Eliot, *Letters* 4.243). Blackwood describes the experience of the novel as similar to viewing an image or reading a collection of maxims; characters "speak and act before us," as opposed, presumably, to interacting in a more realistic manner with each other. Eliot anticipates such criticisms within the novel proper. Esther exclaims to Felix, "You should really found a sect. Preaching is your vocation. It is a pity you should ever have an audience of only one" (*Felix Holt* 125). Despite her ultimate conversion to Felix's way of seeing (paving the way for a similar conversion on the part of the reader), Esther is annoyed that Felix plays the part of didact rather than lover. Critical readers found Felix's speech unnatural. R.H. Hutton writes in the June 23, 1866, *Spectator*, "Felix Holt seems a grand *stump* of a character in an impressive but fixed attitude" and "a mutilated statue of massive mould" (in Eliot, *Critical Heritage* 258–9). Henry James writes that "Felix Holt, in the work which bears his name, is little more than an occasional apparition" (16), and is "marked by the same singular rigidity of outline and fixedness of posture which characterized Adam Bede" (H. James, *Portable* 26). Paternal rhetoric, in Eliot's novels, is more palatable when it comes out of the mouths of women.

In *The Reader's Repentance* (1992), Christine Krueger writes of Methodist women preachers that they "address their patriarchal audience" through "the ethos of prophecy and the ethos of simplicity" in order to "sound sincere, but not enthusiastic; simple, but not uninspired" (61). The stance "reflect[s] the complicated relation of women's oratory to the literary tradition" in that "[p]rophecy generally implies an authoritarian, exclusionary discourse" but "women assumed prophetic authority to call for the liberation of silenced voices" (61). Krueger writes that Eliot, "with her range of authorial stances," embodies "the same contradiction" (61). Eliot, whom Henry James figures as, in the end, "conservative" (James, *Views* 36), transfers the patriarch's prophetic utterances to the woman's mouth, but punishes the woman if she wields this power to undermine domestic ideals. Dinah ceases her preaching after she marries Adam Bede. Dorothea emerges from her role as Casaubon's amanuensis, but her philanthropic schemes are mere wifely hobbies by the end of the novel. In *Felix Holt*, Esther's balanced speech on Felix's behalf saves him from conviction at his trial (448, 463). In this speech she demonstrates *her* ability to "lay hold" of men "by their fatherhood" (130). Her speech leads to "stirring of heart in certain just-spirited men and good fathers among them, which had been raised to a high pitch of emotion by Esther's maidenly fervor" (451). Yet she attributes all she knows about persuasion to Felix's father-focused example: "I think I didn't see the meaning of anything fine—I didn't even see the value of my father's character, until I had been taught a little by hearing what Felix Holt said, and seeing that his life was like his words" (418).

Eventually, Eliot decided to continue Felix's domesticating labors outside of the novel. Felix was so appealing to John Blackwood's sensibilities that he recruited Eliot to write a free-standing speech for her character. The resulting "Address to Working Men" provides a concentrated continuation of the novel's message. Blackwood had just heard Benjamin Disraeli speak to workers, and thought that the fictional Felix could do just as well as the soon-to-be prime minister (*Holt* 483). Blackwood was pleased with politics that he thought would "attract all parties," and wrote to his London manager, "Her [Eliot's] sayings would be invaluable in the present debate" (in Eliot, *Letters* 4.247).

In the review "The Natural History of German Life" (1856), Eliot argued that German novelists "fall into the same mistake as our English novelists" in describing rebellions among the lower classes. Despite a lack of sentimentality and "tender affection" in his family, she says, "The peasant never questions the obligation of family-ties—he questions no *custom*" (62). Disraeli also imagined the laborer classes as having naturally traditionalist leanings, but argued, unlike Eliot's description of an automatic or even unconscious adherence to custom, that their conservatism was rooted in positive feeling for the "hereditary" aspects of shared national identity. He said, in an 1872 speech about his support of reform, that the word "Conservative" is used in "its purest and loftiest sense," to show that the working classes "are proud of belonging to a great country, and wish to maintain its greatness ... that they believe, on the whole, that the greatness and the empire of England are to be attributed to the ancient institutions of the land" (Disraeli 4). The working classes were, according to Disraeli, drawn to "the hereditary, the traditionary policy of the Tory party" (7), and thus less of a threat to the nation's stability than some of the men already voting in England's elections. The working classes connected loyalty to their own families with loyalty toward the nation. The reform Disraeli called for limited suffrage to the male heads of families and to male lodgers who paid at least 10 pounds rent per year. The plan for reform designated the man of family as the ideal working-class voter (McClelland 71; St. John 72, 81).[11]

---

[11] Walter Besant's *All Sorts and Conditions of Men* (1882) advocated for culture as a solution, believing that the "palace of delight" will awaken the lower classes' higher natures (Swafford 34). Works such as Chadwick's *Report ... on an Enquiry into the Sanitary Condition of the Labouring Population of Great Britain* (1842) performed similar rhetorical work. Writes Childers, "By ascribing to a 'hand that rocks the cradle' representation of working-class political power, Chadwick and his informants provide the spectre of a potentially depraved, but also potentially tractable, working class" in order to "impose a normalized code of moral conduct upon the working classes ... through the promulgation of the various forms of domestic ideology that abounded within the middle classes" (118). Ironically, the push for male suffrage via the rhetoric of domesticity held back the question of the woman's vote, because it was assumed that the married woman was "virtually represented" by her husband and that the father represented his young, unmarried daughter (McClelland 96).

The politics of *Daniel Deronda* and *Felix Holt* are closer to Disraeli's emphasis on the importance of race and education than one would expect from Eliot's lukewarm reaction to him in early letters. Eliot differed most from Disraeli about his belief in "Young Englandism," which called for more rapid change than Eliot preferred (Cogtugno 125). Disraeli thought that this group would be crucial in lifting up the lower classes; Eliot thought that reform would come from within.[12] She wrote in a February 11, 1848, letter, "Young Englandism is almost as remote from my sympathies as Jacobitism as far as its form is concerned, though I love and respect it as an effort on behalf of the people" (*Letters* 1.245–6). Her creation, Felix Holt, similarly prefers peaceful and gradual change, based in domestic space. In his "Address to Working Men," Felix Holt argues against taking arms against bad national leadership, because a "too hasty wresting of measures which seem to promise an immediate partial relief" would "make a worse time of it for our own generation, and leave a bad inheritance to our children" (487). Learned sympathy and public education are, instead, his preferred method for policing the delicate social organism. Since men "are sufferers by each other's wrong doing; and the children who come after us are and will be sufferers from the same causes" (488), Felix advocates for the slow distribution of power to the working classes, showing a fear of the hasty abuse of new powers. On this point, Helen Rogers reminds us that although "[e]arly nineteenth-century British radicalism tended to assert a virile, pugnacious model of manliness," by the 1830s "radicals increasingly linked men's political and social rights to the fulfillment of their domestic duties" (157). Similarly, Catherine Hall writes in *Civilizing Subjects* that, by the 1830s, "[t]rue manliness ... encompassed the capacity to establish a home, protect it, provide for it and control it"; in other words, "domesticity was integral to masculinity" (27). "True manliness," therefore, is a precondition for the establishment of domesticity.

Within the "Address to Working Men," Holt uses admittedly "old-fashioned" (494) rhetoric that compares the uncontrolled mob to the descendants of a family led by a drunken father. In the process, he separates his enlightened listeners ("we") from the problem ("they"):

> They are the ugly crop that has sprung up while the stewards have been sleeping ... the multiplying brood begotten by parents who have been left without all teaching save that of a too craving body, without all wellbeing save the fading delusions of drugged beer and gin. (*Holt* 492)

"They," the "ugly crop," are not the products of government policy, but of parents who have been "left without all teaching." Felix hopes to contain a contagion that bubbles from below: "We have all to see to it that we do not help to rouse what I may call the savage beast in the breasts of our generation—that we do not help to poison the nation's blood, and make richer provision for bestiality to come" (492–3). Felix's speech conceives of society as a collective ("the common

---

[12]   See Linda K. Robertson, *The Power of Knowledge: George Eliot and Education* (1997).

estate of society" [494]), but does not require a radical redistribution of resources across its households or a collective assumption of responsibility for the failures of particular individuals. Rather, he looks to displace individual desires away from material advancement and toward "the treasures of knowledge," in order to "break the yoke of ignorance" (495).

In this speech, everything rests on poor fathers getting education for their children: "Let us demand from the members of our Unions that they fulfil their duty as parents in this definite matter, which rules can reach. Let us demand that they send their children to school, so as to not go on recklessly breeding a moral pestilence among us" (497). Felix insists on domestic rhetoric in passages such as the following:

> But now, for our own part, we have seriously to consider this outside wisdom which lies in the supreme unalterable nature of things, and watch to give it a home within us and obey it. If the claims of the unendowed multitude of working men hold within them principles which must shape the future, it is not less true that the endowed classes, in their inheritance from the past, hold the precious material without which no worthy, noble future can be moulded. Many of the highest uses of life are in their keeping; and if privilege has often been abused, it also has been the nurse of excellence. (498–9)

Felix Holt asks his listeners to give "outside wisdom" a "home within us," making a public and politicized issue feel private and domestic. The future is a child in this passage, a nebulous being to be "shape[d]" and moulded." Surrounding this discussion of the future, and the knowledge in the keeping of the "endowed classes," are words such as "nature," "home," "within," "inheritance," "life in their keeping," and "nurse." He hopes to inspire the crowd (this time, readers of the published speech), to disperse to separate homes, rather than to take to the streets. The domestic tone reiterates the point of the speech itself, which is to translate a large political crisis into manageable, family-based units. He uses the idea of fatherhood to move fathers, which in itself is a revolutionary take on paternal authority.

The Reverend Rufus Lyon, from the novel proper, would approve. The call to correct the whole through parts resonates with the sermon he prepared early in the novel, as he paced between the "piles" of books on his floor, "so arranged as to leave narrow lanes between them" (52). The words that emerged from his study crammed with books were an attempt to affect the many rather than the few, but by asking them to do exactly what the more radical voices dismissed as "mind[ing] your pin-making ... a slave's share" (289):

> My brethren, do you think that great shout was raised in Israel by each man's waiting to say "amen" till his neighbours had said amen? Do you think there will ever be a great shout for the right—the shout of a nation as of one man, rounded and whole, like the voice of the archangel that bound together all the listeners of earth and heaven—if every Christian of you peeps round to see what his neighbours in good coats are doing, or else puts his hat before his face that he may shout and never be heard? (53)

The irony, of course, is that Lyon's sermon about independence is contained within the walls of his study as he practices his sermon. At this point, he is heard by no one but the servant who interrupts him. The second irony, of which Eliot was well aware, is that the speech for many was contained not only in a lonely study, but also within a novel, likely held by only one reader. The chapter's epigraph, "A pious and painful preacher," announces his crisis of charismatic authority.

The statements of men gain importance because idealistic women—from Dinah to Esther to Romola to Dorothea to Mirah—appropriate the lessons and rebroadcast them in more effective sentimental appeals. Esther initially thinks ill of Felix's "singular directness and simplicity of speech" (368) because "He loved lecturing and opinion too well ever to love any woman" (173). Ultimately, though, she is drawn to him *because* his words are more substantive than the murmurings of a hero from romance. He wins her with ideas normally conveyed by the father figure rather than the lover figure. However, as lover, his paternal words reach her in a way that a real parent's could not. Her adopted father, Rufus Lyon, has lost his power to convince her: "Esther had been so long used to hear the formulas of her father's belief without feeling or understanding them, that they had lost all power to touch her" (265). Early in the novel, the narrator gently chides Rufus Lyon for spinning an entire sermon out of a verse that should signal an ending rather than beginning, "And all the people said, Amen" (53). And, as discussed above, the content of Rufus's sermon is lost to the crowd as he practices it alone in his study. Felix's way of speaking, in contrast, is tied entirely to beginnings rather than endings. He says to Esther, "I am a man who am warned by visions. Those old stories of visions and dreams guiding men have their truth: we are saved by making the future present to ourselves" (262). In this statement about a collective future, Felix quickly moves from the singular "I" to the plural "we," and from realistic dialect to improbable eloquence. He is less of an individual than a spokesperson for a whole class and way of being. He makes his future, which includes marriage and a son, "present" to his listeners by adopting the father stance in anticipation of the father role.

"That Purifying, Restraining Influence": Felix's Afterlife

Eliot's later novels expand upon *Felix Holt*'s conclusions about the metaphorical power of disembodied fatherhood. *Felix Holt* and *Mill on the Floss* emphasize paternal speech and father-provided education, but *Felix Holt* replaces *Mill's* pessimism with optimism. *Middlemarch* (1871–2) shares the preoccupations of both novels. *Middlemarch* opens under the assumption that "the disappointed father held a strong lever" (568), as Mr. Vincy fears that his son has thrown away the education he provided for him. Fred Vincy's life is determined by his biological father's lack of faith in him, but then by a surrogate father's faith. Eliot allows Fred Vincy to achieve what Tom Tulliver wanted, but through the influence of someone else's father, rather than his own. Caleb Garth begins to train Fred Vincy for a career on the land rather than in a city or library. Unlike Tom Tulliver,

Caleb Garth, the most heroic of Eliot's biological fathers, and widely thought to be based on Eliot's own father, has a knack for finding the right words, as evidenced when he had to break up a fight between workers and railway agents (559–60). Garth's "talents did not lie in finding phrases" (402), and, like Mr. Tulliver, "[i]t always seemed to him that words were the hardest part of 'business'" (338). Yet when Caleb needed to exert his influence, again to encourage men to be calm and rational, "perhaps the greatest orator could not have chosen either his pause or his images better for the occasion" (560).

Middlemarch's orphaned Dorothea Brooke seeks a second father in Causabon and redirects her philanthropic energies upon marriage. The father figure's role as educator becomes unsettling within *Middlemarch*. A delusional Dorothea thinks that "the really delightful marriage must be that where your husband was a sort of father, and could teach you even Hebrew, if you wished it" (10). Dorothea is initially attracted to Causabon because he embodies the wider education denied to the fatherless heroine. He is like a walking lecture: "in talking to her he presented all his performance and intention with the reflected confidence of the pedagogue" (86). Dorothea asks if she can "learn to read Latin and Greek aloud to you, as Milton's daughters did to their father, without understanding what they read?" and, just when Causabon reminds her that they rebelled, she calls them "very naughty girls" who should "have been proud to minister to such a father" (64). Eliot's narrator looks on an abstract faith in an embodied literary patriarch with skepticism, and redirects her heroine toward a man more worthy of her devotion.

From *Mill on the Floss* to *Felix Holt*, Eliot moves away from the embodied father as a negative model for the son, to the absent father as a positive spur. Eliot's appeal to the idea of fatherhood as the key to England's future underlies *Daniel Deronda* (1876) and her final work, *Impressions of Theophrastus Such* (1879). *Daniel Deronda* reflects Eliot's "sense of there being a cultural and spiritual *investment* in, as well as a natural mandate for, the differentiation of sex roles, historically institutionalized in the patriarchal family" (Linehan 336). The Ruskinian point of view in *Daniel Deronda* is exemplified by the conversation between Gwendolen and Deronda about her gambling in which she asks, "But why should you regret it more because I am a woman?" and Deronda responds, "Perhaps because we need that you should be better than we are" (337). *Deronda* proposes that women who rupture family lines must be punished. Using the Jewish patriarchal tradition backed by history and spiritual laws, Eliot hopes to apply a sense of "sacredness" to the English sense of family.[13] Eliot's revisionist project is reflected in the epitaph of Chapter 35:

---

[13] In *Realist Vision*, Peter Brooks presents the possibility that *Daniel Deronda*, unlike the typical father/son focus of many nineteenth-century novels, uses the "matriarchy" of Jewishness (107). I argue that the father is more useful as symbol in *Deronda* than the mother, perhaps because of this very orientation toward the embodied mother. The moral *critiques* in the novel are leveled toward mothers; the positively programmatic statements are phrased in terms of fathers and sons.

[W]hoso wins in this devil's game must needs be baser, more cruel, more brutal than the order of this planet will allow for the multitude born of woman, the most of these carrying a form of conscience ... that hindereth from the prize of serene wickedness, itself difficult of maintenance in our composite flesh. (403)

Here, Eliot adopts the diction of the Bible in what may as well be a new "commandment" for the English people. Given the threat posed by privileging feminist concerns, Eliot paints the patriarchal side of Judaism as the ideal. As Mordecai says, "A Jewish man is bound to thank God, day by day, that he was not made a woman; but a woman has to thank God that He has made her according to His will. And we all know what He has made her—a child-bearing, tender-hearted thing is the woman of our people" (575). This statement is simple and idealized, as is the character who delivers it, but the sentiment seems to be what Eliot is advocating in the Jewish section of the novel.[14] When the narrator quotes the words of a Rabbi who said, "The Omnipresent ... is occupied in making marriages," the moral implications of the word "marriage" become broad in their scope, because "by marriages the speaker meant all the wondrous combinations of the universe whose issue makes our good and evil" (743).

Eliot broached "the Woman question" with reluctance, for, writes Rosemarie Bodenheimer, "she did not wish to confront in public the difference between her ideological commitment to the idea that men and women have naturally distinct spheres of influence and her own gender-crossing career" (177). In a May 1867 letter to acquaintance John Morley, Eliot says in continuation of a dinner debate, "I repeat that I do not trust very confidently to my own impressions on this subject. The peculiarities of my own lot have caused me to have idiosyncrasies rather than an average judgment" (*Letters* 4.364). In the letter Eliot does not specifically explain what makes her case different from that of other women, noting only that human evolution's goal was a "more clearly discerned distinction of function" between men and women "allowing always for exceptional cases of individual organization" (4.364). In discussing "function," she alludes to the natural responsibility to bear and raise children. She includes herself as an "exceptional" case, perhaps because of her own dedication to improving the world through her art or perhaps because of her dutiful service to her father after her mother's death. Overall, though, it seems that the "rearing" of a nation was one that, for Eliot, overrode considerations of personal ambition in all but a few situations. If Eliot was reluctant to go into specifics in her public statements, her novels allow her freedom to advocate this position—to present through an "other" what she may have been reluctant to say explicitly (Bodenheimer 178).

---

[14]   Henleigh Grandcourt, his abandoned mistress, and Gwendolen, a woman who lacks maternal instincts, dominate the "English" section of the novel. Gwendolen marries Grandcourt despite knowing that she would disinherit Lydia Glasher's illegitimate children with Grandcourt were she to produce an heir. Grandcourt therefore joins Godfrey Cass and Arthur Donnithorne as extreme negative examples of fatherhood. Gwendolen's guilt leads her, she thinks, to successfully will Grandcourt's death by drowning.

Leonora Halm-Eberstein ("Alcharisi"), *Deronda's* artist and woman who has failed in her duties on both fronts, comes to represent the greatest threat to the healthy feelings of duty necessary for a strong nation composed of strong families. She says to Daniel, "I know very well what love makes of men and women—it is subjection. It takes another for a larger self, enclosing this one ... I was never willingly subject to any man. Men have been subject to me," to which he replies, with a "grave, sad sense of his mother's privation," "Perhaps the man who was subject was the happier of the two" (*Deronda* 666). She becomes an object of pity rather than empowerment in her son's eyes. The novel encourages its readers to pity Alcharisi, but to also see the poetic justice within the novel's punishment of her. Alcharisi becomes the counterpoint of Gwendolen, the other woman rejected by Daniel, because of her unhealthy relationship with patriarchy. As S.L. Goldberg writes of both women's attempts to defend themselves: "Each speech ... expresses a variant of the *other* woman's state of soul, so that when Gwendolen's cry comes near the end of the book it brings us to think of both women in the one thought: the one who had all too much father, and the other who had all too little" (146). These interlocking narratives announce the insufficiency of the embodied father, returning Eliot to a portion of her concerns in *Adam Bede* and *Mill on the Floss*. However, the turn to the *idea* of fatherhood is Eliot's new solution. The turn is modeled by Daniel in his interactions with his lost father and embodied mother. Although Daniel's mother has lost her "faith" in family, "To Daniel the words Father and Mother had the altar-fire in them" (*Deronda* 469). The act of holding a letter from his mother is a "sacramental moment" (613). Daniel calls the disillusionment of parting with his mother "a disappointed pilgrimage to a shrine where there were no longer the symbols of sacredness" (660). As with *Felix Holt*, *Daniel Deronda* evokes a simpler time when the bodies of the parent recalled duty, but takes comfort in the continued force of the "words."

Even Eliot, in her proposal of a moral system that seems to return to a valuation of patriarchy, allows the other side of the woman question to peek through. Just as she allows the creation of "defective" Jewish characters to contrast with her Jewish "heroes"—for every Mirah there is an Alcharisi, for every Daniel there is a Lapidoth—Eliot surely allows criticisms of female oppression to appear even while advocating for the Jewish version of a benevolent patriarchal society (Linehan 343). Even Mirah, throughout described as the ideal female with the impossibly tiny feet, displays flashes of feminism (Meyer 742). On the one hand, Eliot presents a Mirah who responds with surprise to the question of why women must sit apart from men in services (*Deronda* 362); on the other hand, a desire for independence of feeling emerges when Mirah speaks of why she is not perfect. Describing her friendships with kind Gentiles, Mirah says:

> I think my mother was strict; but she could never want me not to like those who are better to me than any of my own people I have ever known. I think I could obey in other things that she wished, but not in that ... I remember a play I read in German ... where the heroine says something like that. (370–71)

As Daniel points out, the play to which Mirah refers is *Antigone*, a classical example of a woman caught between two opposing systems of morality and duty, one of family and one of state. Antigone sacrifices herself for her brother just as Maggie Tulliver did, and ends up teaching her father something about duty. The allusion implies that Mirah's moral choice is similarly difficult and painful, yet necessary. Mirah is only willing to rebel against the state in the service of the family unit. Mirah's father was a teacher who failed her once he became an actor and decided to use his daughter's and his own voice for profit (*Deronda* 214). But rather than discount him completely, she restores her sense of duty through surrogate patriarchs (brother and husband), through dreams of an absent mother, and through allegiance to a faith and nation. She recuperates duty by translating "father" into "fatherland."

Eliot's first narrator struck readers as "a clergyman—a Cambridge man ... the father of a family— ... a man who had seen a great deal of society etc. etc." (Pinion 106). Eliot's final narrator, Theophrastus, is a London bachelor who is the "author of a book you have probably not seen" (6). Thus, any authority he has comes from somewhere other than fatherhood or authorship. The name Theophrastus harkens back to the student and successor of Aristotle (and thus to an impressive intellectual pedigree), and the name means "Spoken by God." Theophrastus' sketches become manifestoes for the preservation of England. As he expresses in "The Modern Hep! Hep! Hep!," which follows Eliot's great epic of duty to family, *Daniel Deronda*, much as the "Address to Working Men" followed *Felix Holt*,

> Whether we accept the canonical Hebrew books as a revelation or simply as part of an ancient literature, makes no difference to the fact that we find there ... a people taught by many concurrent influences to identify faithfulness to its national traditions with the highest social and religious blessings. (*Impressions* 149)

This class consciousness and national consciousness is tied to minds that think in family terms. In "The Modern Hep! Hep! Hep!" her narrator says of the lessons one can draw from Judaism, "An individual man, to be harmoniously great, must belong to a nation of this order, if not in actual existence yet existing in the past, in memory, as a departed, invisible, beloved ideal, once a reality, and perhaps to be restored" (*Impressions* 147).

In the "Looking Backward" chapter within *Impressions of Theophrastus Such*, Eliot's narrator writes about his father, a country parson in the time of William Wordsworth and Sir Walter Scott (18). He idealizes the pre-Victorian past, describing his "father's England" as "lovable, laudable, full of good men" (23). Yet, he claims, his father's generation lacked "the large sympathetic knowledge of human experience which comes from contact with various classes on their own level" (19). Theophrastus's romantic idealization of his "father's England" clashes with his critique of the "social ignorance" (19) of his father's time. Theophrastus's condition reveals what theorists of satire and sentiment already know, that "the conservative and the revolutionary are more akin then they may realize. The conservative wants to conserve the best of tradition, the radical or revolutionary wants to return to the *roots* to find a purity that has been corrupted" (Griffin 149). Conservatives and Radicals both operate by "looking backward." As do, in many cases, the most effective writers. Theophrastus is aware that he has swerved away from real men and real lives into concepts and ideals, but this is all the better to offer his audience the most effective, and affecting, vision. He writes in the same essay:

> the illusions that began for us, when we were less acquainted with evil have not lost their value when we discern them to be illusions. They feed the ideal Better, and in loving them still, we strengthen the precious habit of loving something not visibly, tangibly existent, but a spiritual product of our visual tangible selves. (26)

The ideals that individuals come to embrace, he argues within his series of essayistic monologues, are, in a way, our own children. The ideals become symbols of what is otherwise only tangible during one limited lifetime. Abstraction allows a writer to transcend the limitations of corporeal inheritances.

Eliot's "radical" family-based conservatism in *Felix Holt* takes her back to the thoughts of 18th century philosopher David Hume. In book 3, part 1, section 1 of his *Treatise of Human Nature* (1739–1740), entitled "Moral Distinctions Not Derived from Reason," Hume rejects human reason as the sole engine of moral action. In one passage, he uses the example of honoring one's parents, and the crime of parricide, to prove his point, drawing on Eliot's favorite metaphor for moral development, the natural or unnatural growth of plants. He argues that "of all crimes that human creatures are capable of committing, the most horrid and unnatural is ingratitude, especially when it is committed against parents" (466), but claims that we cannot reason ourselves to that conclusion, only feel our way to it. The overly rational will take the natural world as a literal, rather than figurative, model, and conclude that parricide is not a crime after all:

> To put the affair, therefore, to this trial, let us chuse any inanimate object, such as an oak or elm; and let us suppose, that by the dropping of its seed, it produces a sapling below it, which springing up by degrees, at last overtops and destroys the parent tree: I ask, if in this instance there be wanting any relation, which is discoverable in parricide or ingratitude? Is not the one tree the cause of the other's existence; and the latter the cause of the destruction of the former, in the same manner as when a child murders his parent? (466–7)

This is Hume's most powerful negative argument in the section. Hume's most powerful positive argument depends on an appeal to feeling rather than to reason. In trying to explain how man knows vice when he sees it, Hume concludes: "The vice entirely escapes you, as long as you consider the object. You never can find it, till you turn your reflexion into your own breast, and find a sentiment of disapprobation, which arises in you, towards this action. Here is a matter of fact; but 'tis the object of feeling, not of reason" (468–9) Hume asks each individual to be his own moral compass, in a passage more powerful than Rufus Lyon's sermon ("My brethren, do you think that great shout was raised in Israel by each man's waiting to say "amen" till his neighbours had said amen?" [53]), but offering a similar suggestion. A moral sense that comes from feeling more than thinking, leads one to honor one's father, but rely on oneself.

In almost uncountable examples within her works, Eliot mirrors Hume's metaphor, reminding us that the cliché of the "family tree" has many roots and branches. She adheres to Hume's imperative, however, by looking to nature metaphorically rather than literally. In "The National History of German Life," to prove that "there is an analogous relation between the moral tendencies of men and the social conditions they have inherited," she discusses the importance of letting the "roots" of the past "remain undisturbed while the process of development is going on, until that perfect ripeness of the seed which carries with it a life independent of the root" (70). To chastise the selfish Hetty in *Adam Bede* for her disregard for "her second parents – of the children she had helped to tend—of any youthful companion, any pet animal, any relic of her own childhood," the narrator simply says "There are some plants that have hardly any roots" (154). In *Daniel Deronda*, during the conversation between the "genial and rational" Gideon and the Zionist Mordecai, Gideon calls for the kind of reasoning Hume abhorred, as a rationale for separating modern-day Jews to Judah and Palestine: "It's no use fighting against facts. We must look where they point; that's what I call rationality" (534). Mordecai, who draws his moral compass from dedication to his family and his race, compares Gideon's reasoning to making a pike staff, "You pluck it up by the roots, strip off the leaves and bark, shave off the knots, and smooth it at top and bottom; put it where you will, it will do no harm, it will never sprout" (534). Chapter 7 of "Janet's Repentance" from *Scenes of Clerical Life* (1858) announces the difficulty of "kill[ing] the deep-down fibrous roots of human love and goodness" (245). And, of course, the metaphor reappears in *The Mill on the Floss*, where the narrator rejects the rational discarding old roots and branches, saying that fondness for "an elderberry bush overhanging the confused leafage of a hedgerow bank" is "an entirely unjustifiable preference to a landscape-gardener, or to any of those severely regulated minds who are free from the weakness of any attachment that does not rest on a demonstrable superiority of qualities" (152). Yet, the narrator argues:

> there is no better reason for preferring this elderberry bush than that it stirs an early memory—that it is no novelty in my life, speaking to me merely through my present sensibilities to form and colour, but the long companion of my existence, that wove itself into my joys when joys were vivid. (152)

Eliot's elderberry bush is valuable, not in itself, but in the human feelings and human memories that one consciousness has connected to it. Rootedness of all kinds leads to right feeling and right action, and right feeling and right action lead one not to parricide, but to a renewed admiration for the idea of fatherhood.

The end of *Felix Holt* echoes Hume's most famous hypothesis, his claim in the same section of the *Treatise of Human Nature* that there should be no connection in moral systems between "is, and is not," and "an ought, or an ought not" (469)—

in other words, that "the distinction of vice and virtue is not founded merely on the relations of objects, nor is perceived by reason" (470). Eliot's novel ends, "There is a young Felix, who has a great deal more science than his father, but not much more money" (428). We get the sense that the second Felix's relationship to the first will not involve substantial material advancement, even though Felix has done his duty in providing his son with education. But perhaps this is the wrong measure of a man after all. Eliot's project for working-class England prefers preservation to advancement, including preservation of both the economic and moral status of the working classes even as they progress in intellect. Describing what *Felix Holt* does for the conventions of descriptive representation, Catherine Gallagher writes in *The Industrial Reformation of English Fiction* that Eliot no longer believes, by the time of *Felix Holt*, "that the 'ought' can grow out of the 'is,' in literature any more than in politics" (224). Yet, in this final sentence, we do find an "ought" within the "is"—"there is a young Felix," and his social similarity to his father is as it should be. Interestingly, Eliot's treatise in favor of the idea of fatherhood ends with a literal father and son. Yet, the relationship is most important as a symbol—a symbol of the domesticated "radical." The man whose well-chosen words discouraged violent social uprising becomes an embodiment of his family-based conservative rhetoric.

One has to wait for the very end of *Felix Holt* to find a father-son relationship that is both biologically and economically positive. The relation between Harold Transome and his subhuman son Harry presents anxiety about race-mixing and its implications for the health of nations. His son was conceived with an Eastern slave because Harry disliked the English woman's "transition from the feeble animal to the thinking being" (16). Since he was conceived *against* the "future," it is no surprise that the "savage" (95) boy bites his grandmother and replaces language with "trotting feet" and "puppy-like noises" (457). Harry and his son embody the threat of *excessive* feeling—sensuality and hedonism leading to the decline of the English race. Esther and Felix, in the idea-based romance between the girl and the man who "should really found a sect" and should never "have an audience of only one" (125), become the antidote. In taking in an orphan named Job, Felix draws attention to moral responsibility and cycle. He suggests that biological fatherhood has moral weight only when it is linked to ideals of duty—when the relationships enact Eliot's preferred modes of sympathy. Esther learns of her birth father and her ties to the Transome fortune, but renounces the connection, and rejects her own chance for material advancement, on moral grounds (361). The brand of fatherhood she embraces instead relegates it to a rhetorical device. Rufus Lyon does not want to tell Esther that he is not her biological father because "he had not the courage to renounce that hold on her tenderness which the belief in his natural fatherhood must help to give him" (79). He is, of course, wrong, as Esther's life-long connection with Rufus Lyon, as with Eppie's to her adopted father in *Silas Marner*, presents the word "father" as a matter of feeling.

PART III
Legal-Rational Authority

"... and, finally, worldly power"

Chapter 5
Samuel Butler at the Museum

As we transition from the father's charismatic authority, which depends on his personal attributes, to the legal-rational authority emerging from his position as an "official," or as part of a bureaucratic structure, let us take a final glimpse of the father at prayer. Samuel Butler's famous painting, *Family Prayers* (1864), depicts a father holding a book in a quiet drawing room, surrounded by his apathetic household. Here, the book—in this case the Bible—is not competing with other texts, but is unsuccessfully competing for the attention of the people in the room. The painting is in the "naïve or primitive style" (Shaffer 39) that Butler saw as an escape from the exacting professional instruction he received as a burgeoning painter. He wrote on the top of the image, in pencil, "I did this in 1864 and if I had gone on doing things out of my own head instead of making studies, I should have been all right" (qtd. in Shaffer 39). Butler sees *Family Prayers* as an original creation, despite taking his own family as its source material. The 1864 image is later "captioned" by Chapter 23 of *The Way of All Flesh* (1903).

Butler's first editor deleted the following lines from the novel: "How is it, I wonder, that all religious officials from God the Father to the parish beadle shall be so arbitrary and exacting?" (qtd. in Shaffer 41). The omitted lines turn Mill's second category, "the power of addressing mankind in the name of religion" (Mill, *Spirit* 27) toward his third, "worldly power" (27). Mill argues that for Protestant denominations, the power of the minister is closer to the legal-rational than the charismatic in any case: "in the Protestant sects, you resorted to the teacher, because you had already decided, or because it had been decided for you, that you would adopt his religion" (36). So, the Protestant minister gains his power from a congregation's acceptance of the church's creeds, rather than from his individual influence over the hearts of the people. His power is therefore easily usurpable, writes Mill: "Every head of a family, even of the lowest rank, in Scotland, is a theologian," and that "[w]hat I have said of the Scottish church, may be said of all Protestant churches, except state churches" (36). In "state religions" the minister's power is what Mill calls "worldly" and what Weber would later call legal-rational: "your creed was chosen by for you by your worldly superiors, and you were instigated by conscience, or, it may be, urged by motives of a more worldly nature, to resort for religious instruction in the minister of their appointment" (36).

Samuel Butler confirms the impression that what is initially perceived as charismatic authority may be "worldly power" in disguise, in the scene from his posthumously published novel that reproduces his 1864 painting. This patriarch leads his household in family prayer after having beaten and then banished his son, a toddler, for his inability to pronounce the word "come" correctly. The narrator, a family friend, remembers the scene this way: "they filed in. First Christina's maid, then the cook, then the housemaid, then William, and then the coachman. I sat opposite them, and watched their faces … They were nice people, but more absolute vacancy I never saw upon the countenances of Human Beings" (110–11). The father's "job," as amateur theologian, is to reach many others of diverse rank, from maid to cook to heir apparent. Yet they all respond mechanically to his mechanical exercise. In his notebooks Butler imagines his father as a machine with a specific purpose: "A bad sleeper should have a phonograph to lull him to rest by preaching, we will say, my father's sermons. If I survive my father I will keep some of his sermons for this purpose. The machine should be placed on a high shelf to imitate a pulpit" (*Notebooks*, ed. Breuer 266).[1] In another entry, under the heading "Titles for Unwritten Articles," Butler proposes his own book of "Family Prayers" that will offer "A series of perfectly plain and sensible ones asking for what people really do want without any kind of humbug" (*Notebooks*, ed. Festing-Jones 231).

The narrator of *The Way of All Flesh* chuckles at Theobald's prayer that his family becomes "truly honest and conscientious" (112), and his mind wanders to an analogous event he witnessed—swarms of bees trying to pull nectar from wallpaper flowers (112). In the narrator's eyes, Theobald's household becomes like those hopeless bees, trying to draw nourishment from a flat image. The novel follows Ernest as he begins to realize that his father's power over the household is as illusory as the wallpaper flowers. *The Way of All Flesh*, according to Susan Haack's study of it as concerned with "intellectual integrity," requires "thinking about the role of the will in belief and pseudo-belief; and about the differences between inquiry and advocacy, and what happens when the two are blurred" (Haack 363). Ernest learns that the poor preacher is a cousin to the poor scholar, and that "pseudo-belief and pseudo-inquiry are ubiquitous" (367).

Butler's notebooks begin with a request that readers disconnect his books from the people who gave him life: "These are the sayings of me Samuel Butler and of my friends—the prophecyings which my mother did not teach me at all, nor my father, nor any of my uncles and aunts, but altogether otherwise" (*Notebooks*, ed. Breuer 56). Yet the same notebooks, which were carefully edited over several years and intended for publication, are full of reflections about his father. One of the most effusive entries, titled "My Father and Myself," embodies the struggle between fascination and aversion:

> He never liked me, nor I him: from my earliest recollections I can call to mind no time when I did not fear him and dislike him; over and over again I have relented towards him, and said to myself that he was a good fellow after all; but I had hardly done so when he would go from me in some way or other which soured

---

[1] In this chapter, I draw from three different editions of Samuel Butler's notebooks, which all contain different extracts in different orders. I distinguish between the volume edited by Henry Festing-Jones (1917) and that edited by Hans Peter-Breuer (1984), by indicating the editor's last name within the parenthetical citation. The third edition, edited by A.T. Bartholomew, I note using the first word of its title, *Further Extracts from the Notebooks of Samuel Butler* (1934).

me again … There can be no real peace and contentment for me until either he or I are there where the wicked cease from troubling. An unkind fate never threw two men together who were more naturally uncongenial than my father and myself. (*Notebooks*, ed. Breuer 231–2)

Butler was dependent on his father for income, and desirous of his father's approval. He was also certain that he would never gain that approval in his lifetime. Countless critics argue that this struggle permeated all of his writings. "As Butler imposed his own pattern on the outside world so he imposed a pattern on the life within him," Malcolm Muggeridge writes, "He hated his father, and therefore fatherhood was hateful. It was the Law that sons should hate fathers and fathers sons" (xiii). My goal in this chapter is to complicate this vision. Butler built his literary and intellectual legacies with the ashes of the patriarch scorched in his writings. He hated his father, but loved that his father fueled his writing, both logistically and personally. Parents ensure that the children can find their own callings in the secular spaces of the world. Butler was aware that so much of what a man is relates to what he does. His escape from "the professional treadmill first by becoming a sheepherder … and then by returning to England to study painting" was financed by his father (Jeffers 84). Ernest, similarly, need only dabble in a profession—tailoring—until his father's wealth saves him (84). Butler and Ernest's greatest conflicts with their fathers come from the father's role in suggesting, or rather, imposing, a career path. Samuel Butler, unlike his protagonist Ernest Pontifex, refuses his father's plan, does not become a minister, never marries, and never fathers a child. Yet his writing never escaped his father's influence. Butler earns enough money raising sheep, painting, and writing to subsist until his father dies and he inherits his fortune. Butler's belief about a parent's duty, writes Thomas Jeffers, drawing from Butler's final novel and from his notebooks, is that "Parents should give their children lots of money, or if no large legacy can be brought together, give them the sort of training that will put them in the way of making money for themselves" (93). The father, therefore, is the source and fount of what John Stuart Mill calls "worldly power" and what Weber calls "legal-rational" authority.[2]

"Legal-rational Authority," as Max Weber imagines it, is the authority of the bureaucrat as opposed to that of the king or the priest (Spencer 125). Thus, it is the least mystical, and most modern, of his three forms of authority. It is also the most "worldly." This mode of authority depends on the laws, codified in official documents, and on individuals charged with promoting official rules performing their professional duties. Since the laws governing parenting in Victorian Britain were oriented toward the husband, it seems that paternal authority would blossom

---

[2]   Samuel Smiles presents more idealism than either Mill or Butler in the role money plays in the wielding of authority. Speaking strategically to a potentially working-class audience, he writes, "The power of money is on the whole over-estimated. The greatest things which have been done for the world have not been accomplished by rich men, or by subscription lists, but by men generally of small pecuniary means" (305).

within a category that depends on codified rules. In the Victorian period, children were the legal property of their fathers. The 1839 Custody of Infants Act merely allowed a woman "of good character" "access to her young children and, potentially (although it was unlikely) temporary custody of children under seven years of age" (Berry 99). An 1873 revision allowed for temporary custody of children under the age of 16 (99–100), but it was not until the Guardianship of Infants Act in 1886 that the mother became the default caregiver after a father's death. Even then, her rights could be stripped if there were any "question concerning her suitability" (100).

Yet, as has been noted by several scholars of Victorian jurisprudence, and scholars studying the increasing "feminization" of some professions during the period, institutions and laws can also test paternal authority. Monica Cohen analyzes the tendency in Victorian novels to "unveil domesticity as an elected vocation" (7), thus not excluding women from discourses related to professionalization. Indeed, in works by Dickens, Eliot, and Brontë, as well as in the larger social conversation, "home emerges as an occasion for serious and often divisive discussions about how society should be organized, managed and reformed" (71). Although the "monarch as father" model had eroded with the same speed as "monarch as god," Herbert Spencer, writing in 1859, could still, "with an almost casual familiarity, lin[k] the welfare of the individual family with that of all society" in his essay "What Knowledge is of Most Worth?" (Berry 1). On the other hand, domestic legal disputes were increasingly subject to "endless fascination and comment in newspapers, periodicals, and novels, a circumstance that worked to disseminate knowledge of contractual complexity widely throughout Victorian society and culture" (Finn 165). The home became "increasingly subject to such diverse and evolving authority as the educational and legal systems, the medical establishment, and the apparatus of social welfare" (Berry 2). Margot Finn writes of the fall and subsequent rise of the family as a legal unit, the fall during the "mid-Victorian triumph of contractual individualism," and the later "reassertion of collective values and social rights with the emergence of the early welfare state" (159).

In Chapter 4, I discussed how George Eliot and her contemporaries figured the rise of print as a potential crisis for paternal authority, as knowledge that once passed from father to child could now be acquired by the child without the father's help. Butler voices a similar suggestion in the journal entry "On Trail and Writing," saying that "[b]efore the invention of writing the range of one man's influence over another was limited to the range of sight, sound and scent; besides this there was trail, of many kinds" (*Notebooks*, ed. Festing-Jones 92). Although literal trails were "unintentionally left," literature becomes a trail "left intentionally" (92). Literature contains "that power of extending men's influence over one another," and thus enabled "the development of modern civilization" (92). The bindings imposed by documents are not comfortably accepted by the "enfant terrible" (182), unless, as I will discuss, he composed the documents himself. Moreover, Butler writes, playfully, of "The Law," that formal and informal rules can bind one equally tightly:

> The written law is binding, but the unwritten law is much more so. You may break the written law at a pinch and on the sly of you can, but the unwritten law—which often comprises the written—must not be broken. Not being written, it is not always easy to know what that is, but this has got to be done. (91)

Butler writes as a man who is increasingly frustrated with the conventions that surround him, in and outside of literature. But, as so many of the offspring have realized, and as I describe in the other chapters of this book, it is difficult to write one's way out of a system of power when one's own writing draws from the same vocabulary.

Elizabeth Gaskell and George Meredith considered fathers who attempted to gain authority *as* writers and editors, while George Eliot and William Makepeace Thackeray connected patriarchal power with charisma, as displayed in persuasive speech and *supported* by documents. Samuel Butler, however, begins to see fathering and writing as professions with parallel structures, but opposed in that the energy required for one is usurped by the other. Butler characterizes fathering as the more difficult job of the two. He writes in his notebooks that "the man who has educated one child, and done him fairly well from first to last, has done a harder thing than writing all my books put together" (*Further* 200). Prolific authorship seemed to be easier than effective fathering, although both enterprises have the same goals of self-preservation.[3] Butler writes elsewhere, "Bodily offspring I do not leave, but mental offspring I do," joking, "Well, my books do not have to be sent to school and college and then insist on going into the Church or take to drinking or marrying their mother's maid" (*Notebooks*, ed. Festing-Jones 373). Books, then, seem to respond to their makers with more obedience than do living children. Elsewhere, however, he is less sure about his control over his mental offspring, writing in the entry "My Books" as if they are made of organic, changeable, material, just as with bodily offspring: "I never make them: they grow; they come to me and insist on being written, and on being such and such ... as I did like the subjects and the books came and said they were to be written, I grumbled a little and wrote them" (102).[4] Butler figured writing as a way for a childless bachelor to create a lasting lineage for himself, and, as I will discuss, saw his own writing as a way to counter his father's influence. Yet his overt presentation of his writing as opposed to his father belies an obsession with understanding the one via the other.

---

[3]   He voices this explicitly in another entry: "If the literary offspring is not to die young, almost as much trouble must be taken with it as with the bringing up of a physical child. Still, the physical child is the harder work of the two" (*Notebooks*, ed. Festing-Jones 103).

[4]   This entry bears a striking resemblance to the entry "My Son" (*Notebooks*, ed. Festing-Jones 373) that I discuss at length later in the chapter. In the latter passage, Butler imagines an argument between himself and an unborn child about whether or not the son should be conceived. His books insisted on birth, and so they were born, but a biological son fails to make enough of a compelling case to be worth the aggravation.

In confronting an increasingly bureaucratic world, Butler figured himself as a rule breaker and dissenter. "I am the enfant terrible of literature and science," he announces in his notebook entries, "If I cannot, and I know I cannot, get the literary and scientific big-wigs to give me a shilling, I can, and I know I can, heave bricks in the middle of them" (*Notebooks*, ed. Festing-Jones 182). This chapter is divided into sections based on these two major battles with "big-wigs." The first section, "Greetings from 'Block B,'" unfolds the British museum reading room as a site for his attempts to understand literary inheritance. The second section, "The Science of Disinheritance," discusses how his ambivalent relationship with the Reading Room plays out in his thoughts about natural history and memory. The two targets of his bricks, literature and science, have fatherhood in common. He understands writing within a literary tradition in terms of dictatorial fathers and rebellious sons, and repeatedly describes his books as his own wayward children. In his writing about science, the connections between ancestors and offspring that are resisted in other contexts are embraced, as, I will argue, a radical method of subordinating fathers in favor of more distant ancestors, and promoting a narrative in which offspring inevitably improve upon parents.

The museum becomes Butler's controlling image. In his frequent visits to the British Library Reading Room (three mornings a week, starting in 1877), Butler would always sit in block "B," as if he wanted to place himself properly within the collection. He would surround himself with ideas that were, sometimes literally, related to him (Raby 162), yet his primary action within the Reading Room was writing, rather than reading. The tension in Butler between a desire for connection and a desire for independence appears in his science writing, as he embraces Lamarckian inheritance as a form of radical disinheritance. It appears in his research tasks, as he translates the Odyssey and rejects received stories about its authorship. It appears in his fiction, which draws heavily on his own family while denying that it does so. This chapter attempts for Butler's writing what he attempted for his life—to understand how a man claims, and loses, his professional authority, as intellectual inheritances simultaneously shake him and shape him.

Greetings from "Block B": Butler and Literary Inheritance

It is a commonplace, in contemporary assessments of Butler, to see "hate in every reference Butler makes to his childhood" (Muggeridge 9) and to call his final novel "the most devastating and relentless literary assault by a son upon a father ever written" (Daniels 11). Was the assault fully successful? Did Butler successfully erase his father, or did antipathy reinforce, or even duplicate, his brand of influence? Butler's failure to find an audience started with his own family. His sister May is the only person in his family who read all of his books (*Correspondence* 25). His father limited his reading to Butler's first publication, *A First Year in Canterbury Settlement* (1863). The memoir as self-help tome was his father's idea, and his father composed the Preface. Butler later wrests his New Zealand experiences out of his father's hands by using them as the backdrop for his mock utopian narrative *Erewhon*.[5] Textual battles recur across Butler's oeuvre. When collecting his letters for publication, Butler added angry annotations to the letters from his father. Comments such as "Whoever said it was? S.B.," or "This is just enough. S.B.," or "I had not talked of doing so," pepper letters in which his father tries to influence his son's professional and personal movements (*Family Letters* 121).

His father discouraged his desire to write for a living. He wrote to his son on March 12, 1859, "By writing you might pick a poor and scanty subsistence. School books are the only ones that pay, and it may be you won't be read" (*Family Letters* 68). His son's professional future was of both "thematic" and "formal" concern to his father. As with all of the paternal authorities we have discovered in this book, Butler's father wanted the narrative of his son's life to have a distinct form and trajectory. "Do pray put life into some practical shape," he writes to his son, "You refuse the plan I had looked to—and refuse it at the 11th hour when time and education had been laid out for it. Still I don't quarrel with that but it rests with you to find a substitute" (*Family Letters* 72).

The "shape" of family narrative was a recurring preoccupation, as if his father's admonitions continued to haunt his pen. His mock religious tract, *The Fair Haven* (1873), is preceded by a mock memoir in which one brother talks about "the most deplorable confusion" within his brother's papers, and his painstaking attempts to offer the ideas in "a presentable shape" (49). Before encountering his grandfather's written "remains," Butler had no use for the man, who died when Butler was four and who he reimagined as *The Way of All Flesh*'s George Pontifex (*Notebooks*, ed. Breuer 6–7). After holding his grandfather's papers in his hands, and then interviewing his former students, Butler was inspired to write a two-volume biography of the man. During one of his frequent trips to the British Museum, he pored over his grandfather's journal, and was inspired to check the date of a storm that his grandfather narrowly missed due to a delay at the port at Lerici (Raby 214). Butler hoped for the poetic coincidence of his grandfather escaping the storm that killed Percy Shelley, but was disappointed (*Family Letters* 220–21; Raby 214). Butler was determined, however, to offer a poetical vision of his grandfather to the world, in stark contrast to the satirical vision he offered elsewhere. This experiment in ordering his grandfather's remains would inspire much of the work he conducted afterwards. Writes Hans-Peter Breuer, "It was an unexpected revelation and must have brought home to him the importance of leaving behind personal memorabilia (preferably in a state of orderliness), especially if he was to have the posthumous hearing he devoutly yearned after" (*Notebooks*, ed. Breuer 7). Butler spent more than a decade writing and revising his Notebooks, and the last decade of his life collecting and rearranging his other varied writings for posterity (*Notebooks*, ed. Breuer 7).

---

[5]   He was so eager to erase *Canterbury Settlement* from his memory that he writes in his notes for *Erewhon Revisited*, "I rather think I have told this [a hiking story] in *A First Year in Canterbury Settlement*, but am so much ashamed of that book that I dare not look to see" (*Notebooks*, ed. Festing-Jones 291).

Butler had a multilayered response to his father's request for a "shape" to his son's life. Butler spent close to a decade fictionalizing his life in the posthumously published novel, *The Way of All Flesh*. This *künstlerroman*, as with *Pendennis* and *David Copperfield*, memorializes the struggle of father and son, but also memorializes the work a son can do to author himself. Since "the protagonist, Ernest Pontifex, and the narrator, Mr. Overton, are Butler" the book "allows Butler to portray himself both as a young and as a mature man, the seed and the fruit" (Daniels 11). As narrated by Overton, the "mature" Butler, the lives of Samuel Butler and Ernest Pontifex are identical until one "refuses the plan ... at the 11th hour" (*Family Letters* 72) and one does not. Ernest Pontifex becomes a minister, per his father's design, and his life devolves into farce from there, a farce that includes imprisonment after mistaking an honest woman for a prostitute, and the domestic nightmare of selecting a bigamous alcoholic as his wife.

Butler insisted that *The Way of All Flesh* did not contain a portrait of his father, and indeed that he had "written no book in which any single character is drawn from life" (*Family Letters* 65). He promises May, who was on the receiving end of the letter, that he had not and would not write in an autobiographical vein, nor would he publish anonymously (65). Despite this protest, the *Way of All Flesh* is now read as scathing *roman à clef*, especially especially given Butler's direct quotations from his father's letters within the satire of the patriarch in that novel.

The fictional and real Samuel Butler diverge due to the father's professional prodding, and their fates reconverge when, to paraphrase Butler's statement from the notebook entry "My Father and Myself," one is "there where the wicked cease from troubling" (*Notebooks*, ed. Brueur 231–2). Ernest becomes the absentee father of two children, and is only redeemed when his father dies and he inherits his fortune. Ernest is free to write once he has both orphaned himself and disinherited his offspring, just as Butler unapologetically attributed his freedom to write to his material inheritance from his father. Ernest's escape from the narrative his father set out for him "requires luck, in both its circumstantial and its biological aspects" and "cunning—the power of intelligence which a) is one form of biological luck, b) is activated by circumstantial luck, and c) is free to improve upon both" (Jeffers 88). His children, rendered illegitimate when his marriage with an alcoholic bigamist is revealed as a sham, are raised by surrogates, people they call "uncle and aunt" (403). Ernest's first book, *Essays and Reviews*, becomes a fictional counterpart to Butler's *Erewhon*. Ernest's book is published to great acclaim because it is published anonymously. The anonymity "made many turn to it who would never have looked at it otherwise" (Butler, *Way* 409). By writing anonymously, Ernest is not weighed down by his surname, or by the expectations that come from being the "son of" anyone. Ernest is able to claim what Samuel Butler hopes to claim in the opening page of his *Notebooks*, that these are "the prophecyings which my mother did not teach me at all, nor my father, nor any of my uncles and aunts, but altogether otherwise" (*Notebooks*, ed. Festing-Jones 56).

In his extended study of the shape of Samuel Butler's writing, Ralf Norrman calls him a "chiasticist," in that his "fondness for chiasmus is so extreme that it deserves to be called obsession" (3). For Butler, Norrman argues, symmetry was a "psychological necessity" (3). He attempted to "arrange things in such a way that he could structure reality dualistically. If there was more than two of something he would see this larger number as forming two groups (usually in opposition to each other)" (5). Butler's works ask, for example, how does *The Iliad* oppose the *Odyssey*? How does Jean-Baptiste Lamarck oppose Charles Darwin? Man oppose Machine? *God the Known* relate to *God the Unknown*? (6–7, 11, 17). The oppositional structure has embedded within it, however, a desire for connection, as "[c]hiasmus both creates and frustrates the longing for fusion" (23). When applied to his father, we see the conundrum: "A chiasticist cannot love someone until this someone loves him. Moreover, if someone hates a chiasticist, the chiasticist has to hate that someone" (26).

The museum became a useful structuring principle in Butler's life and writing. Only a place like the British Museum could contain, under one roof, all of Butler's intellectual interests, and simultaneously embody the utter necessity to keep the different parts segmented and organized. He turned to the museum when asked to explain the way that he organized his life. Yet, he often contrasted the museum with life and creativity, criticizing the ways in which the spaces are accessed. See, for example, a speech he delivered in 1895, entitled "How to Make The Best of Life":

> In the wreckage that comes ashore from the sea of time there is much tinsel stuff that we must preserve and study if we would know our own times and people; granted that many a dead charlatan lives long and enters largely and necessarily into our own lives; we use them and throw them away when we have done with them. I do not speak of these, I do not speak of the Virgils and Alexander Popes, and who can say how many more names I dare not mention for fear of offending. They are as stuffed birds or beasts in a Museum, serviceable no doubt from a scientific standpoint, but with no vivid or vivifying hold upon us. They seem to be alive, but are not. (*Essays* 79–80)

Here, he is describing the past "stuff" of literary history as a necessary evil—part of understanding the "mechanics" of everyday life, but not part of the creativity that emerges from one's own time. It is a puzzling stance, coming from a man who labored diligently over prose translations of the *Iliad* and the *Odyssey*, and conducted painstaking research into the poem's origins. The resolution comes when one sees how he describes that work. His distinction between literal and loose translation recalls the comparison, in "How to Make the Best of Life," between past literary greats and "stuffed birds or beasts in a museum." After receiving a scathing review of his translation of the *Odyssey* from Andrew Lang, he compared his common English prose translation to Lang's more traditional take via a contrast between "making a mummy and a baby" (*Notebooks*, ed. Festing-Jones 197). Thus, Butler's disdain is not toward the preservation of previous generations of authors, but toward preservation that does not take modern advance into account. "If you wish to preserve the spirit of a dead author," he writes in his response to Lang, "you must not skin him, stuff him and set him up in a case.

You must eat him, digest him, and let him live in you, with such life as you have, for better or worse" (*Notebooks*, ed. Festing-Jones 197). His positive, active model of inheritance is compared with "making ... a baby," with communion ("eat him, digest him"), and with marriage ("with such life as you have, for better or worse"). He uses the language of family and faith to theorize the right relationship between generations of authors. In this formulation, the museum is more of a mausoleum than a hearth. Yet he returned there daily, embodying the same chiastic dynamic that fueled his intellectual life.

The British Museum was founded as a "national" museum rather than a "nationalist" one (Cuno 13), containing "collections not of imperial foundation but assembled by individuals, chief among them the London physician Sir Hans Sloane" (11–12). Its "guiding principle" was to find unity in difference, to show, through the elevation of "discoveries in Natural Philosophy and other Branches of speculative Knowledge" that "all Arts and Sciences have a Connexion with each other" (13), and part of the work of connection involved a bit of chaos. Art collided with "antiquarian and ethnographic artifacts" and past collided with present, in "a vast, confused array of modes of display" (Bohrer 200).[6] The function of the museum is to make confusion seem like order, through processes of classification, contextualization, and the careful defining and policing of the museum's public (Sherman and Rogoff x–xi, xiv).

The British Museum's famous round Reading Room became the "mecca of literary research works" (Hoberman 495) from the 1870s until 1901. Samuel Butler, in his regular visits to the newest version of the reading room (opened in 1857), was joined by Thomas Hardy, Arnold Bennett, Leslie Stephen, Bram Stoker, W.B. Yeats, and many other men and women, as has been well documented by Ruth Hoberman and Susan Bernstein's feminist readings of the space. The reading room was as crowded as the most popular museum display rooms. The reading room became its own kind of exhibit space. Periodical articles described the "triflers" (Hoberman 496), dawdlers, and refugees from other lands who rubbed shoulders with the British literati.[7]

---

[6]   Georgel writes:
As heir to the cabinet of curiosities and bearer of the ideals of the Enlightenment and the Revolution, the museum needed to be able to represent itself as a world in microcosm. The entrance examination of the Royal Academy of Architecture made the point in 1778: "A museum is an edifice containing the records and achievements of science, the liberal arts and Natural history—in short, the totality of human knowledge and practical skill." (115–16)

[7]   Susan Bernstein outlines how it was seen and described as a "vulgar" place, a space full of distracting women, "political refugees, like Panizzi and Karl Marx, and for other foreigners and Londoners of insecure social classes" (107). Marx wrote *Kapital* there (107). Part of the attraction was due to the fact that admission was free, unlike the more exclusive London Library. Admission required "a brief application with a letter of sponsorship from a householder" which just meant "head of household, not necessarily a property owner" (Bernstein 103, 103n3).

The reading room was a space to request texts, digest texts, and create texts, but in this the room was not as different from a museum gallery as one may think. In the 1888 essay *Museum-History and Museums of History*, George Brown Goode contrasts a museum exhibit space and a library space, arguing for the superior pedagogical utility of the former. He writes of the library that its holdings "must be examined one at a time, and by one person at a time," that "[t]heir use requires long-continued attention, and their removal from their proper places in the system of arrangement," and that "[i]n the library, one studies the impressions of others" (266). By contrast, the treasures of a museum "are displayed to public view in groups, in systematic sequence, so that they have a collective as well as an individual significance," that unlike the "long-continued attention" required in a library, in a museum "much … meaning may be read at a glance," and that rather than "stud[ying] the impressions of others," the museum-goer "makes discoveries for himself, and, under the guidance of labels, forms his own impressions" (266). Goode, in these remarks to the American Historical Association, argues for the museum as more democratic than the library in its ability to reach individuals of varied levels of education: "the library is most useful to the educated; the museum to educated and uneducated alike, to the masses as well as to the few" (266). But, as Tony Bennett outlines in his deconstruction of Goode's argument in *Pasts beyond Memory*, labels were "merely the tip of the textual iceberg" (*Pasts* 167) in gallery spaces.

Those who experienced the British Museum reading room were often tempted to metaphorize it, as Virginia Woolf famously did in *A Room of One's Own* (1929), describing how a visitor may feel oneself "a thought in the huge bald forehead which is so splendidly encircled by a band of famous names" (44).[8] "If truth is not to be found on the shelves of the British museum," she asks in the second chapter of her book, "where … is truth?" (43). Even when museums did not house reading rooms, they were still often described in terms of reading. Common descriptions of "the museum" as concept included the museum as a "library of objects" (Bennett, *Pasts* 169), or the museum as a book with the labels "functioning as its index" (168). Chantal Georgel's article in the book *Museum Culture* outlines the concept of the "printed museum" that dominated periodical publishing in 19th century France (113–14), arguing that the periodicals borrowed "their purpose … 'table

---

8   The names were added in 1907 (Hoberman 490), so Butler would not have seen them. The list of male names was added, not coincidentally, just as the seats reserved for women were removed (507). The room Woolf describes was the seventh different reading room (492). Woolf, after collecting her pile of books in the Reading Room and creating her own index from the works, with the header, "WOMEN AND POVERTY, in block letters" (*Room* 48), finds herself writing "in the margin, Why does Samuel Butler say, 'Wise men never say what they think of women'?" (Woolf, *Room* 49). Woolf may not have known, as she scribbled a note about Butler in her own notebook, as she tried to make sense of literary history within the British Museum reading room, that she was performing, on behalf of women in history, the same work he performed in the Reading Room for his own place in history.

of contents'… conceptual categories, and even their layout" from museum gallery spaces (113–14). Visiting a great museum was sometimes compared with the privilege of reading a rare book. Painter and journalist William Hazlitt writes in *Sketches of the Principal Picture-Galleries of England* (1824):

> A visit to a genuine Collection is like going a pilgrimage—it is an act of devotion performed at the shrine of Art! It is as if there were but one copy of a book in the world, locked up in some curious casket, which, by special favour, we had been permitted to open, and peruse (as we must) with unaccustomed relish. (Hazlitt 6)

A museum can create the feeling of exclusive ownership even when one is surrounded by other viewers. And, it is a feeling that can be refreshed when necessary. "Our intercourse with the dead is better than our intercourse with the living," Hazlitt writes, "There are only three pleasures in life, pure and lasting, and all derived from inanimate things—books, pictures, and the face of nature … All other pleasures are as false and hollow, vanishing from our embrace like smoke, or like a feverish dream" (Hazlitt 51). Hazlitt's idealized vision of the museum as a joyous "intercourse with the dead" contrasts with Butler's fear than the museum can easily become a mere mausoleum.

Samuel Butler's British Museum routine was so visible and regular that several of his eulogists commented on the practice. The memorial of his life published in the Cambridge paper *The Eagle* (December 1902) outlined his process once he arrived at his customary seat:

> He sat at block B and spent the first hour "posting his notes"—that is reconsidering, rewriting, amplifying, shortening, and indexing the contents of the little note-book he carried in his pocket. The rest of the morning till 1:30 he devoted to whatever book he happened to be writing. (Streatfeild 51)

The trips replaced equally regular morning trips to the painting rooms at Heatherley's, rooms that Butler satirized in his most popular painting, *Mr Heatherley's Holiday: An Incident in Studio Life* (1874). The image, now at the Tate Gallery, shows the owner of the painting studio taking a break from his normal work in the pleasant labor of mending a human skeleton. The painting, notes its Tate Gallery caption, "satirises the dusty, macabre jungle out of which 'grand style' Victorian classicism was expected to arise" (*Mr. Heatherley's Holiday*). Art Historian Graham Reynolds calls *Mr Heatherley's Holiday* "an example of Butler's academic manner and the dryness which overcame him when painting to a formula" (Shaffer 22). The Heatherley model of art training followed "the programme of copying: from engravings, prints, and drawings; from casts; and finally from the live model" (20). Both *Mr Heatherley's Holiday* and his poem "A Psalm of Montreal" portray "the modern misuse of the classics" (25).

Butler's tendency toward self-deprecation when discussing his own legacy was mirrored by his discussions of the museum as national project. He wrote of history in one of his essays:

> When a thing is old, broken, and useless, we throw it on the dust heap, but when
> it is sufficiently old, sufficiently broken and sufficiently useless, we give money
> for it, put it into a museum, and read papers over it which people come long
> distances to hear ("Aunt," in *Essays* 45)

This tendency to celebrate what is useless in practical, material terms, is at least
preferable to the waste that occurs when the valuable item is overlooked due to the
glut that surrounds it. The latter is the case in "A Psalm of Montreal," a mock ode
to a museum storeroom that Butler published in *The Spectator* on May 18, 1878.
The prefatory notes describe a mass of waste that resembles the spaces of Mr.
Heatherley's art studio, as depicted in *Mr. Heatherley's Holiday*. He writes about
two plaster casts "banished from public view to a room where were all manner of
skins, plants, snakes, insects, etc., and in the middle of these, an old man stuffing
an owl" (*Notebooks*, ed. Festing-Jones 392). When natural science specimens are
not correctly distanced from fine art specimens, or when the latter is "shelved" to
make way for the former, the elegant economy of the museum is lost. Opposing
narratives exist about knowledge acquisition and the trajectory of intellectual
history. One narrative of information acquisition suggests a positive brand of
proliferation in which new knowledge offers a productive expansion of what
came before. Another suggests increasing glut, excess, clutter, and confusion. If
information accumulates in a haphazard manner, the best is lost within the detritus
of the rest. If the caretakers of the past are selective and strategic, however, the
march of history is a process of streamlining and clarifying. As I will discuss,
Samuel Butler wrestles with these options in terms of art and literature, and also
as relates to memory and scientific knowledge. His conclusions about the former
are less optimistic than those about the latter.

Butler replaced his regular visits to Heatherley's with regular visits to the
British Museum. Butler's Reading Room activities could have been conducted
anywhere, because his labor, for the most part, consisted of improving his own
work rather than active acquisition of external knowledge. Butler returned to the
museum to perform a unique brand of reading, reading influenced by the copying
he performed in the studios at Heatherley's. Butler read and annotated numerous
diverse texts, but also copied and rearranged his own sayings, as recorded in
notebooks he carried with him. Thus, he ingested his own ideas as if he were
editing another writer. Writes Jodie Nicotra, in her analysis of Butler's "rhetorical
agency," "unlike other purposes for reading, imitatio, a practice in which pupils
of rhetoric hand-copied texts of speeches, is a type of reading practice that is used
not to interpret or understand the text but rather as a form of rhetorical production"
(49). She sees in Butler's strategies for engaging with inherited knowledge
something akin to imitatio:

> When pupils hand-copied texts, they did so not to understand the texts or to
> study their meaning but to (among other things) identify rhetorical strategies,
> learn style, and inculcate within themselves a body of common topics that would
> increase their ability to respond to any given rhetorical situation. (49)

Butler copies texts (including his own past ideas) in order to experiment with them, claim them, reinvent them. Butler described his process of retranscribing his previous notebook entries in terms of creation (and conception and birth), writing, "My notes always grow longer if I shorten them. I mean the process of compression makes then more pregnant and they breed new notes" (*Notebooks*, ed. Festing-Jones 97). Nicotra adds, "what is most important about Butler's logic of textual engagement is that he does not automatically know what the text is or what should (or can) be done with it" (47).

Butler rewarded himself for diligence in writing by sketching or walking in the country on Thursdays and weekends. One of Butler's obituary notices, from the *Monthly Review* (September 1902), was eager to describe this latter Butler, out in the world rather than trapped amongst other people's work. "It was characteristic at once of his independence and of his sincerity that when he attacked a subject it was at the fountain-head," the eulogist wrote, and continued:

> His investigations into the Trapanese origin of the Odyssey were conducted not in the Reading-room of the British Museum, but in Sicily itself, and when he devoted himself to the study of Shakespeare's Sonnets he began not by reading the lucubrations of his innumerable predecessors, but learning the entire series of the Sonnets by heart. (Streatfeild 28)

Butler's preoccupation within the museum involved—sometimes jokingly, sometimes in earnest—maintaining the borders between his personal "record" and that of others. He wrote a humorous piece for the *Universal Review*, called "Museum Grievance," that reminded his readers of the thin borders between one's personal identity and those who share one's name. He described his "literary grievance against the authorities of the British Museum," in that the catalog lists, under "Samuel Butler," "three sermons on infidelity in the year 1820" (Streatfeild 24). His mock grievances receive the imagined reply, "they would change the description if I would only tell them what I was" (23–4). In explaining that he was only a "Bachelor of Arts," they reply that she should try "Masters," or at least "something between a bishop and a poet ... anything I liked in reason, provided I showed a proper respect for the alphabet" (24).[9] Butler settles upon "philosophical writer" as the best way to sandwich himself between the various men who share his name, without preceding all of them, "as b-a-chelor comes before b-i-shop" (24). This preoccupation with ordering and positioning oneself in "relation" to other practitioners of his craft appears in all of his writing, for example, in *The Way of All Flesh*, when grandfather and grandson visit the same convent, on the same European tour, at the same time in their lives. The records that remain differ greatly, the grandfather voicing wonder and novelty, and the grandson brevity in his ennui. The grandfather writes in his diary, "The thought

---

[9]   He echoes this category of "grievance" in "Quis Desiderio," alluding to the famous poet Samuel Butler: "If I could get a volume of my excellent namesake's 'Huidibras' out of the list of my works, I should be robbed of my last shred of literary grievance" (*Essays* 15).

that I was sleeping in a convent and occupied the bed of no less a person than Napoleon, that I was in the highest inhabited spot in the old world and in a place celebrated in every part of it, kept me awake some time" (*Way of All Flesh* 15). The grandson writes in his diary, "I went up to the Great St. Bernard and saw the dogs" (15). What has been lost, and what has been gained? Do the grandfather and grandson's writings represent a move from romanticism to realism, from poetry to prose, from meaning to meaninglessness, or from meaninglessness to meaning? The grandfather waxes poetic, imagining himself in close proximity to a hero of the past in a heroic locale. The grandson offers more practical information. The grandfather offers literature, and the grandson offers "science."

The man who sat at "B" three mornings a week was, seemingly, of two minds. He revered the Reading Room and chafed at its limitations. He tried to find his grandfather within its walls, and tried to escape his father there. He criticized excessive order when he saw it, and criticized excessive disorder when he saw that. He chafed at its expansiveness and its narrowness. The contradictions in his thinking about the museum and literary inheritance mirror, with exactness, his thoughts about the body and biological inheritance. When pairing his writing about fathers and books in fiction and journal entries with his science writing, we see how his theories about memory inform his method for writing against literal and literary habits of mind.

The Science of Disinheritance

Defenses of museum collections often linking the value of the space to the value gained by connecting with personal or national ancestors. In the book *Old England: A Pictorial Museum of Regal, Ecclesiastical, Municipal, and Popular Antiquities* (1850s), editor Charles Knight claims that "the Antiquities of a Great Nation" are the "richest treasures that we have derived from a long line of ancestors" (1). They are often the only method of recovering knowledge of "dim periods that have bequeathed to us no written explanation of the origin and the uses of their indestructible monuments" (1). The artifacts preserved in the books are themselves texts, and "every fragment has its own lesson, which cannot be read unprofitably" (51). In *Older England*, a series of six lectures given by J. Frederick Hodgetts at the British Museum, he calls citizens to that space to find "carefully preserved chronicles, sagas, and lays of incalculable wealth to us" (24).

Fitting, therefore, that Samuel Butler dedicates his most ambitious piece of science writing, *Unconscious Memory* (1880), a text about the transferal of mental experiences from one generation to the next, to the British Museum's Richard Garnett, "in grateful acknowledgement of the unwearying kindness with which he has so often placed at my disposal his varied store of information" (v). In a notebook snippet entitled "Myself and Garnett in the British Museum," Butler explains his admiration for the collections in detail that reveals the connection, for Butler, between personal and national legacies. "Here is a way," he writes, contrasting wholly imaginative art with photographs and non-fiction prose, "in which a man with no very unusual power may make himself enjoyed long after he is dead, and that too with no great strain upon himself—I shall certainly go in for it" (*Notebooks*, ed. Festing-Jones 216).

Science writing was another realm in which Butler sought a specific brand of independence. He credited the British Museum and its director, but refused to give his father any credit for his scientific interest or aptitude.[10] He writes in his notebooks:

> Because my father has made a collection of plants people may perhaps say I got my taste for biological study from my father. I do not think it was so. My father never to the best of my belief gave me the smallest encouragement in this respect, nor does he care about the study of living forms. He cares only about making a complete collection, but what he cares most about is the strapping of the specimens down with little strips of paper. (*Further Extracts* 99)

In this critique of his father, he also offers his philosophy about acts of collection. As with the contrast he draws between his literary translation and Andrew Lang's, he sees the "mummy" in his father's approach to biology, and the "baby" in his own. His father's collecting asserts control, whereas his own is a process of discovery that liberates, rather than shackles, its specimens. The paradox, however, is the same as with his philosophy of the museum. In the museum, Butler is able to see the possible passivity of the viewer in the face of the curator's control, but he also acknowledges the capacity for the viewer to read against the institutions' directives, seeing the old objects with new eyes. In his considerations of museum culture, Butler has specific requirements that turn potential waste into treasure. The same applies to his theories about the intellectual inheritances passed from person to person.

In his writing and thinking about biology, he continues to find ways to loosen himself from his father's influence. This involves dealing with another seeming contradiction. In all of his nonscientific writing—his novels, his journal entries, his art and literary criticism—having a mind patterned after a parent is something

---

[10]   In contrast, as I will discuss later, part of Butler's annoyance with Charles Darwin and his *Origin of Species* came from Darwin's refusal to credit his father, grandfather, and contemporaries for the content of his work. He writes in the 1882 preface to the second edition of *Evolution, Old and New* (1879), "I have always admitted myself to be under the deepest obligations to Mr. Darwin's works; and it was with the greatest reluctance, not to say repugnance, that I became one of his opponents" (iii–iv). In the 1879 preface, he again credits Garnett of the British Museum, "for having called my attention to many works and passages of which otherwise I should have known nothing" (vii). The gestures are surely in anticipation of the contradicting goals of *Evolution, Old and New*. One goal is to argue, against a *specific* divine or human figure as author of the universe, that man is his own "designer," "not man, the individual of any given generation, but man in the entirety of his existence from the dawn of life onwards to the present moment" (30). Another is to chastise Charles Darwin for pretending to be the sole author of his ideas, omitting references to Dr. Erasmus Darwin from the first edition of *Origin of Species* (195–6).

to be avoided. In a journal entry entitled "The Family" he writes, "I believe that more unhappiness comes from this source than from any other—I mean from the attempt to prolong family connection unduly and to make people hang together artificially who would never naturally do so" (*Notebooks*, ed. Festing-Jones 24). He admits to never wanting to see his father again, and posits that his father did not want anyone to write a biography of his grandfather (24–5). He speculates that his father "after he was 40, did not wish to see my grandfather any more" and that his grandfather and great-grandfather were avoiding each other in heaven (24–5). In "The World of the Unborn" chapter of his most famous work, the satirical utopian narrative *Erewhon* (1872), his narrator describes the movement from preexistence into existence as a transition from intellectual freedom to intellectual captivity. The potential child signs a contract that makes him a slave to the circumstances into which he was born. Butler describes the Erewhonian's belief that the unborn must "take a potion which will destroy their memory and sense of identity; they must go into the world helpless, and without a will of their own" (169).

Yet, the first and most important point within Butler's 1877 treatise *Life and Habit*, a thesis that he would repeat in his other scientific writing, involves "the oneness of personality between parents and offspring" (19). The rest of the thesis relates to the concept of organic memory, which is, as he describes it, "memory on the part of offspring of certain actions which it did when in the persons of its forefathers; the latency of that memory until it is rekindled by a recurrence of the associated ideas; and the unconsciousness with which habitual actions come to be performed" (19).

Butler's beliefs transform instinct from a passive physical reflex into an active mental action. He writes in *Unconscious Memory* (1880), "A better definition of instinct would be that it is inherited knowledge in respect of certain facts, and of the most suitable manner in which to deal with them" (137). In other words, even the simplest actions constitute more than just nerves responding. Instead, the actor is remembering his ancestors' acquisition of that knowledge. Germ cells, even before they unite at conception, act as recording devices, storing the acquired knowledge of the host body. A pessimistic philosopher, responding to this belief, would argue that the child's identity is thus subsumed into the parents. Butler's more optimistic take asserts that unconscious memory propels children ahead of parents, as they capitalize on, and improve upon, the parent's intellectual labors.

His science writing, which draws from contemporary discussions of organic memory and the inheritance of acquired characteristics, argues that having a mind patterned after one's parent is inevitable, socially useful, and ethical. If germ cells can learn from the actions performed by a parent during his lifetime, then the parent's labor is not wasted. In "The Deadlock in Darwinism," Butler writes that if the "extreme Charles-Darwinians"—those who focus entirely on mutations, on swerves away from the parent—have their way, "habit, effort, and intelligence acquired during the experience of any one life goes for nothing. Not even a little fraction of it endures to the benefit of offspring. It dies with him in whom it is acquired, and the heirs of a man's body take no interest therein" (308). That, to

Butler, would be a tragedy. "To state this doctrine is to arouse instinctive loathing," he writes, "it is my fortunate task to maintain that such a nightmare of waste and death is as baseless as it is repulsive" (308).

Belief in organic memory, or that "one inherited memories from ancestors along with their physical features" (Otis 2), suggests, writes Laura Otis, that "the first step towards gaining control over the past is locating it in a body" (2). The rise in interest in organic memory in the last decades of the nineteenth century was in part a backlash against the random, haphazard, and brutal feel to the most extreme accounts of evolution. Belief in Lamarckian inheritance theory, that one can inherit characteristics acquired by the parent during his or her lifetime, similarly restores the parent as an active shaper of the child rather than as a passive carrier of unchanging genetic material. Both theories have been largely debunked, though vestiges exist in certain strains of philosophy and psychology (for example, in concepts of the collective unconscious), and even, as Jay Clayton contends, in modern epigenetics (Clayton, n.p.). In 1912, James Ward, professor of Mental Philosophy and Logic at Cambridge, drew from Butler's theories in his argument about complex human activities. He writes of "the knowledge we know so thoroughly that, as Samuel Butler said, we have ceased to know that we know it at all" (257). In discussing, subsequently, "genealogical ascent," "permanent advance," and "a structure which has been perfected by practice" (257), Ward confirms Butler's narrative of continuity paired with progress.

How, then, does Butler's insistence on the most intimate connections between his brain and his father's brain become a liberating and radical form of disinheritance? How do we reconcile his insistence on "oneness of personality between parents and offspring" with the "naturally uncongenial" connection between Butler and his father?

The first step is to make immediate inheritance equivalent to distant inheritance. Butler negates the patriarch by multiplying him. He does so by drawing a distinction between the "common sense" and "high philosophy" methods of thinking about inheritance. He writes in "The Deadlock in Darwinism":

> The common-sense view of the matter to people who are not over-curious and to whom time is money, will be that a baby is not a baby until it is born, and that when born it should be born in wedlock. Nevertheless, as a sop to high philosophy, every baby is allowed to be the offspring of its father and mother.
>
> The high-philosophy view of the matter is that every human being is still but a fresh edition of the primordial cell with the latest additions and corrections; there has been no leap nor break in continuity anywhere; the man of today is the primordial cell of millions of years ago as truly as he is the himself of yesterday; he can only be denied to be the one on grounds that will prove him not to be the other. Every one is both himself and all his direct ancestors and descendants as well; therefore, if we would be logical, he is one also with all his cousins, no matter how distant. (330)

The vastness of Butler's vision allows him to pick his own father, and indeed to link his identity, selectively, to anything else in the universe that he admires.

Each body becomes like a comprehensive encyclopedia, containing entries that span the gamut of history. He writes in *Unconscious Memory* that a newborn baby is just as connected to his parents via memory as a "man of eighty" is connected to his past self via memory. When either being looks to his ancestry he should feel free to "claim identity with each generation of [his] ancestors up to the primordial cell inclusive" (17). To fully grasp the essence of a person, therefore, one has to look to every consciousness on which his consciousness draws, not only at his birth father and mother. Butler is also careful to think of inherited memories as belonging to the child as a co-owner, rather than as an heir to the parent. The infant says "I was you only a few months ago" (17). In *Life and Habit* Butler speaks of the child "profiting by all the experiences, which are, in fact, his own" (51).

After replacing immediate material inheritance with an expansive, cosmic vision, Butler describes the relationship between the parent's mind and the child's mind as one of inevitable improvement. The newest cells are "fresh edition[s] of the primordial cell with the latest additions and corrections" ("Deadlock" 330). The son's brain has everything positive that the father's brain offered to it, but adds its own advances. Butler turns to analogies with machines to solidify his point. In a passage from *Book of the Machines* that later migrated to *Erewhon*, Butler uses the grandfather clock and the watch to describe human evolution as progress: "Take the watch, for example; examine its beautiful structure; observe the intelligent play of the minute members which compose it; yet this little creature is but a development of the cumbrous clocks that preceded it; it is no deterioration from them" (*Book* 5). He argues that, as material culture marches on, the watch will be the only evidence that grandfather clocks used to exist. The passing of the latter is cause for celebration, because the watch has all of the features of the grandfather clock, but in a superior form.

The stress on "development" rather than "deterioration" gives way to Butler's third strategy for turning inheritance into disinheritance. He authorizes the germ-plasm as an agent in its own making. As he summarizes in "Deadlock in Darwinism,"

> The question is one of cognisance or non-cognisance on the part of the new germs, of the more profound impressions made on them while they were one with their parents. Those who accept the theory put forward independently by Professor Hering of Prague (whose work on this subject is translated in my book "Unconscious Memory" and by myself in "Life and Habit," believe in cognizance, as do Lamarckians generally. (322)

The "stuff" of heredity, the material that contains the DNA, is able to think as well as remember, even before its pieces combine in the body of the mother. The germ records and remembers what each parent records and remembers. Where that recording involves progress, the germ-plasm conserves energy and effort by learning the skill alongside the parent. Where that recording involves mistakes, accidental or intentional mutations send the offspring on a superior path. The final expulsion of the germ from the father's body marks the beginning of his freedom from the father's mind.

One critical reading of *The Way of All Flesh* in light of Butler's science writing focuses on narratives of trauma. Danielle Nielsen, comparing *Life and Habit* with Butler's novel, argues that the child is a slave to memory until trauma leads to new experiences for which he has no stored memories. She thus links Butler with Herbert Spencer in "hypothesiz[ing] little room for volition in the development of personality" (87). She claims that for Butler decisions are only conscious when entirely "unmediated by memory" (87). Yet Butler's description is more nuanced elsewhere. For example, in "The Deadlock in Darwinism," he describes a gradual decline in the influence of ancestral memory. As a man approaches the age of his parents when he was conceived, or the age of "the parent's ceasing to contain the offspring within himself," his mind becomes increasingly disconnected from that of his parent:

> From the average age, therefore, of reproduction, offspring should cease to have any farther steady, continuous memory to fall back upon; what memory there is should be full of faults, and as such unreliable. An organism ought to develop as long as it is backed by memory—that is to say, until the average age at which reproduction begins; it should then continue to go for a time on the impetus already received, and should eventually decay through failure of any memory to support it, and tell it what to do. This corresponds absolutely with what we observe in organisms generally, and explains, on the one hand, why the age of puberty marks the beginning of completed development. ("Deadlock," in *Essays* 336–7)

The "failure" described in the passage is that of the hold of memory on the offspring. The farther the germ-plasm travels from the body of the parent, the less likely that memory plays a role in "tell[ing] it what to do." Here, the rupture from the parent is a natural process of evolution rather than a traumatic rupture.

No passage from Butler's writing captures his desire to empower the germ-cell as well as his reflections about his own hypothetical child. As mentioned previously, this child chose never to be born. Butler's description of the imaginary boy in his Notebooks, under the heading "My Son," is infused with his belief in the "germ" as agent. The potential child must actively decide to participate in the making of himself:

> I have often told my son that he must begin by finding me a wife to become his mother who shall satisfy both himself and me. But this is only one of the many rocks on which we have hitherto split. We should never have got on together. I should have had to cut him off with a shilling either for laughing at Homer, or for refusing to laugh at him, or both, or neither, but still cut him off. So I settled the matter long ago by turning a deaf ear to his importunities and sticking to it that I would not get him at all. Yet his thin ghost visits me at times and, though he knows that it is no use pestering me further, he looks at me so wistfully and reproachfully that I am half-inclined to turn tail, take my chance about his mother and ask him to let me get him after all. But I should show a clean pair of heels if he said "Yes." Besides, he would probably be a girl. (*Notebooks*, ed. Festing-Jones 373)

Here, Butler mixes wistfulness with sly irreverence. The relationship between hypothetical father and hypothetical son has too many strikes against it, including the possibility, to preview Dickens's formulation, that Father and Son could become Father and Daughter after all.

"Nothing to Mark the Spot"

Butler knew that his thoughts about mental inheritance were radical and problematic, and knew also that he was on the fringes of the scientific community in his mode and methods for presenting them. That is why he often presented himself not as a professional scientist, but as an interested amateur speaking to other amateurs. He prefaces *Life and Habit* with:

> my aim is simply to entertain and interest the numerous class of people who, like myself, know nothing of science, but who enjoy speculating and reflecting (not too deeply) upon the phenomena around them ... It is plain, therefore, that my book cannot be intended for the perusal of scientific people. (1)

The stance is part self-protection and part sour grapes, as Butler really did aspire for legitimacy within the science community. In lieu of that acceptance (which never came), we still find that the theories affected Samuel Butler's thinking about art and religion, as well as about science. Most writings for or against Lamarckian inheritance and organic memory turn to the arts for key examples. Painting or playing the piano, for instance, are often described as heritable skills that are deployed unconsciously when mastered. Some individuals acquire advanced proficiencies in these difficult mental and motor tasks, these theories go, because they are capitalizing on skills acquired by parents during their lifetimes. Good pianists breed great ones; skilled painters breed expert painters. One can see, however, the pressure for a fledgling scientist, or novelist, or artist, who does not want to attribute his talents to his parent's labor.

Butler's paradoxical feelings about his father's directives play out within his paradoxical feelings about the museum. He sees spaces full of inherited ideas as both a boon and a burden. The paradox in this thinking about the museum mirrors his thoughts about the body. Memories inherited from a parent can be a burden and a blessing. When he considers literary originality, the same contradictions appear. In his work with the classics, Butler attempts to "deauthorize" monolithic texts that otherwise provide a daunting challenge to modern authors. On the other hand, Butler insists that authors (other than himself) credit all predecessor texts. Indeed, writes Jeffers: "Butler was very scrupulous about citing sources; indeed he knew he couldn't think at all without borrowing, digesting, and transforming other people's ideas. He wanted to think for himself, but never by himself. The people whom he explicitly acknowledges as sources, however, are desolately few" (1–2).

Butler's work *Evolution, Old and New* (1879) chastises Darwin for not crediting his father and grandfather for the ideas in *The Origin of Species*. In letters and essays, he accuses George Eliot of cribbing ideas from *Erewhon* for *Impressions of Theophrastus Such* (*Further* 90). In *The Authoress of the Odyssey* (1897), Butler claims that the *Odyssey* and the *Iliad* must have had different authors, because they do not display the continuity that one expects from a single consciousness. In his introduction, in which he anticipates the outcry that will emerge from his attempt to topple Homer as author of the *Odyssey*, he quotes from the January 2, 1892, *Spectator*: "That the finest poem of the world was created out of the contributions of a multitude of poets revolts all our literary instincts" (*Authoress* 2). Butler hopes to cut Homer down to size as an ancestor. He writes in *The Humour of Homer*, "No poet ever made gods in his own image more defiantly than the author of the *Iliad*. In the likeness of man created he them, and the only excuse for him is that he obviously desired his readers not to take them seriously" (61).

His constellation of paradoxical ideas about inheritance transformed Samuel Butler's theories about the imaginative creation of other minds. The germ that becomes a person, or the "germ" of an idea that leads to a fictional character, becomes, for Butler, an active agent in his own making. In a notebook entry entitled "Quarreling with One's Father," he writes that "a man begins to do this about nine months before he is born" (103). In his science writing, he describes a conversation between parent and child that begins long before conception, all the way back to that primordial cell.

The energies spent by Butler on shaking the influences of his father extends to the most domineering patriarch of them all. In the mock-memoir portion of *The Fair Haven*, Butler's narrator calls it "an almost invariable rule that children's earliest ideas of God are modeled upon the character of their father ... this conception will stick to a man for years and years after he has attained manhood— probably it will never leave him" (*Fair* 7). God, after all, does not meet Butler's test of a great author. He writes of God:

> He was satisfied with his own work, and that is fatal. Hence the same old "As it was in the beginning, is now and every shall be, world without end, amen" from everlasting to everlasting, without a sign of any effort at amendment of life on God's part. (*Essential* 503–4)

Butler instead bypasses God the Father, and the traditional accounts of his creation, with the same determination that he used to bypass his own father. He recalls Browning's *Caliban upon Setebos* (1864) in saying that "we are members indeed of a God of this world, but we are not his children; we are children of the unknown and vaster God who called him into existence" (85).

Finally, Butler expressed some concern about his own status as father. He begins *Ex Voto*, his analysis of sacred Italian art, with the assertion, "To write a preface is, as it were, to make a will," he writes, "it gives one the feeling of being on one's literary death bed. This is the time at which the ghost of a man's past writings rise up before him and threaten him with its forbidding aspect" (xvii). Samuel Butler, who certainly left a rowdy crowd of diverse literary children, was a curiosity in his own time but is gaining increasing prominence in ours. *The Way of All Flesh* influenced "Bennett, Maugham, Lawrence, Forster, and a host of other writers who continued to explore the realities of family life" (*Family Letters*, ed. Silver 24). Edmund Gosse, the author featured in my conclusion, called Butler's notebooks "excessively interesting" (Raby 298). Butler's approach influenced Gosse's autobiography, *Father and Son* (1907).

According to many of Butler's eulogists, the dizzying diversity within his oeuvre meant that his section of the library sadly needed reordering. If the texts he left behind reflect his life, then his disconnection from his ancestors was incomplete. The *Times* obituary skips over the years before *Erewhon*, saying that Butler had "done nothing to win a reputation, though, 14 years earlier, he had passed with some distinction through St. John's College, Cambridge, like his grandfather and father" (Streatfeild 4). The obituary writer describes "a sense of disappointment at the inadequacy of what is left of permanent work to represent the man" (6) because "he dissipated his strength in grappling with so many diverse subjects" (3). Similarly, O.T.J. Alpers, who wrote a remembrance in the *Press* of Christchurch, New Zealand, writes that

> his versatility was, in a sense, his bane. One contemplates with regret a man who could write a satire like *Erewhon*, devoting his splendid gifts to compiling two bulky tomes of his grandfather's biography, or giving years of work to prose translations of the "Iliad" and the "Odyssey," books which, it must be confessed, filled no want, and in point of style are not worthy of his great abilities. (qtd. in Streatfeild 20)

Alpers argues that Butler spent too much time paying homage to the past, and he is thus unsure about the future location of Butler's literary offspring: "Many of his books will die the death; some will survive only in the libraries of the curiously learned" (Streatfeild 26). In these comments, one hears echoes of Butler's father: "By writing you might pick a poor and scanty subsistence. School books are the only ones that pay, and it may be you won't be read" (*Family Letters* 68) and "Do pray put life into some practical shape. You refuse the plan I had looked to" (72).

Modern critics have fallen into the same critiques as his contemporaries, again because he seems to defy classification and categorization. Writes Schaffer, "general criticism of Butler's literary work (as opposed to professional editing) has faltered and ground to a halt on account of the difficulty of 'placing' him" (xiv). Jeffers adds:

> The imperfections of his work are one with those which marked his life," such as "his foot-tapping tolerance for institutions like the family which take so long to die their natural deaths, and finally his misconceptions about where his most important work lay—the misconceptions which sent him tilting in defense of Tabachetti and Gaudenzio di Ferrara when he ought to have been rewriting the last third of *The Way of All Flesh*. (122)

But the fragments he left behind offer an important model for modernist and postmodernist writers. Virginia Woolf calls *The Way of All Flesh* the harbinger of a "change in human character" starting in 1910 (*Collected Essays* 1.320). V.S. Pritchett called *The Way of All Flesh* "one of the time-bombs of literature" and said, "One thinks of it lying in [his] desk for thirty years, waiting to blow up the Victorian family and with it the whole great pillared and ballustraded edifice of the Victorian novel" (qtd. in Haack 361).

Butler anticipated the world's reaction to his response to his father. He argued for a "practical shape" to his life that resembled a beloved piece of music. In a letter to Henry Festing-Jones (December 1902), he offers an alternative model of his career:

> I am much better today; I don't feel at all as though I were going to die; of course, it will all be wrong if I do get well, for there is my literary position to be considered. First I write "Erewhon,"—that is my opening subject; then after modulating freely through all my other books, and the music and so on I return gracefully to my original key and publish "Erewhon Revisited." Obviously now is the proper moment to come to a full close, make my bow and retire; but I believe I am getting well after all. It's very inartistic, but I can't help it. (qtd. in Streatfeild 56)

This act of revision depends upon erasing his first published work, *Canterbury Settlement*, the one commissioned and edited by his father. It also depends on erasing his last incomplete work, *The Way of All Flesh*, that immortalizes his father within a work of fiction. Butler seeks to reclaim the story of his professional life— to erase his father's influence while still immortalizing him by responding to his ghost at every turn. He also figures writing as a process of negotiation between fathers and sons.

Butler refused his father's final writing assignment, one that would offer a final remark about the shape of his father's life. He says, ruefully, that his sisters never approached him for input about his father's gravestone. He reflects as well about his lack of participation in the entire process:

> No doubt I ought to have gone to the cemetery and seen what they had done and what epitaph they wrote, but have always put off a task which was painful to me, and which I knew I could do at any time. Probably I shall never do—and perhaps as well. (*Family Letters* 288)

His friend and biographer Henry Festing Jones was not surprised that Butler did not want a similar memorial, despite knowing that "epitaphs always fascinated him" (in Butler, *Humour* 55). "Long before he died" he forbade a tombstone, and he was cremated, "his ashes under the shrubs in the garden of the crematorium, with nothing to mark the spot" (55).

In the next chapter, "Preserve the Shadow of the Form: Hardy's Palimpsests," I turn to Thomas Hardy, whose approach to the "professional father" within print culture expands upon Butler's skepticism. Butler, the "enfant terrible of literature and science" hoped to "heave bricks" at all of the "big-wigs" (*Notebooks*, ed. Festing-Jones 182), belying his desire to become a big-wig himself. He was especially invested in attempting to acquire power through writing that would match that of a father, minister, scientific authority, or divinity. In Thomas Hardy's writings, the authority of the science writer and historian gives way to the work of the philologist and antiquarian, yet the conclusions about the letter of the law remain consistent, as embodied most forcefully in his epigraph to *Jude the Obscure* (1895), "The Letter Killeth."

Chapter 6
"Preserve the Shadow of the Form": Hardy's Palimpsests

Thomas Hardy's final novel, *Jude the Obscure* (1895), begins with the inscription "The Letter Killeth," which refers to the legal and biblical conventions that stifle Hardy's proto-modern protagonists. Weber defined legal-rational authority as based in "a belief in the 'legality' of patterns of normative rules and the right of those elevated to authority under such rules to issue commands" (215). As Hardy wrote in his Postscript, published 16 years after the novel's serialization, marriage laws and conventions, drawn from secular and religious traditions, are "the tragic machinery of the tale" (xxxvii). What happens, though, when modern readers take the "letter" of Hardy's motto more literally? In linking inscription and print culture to Hardy's concepts of inheritance and family curses, I hope to supplement readings of *Jude the Obscure* that have considered the fraught symbolism of the Phallus in this novel and the Symbolic language that reinforces patriarchal systems (Devereux 126; Musselwhite 184). Such readings, following Lacan's "The Signification of the Phallus" (1958), figure gender concerns as questions of genre and language. When Arabella throws the famous pig penis at Jude as part of her rustic courtship ritual, she throws a tool that rivals the power of the pen Jude hopes to hold in his hand. His attraction to her replaces books and pens, and material advancement, with the tools of a stonemason, indicating his social stasis. This chapter builds upon these established readings by discussing Hardy as philologist, an interest that paralleled his fascination with architecture and archaeology, but at the level of the page.[1] This chapter will begin with an overview of how palimpsestic erasure and rewriting is figured in the novels that precede *Jude*, and then I will turn to the final novel. In his novels, Hardy uses the history of the family to reconsider history itself, especially as imperfectly recorded, and incompletely erased, by texts.

In contrast with modern book historians, who move from "the dry details of texts" to "the syntheses based on these texts" (Netz 30), the painstaking initial acts of recovery fascinated nineteenth-century researchers (29). The job of the "palimpsest editor" was "like an archaeologist, to 'dig up' the fragments of the former text and carefully piece them together to reconstitute the original artifact" (McDonagh 211).

---

[1]   In a brief example of Hardy's interest in print culture, his notebooks contain a cutting from the London *Times* account of William Morris's talk "On the Printing of Books." In the lecture, delivered for the Arts and Crafts Exhibition Society, Morris displayed and discussed texts as old as "a manuscript Bible written probably about the year 1290" (Hardy, *Literary* 2.253), and carried his listeners through transformations in books and printing up to the present day.

The Royal Society of Literature hosted the occasional discussion of "Palimpsest or Rescript manuscripts" ("Palimpsest" 234), and a modern researcher can easily locate published reports about specific finds.[2] Such documents, records a brief proceedings note from 1824, "have a value hitherto unsuspected" in offering "portions of important works supposed to have perished" (234). "Much may be hoped," the report suggests, "from the further pursuit of a species of research which has already, within so short a period, produced such truly valuable fruits" (235). Some palimpsest manuscripts gained value as holding, underneath new writing, some of the oldest fragments of the Old and New Testaments. Others instead offered traces of classical writings underneath religious texts. In either case, writes one commentator from the *Saturday Magazine* (1841), "The subject has greatly attracted the attention of *philologists*, or lovers of literature, for some years past," as "the search for remains of classic learning has directed the attention of the most erudite scholars to these hidden treasures" ("Palimpsests" 239).[3]

The concept of the palimpsest also bled into metaphor for Carlyle, De Quincey, G.H. Lewes, the Romantic Poets, and many others, due to what it offered in thinking about the layers of an individual's identity or experience.[4] The poem "The Palimpsest," by M.G. Watkins (1874), uses the textual palimpsest as a figure for revelation, as a human religious text obscures a divine one. A beleaguered monk, reading a hymn on an old scroll, is encouraged to look again:

> He holds it to his lamp, blurred specks
> Start forth beneath the hymn:
> Like images the soul collects
> From dreams all faint and dim.

---

[2]   For example, see one review of Tregelles, *The Codex Zacynthius: Greek Palimpsest of Fragments of St. Luke,* published in the *Dublin University Magazine* in 1862. This essay offers a glimpse of one convention of translation and recovery that resonates with Hardy's final novel, the occasional denigration of the idealism of the researcher, and his confidence in letters: "We fully sympathize with the patient scholar who has been obliged to accompany his really satisfactory delineation of the obliterated characters with the current apology to *nearly* every page—'obscure'" (308).

[3]   The author explains that classical writing was replaced with religious texts when "the scarcity and expense of parchment ... frequently induced the monks to erase or wash out the writings of the classical authors, to make room for those of the Fathers" ("Palimpsests" 238).

[4]   See Josephine McDonagh's "Writings on the Mind: Thomas De Quincey and the Importance of the Palimpsest in Nineteenth Century Thought" (1987). McDonagh offers extensive commentary on the "Palimpsest" chapter of Thomas De Quincey's *Suspiria de Profundis* (1845), especially his characterization of the palimpsest as "the 'library' or 'archive' through which 'the secrets of ages remote from each other have been exorcised'" (208). She also discusses metaphorical connections between the palimpsest and the brain in De Quincey and in Lewes's *Problems of Life and Mind* (1874). Lewes also figures the palimpsest, she argues, as "a model of social incorporation" (McDonagh 208), while for Thomas Carlyle it becomes a metaphor for history (211).

Spelling, his soul within him stirred,
He now the text can see—
"IF YE CONTINUE IN MY WORD,
THE TRUTH SHALL MAKE YOU FREE." (33–40)

The monk interprets the message underneath the hymn as a reminder to "prize" the "old pure wisdom" (44), since "time can show / no new truths like the old" (47–8).

When the palimpsest was not a direct intervention by the divine, a reminder to value "the old pure wisdom" as a possible source for "novel truth" (line 28), it was a way to imagine the individual consciousness. In *Suspiria de Profundis* (1845) Thomas De Quincey offers the image of "the palimpsest of the brain" (*Confessions* 136) to narrate an altered state in which, for one who experiences it, "every act—every design of her past life lived again – arraying themselves not as a succession, but as parts of a co-existence" so that "her consciousness became omnipresent at one moment to every feature in the infinite review" (136). The woman he describes, who has a near-death experience when she falls into a "solitary brook" (136), becomes the ultimate omniscient narrator of her own life for one moment—seeing, with god-like accuracy, the entire structure of her narratable existence. De Quincey promises that such experiences are available to those who find the correct external stimulation, in trauma, in illness, in opium, in near-death experiences: "Yes, reader, countless are the mysterious handwritings of grief or joy which have inscribed themselves successively on the palimpsest of your brain ... the endless strata have covered up each other in forgetfulness. But ... [t]hey are not dead, but sleeping" (137). For De Quincey, it is impossible to read one's own mind without finding a way outside of oneself.

Watkins and De Quincey both see "legibility" as unusual experiences, sparked by revelation or extraordinary alterations to the brain and mind. Uncovering a spiritual or psychological layer hidden underneath another one can be as painstaking as finding one text under another in a codex manuscript. As Sarah Dillon writes in her study *The Palimpsest* (2007), "there is no necessary relationship between the texts that cohabit the space of a palimpsest—one text is not derived from the other, one does not serve as the origin of the other—the palimpsest does not *properly* figure the relationship between a text and its sources, including *its own earlier drafts*" (Dillon 47). So, a text, or a brain, that exhibits palimpsestic qualities is literally of two minds, and those two minds may be antithetical to each other. When considering the palimpsest in terms of competing authorities, opportunities for figuring gender and generational conflicts arise. Gilbert and Gubar, for example, claim that women's writing in the Victorian traditions led to "literary works that are in some sense palimpsestic, works whose surface designs conceal or obscure deeper, less accessible (and less socially acceptable) levels of meaning" (Dillon 102; Gilbert and Gubar 73). Such documents come to resemble Roland Barthes's definition of the "plural text," in which "systems of meaning can take over ... but their number is never closed, based as it is on the infinity of language" (5–6). Not only can texts be themselves palimpsestic, but acts of rereading are additional ways to obtain "a plural text: the same and new" (16).

These multiple uses of the concept—material, social, and psychological—all became a crucial part of Hardy's works, his final novel in particular. As Joanna Devereux writes in *Patriarchy and Its Discontents* (2003), "the basic unit of *Jude* is the Word" (121).[5] In a note in his journal, dated March 15, 1889, Hardy insisted that "What has been written cannot be blotted. Each new style of novel must be the old with added ideas, not an ignoring and avoidance of the old. And so of religion, and a good many other things!" (*Life* 227). The quote, on first reading, seems to be an antipalimpsest, in that it denies that existing documents can be permanently obscured. Instead, it confirms the legibility of palimpsestic texts. After all, in order to recognize a document, idea, belief, or experience as a palimpsest, there must be a trace of what was overwritten. In other words, to identify erasure, the erasure must be imperfect. The language of "blotting" is in part biblical ("and so of religion"), as the Old Testament Yahweh often promises the "blotting out" of sinners and opponents of his chosen people.[6] The language of "blotting" refers also to Hardy's sense of precursor texts and his acts of self-revision.[7] In most of his works, including *Jude the Obscure*, material was removed or restored between the serialized and volume versions (Kramer 167–8). Hardy sees his novels as evolving organisms that respond to their older forms. In his prefaces, themselves often rewritten, Hardy discusses his novels in terms of birth, growth, and development. For example, he introduces the first volume edition of *Tess of the D'Urbervilles* by describing his work to "piece the trunk and limbs of the novel together, and print it complete, as originally written" (viii). Joanna Devereax sees such references as a sign of "Hardy's sense of the text as a human body" (113). They also reveal Hardy's interest in how organic materials can be "read" as texts, as can inorganic materials that are "printed" with things other than words. Hardy wrote in 1893, "The worst of taking a furnished house is that the articles in the rooms are saturated with the thoughts and glances of others" (*Life* 270),[8] implying that the histories of things are always connected with the history of people. In his novels, I will argue, Hardy turns to material possessions, especially books, to figure fatherhood. Fatherhood, in turn, allows Hardy to reconceptualize authorship, ownership, and power.

---

[5]   Devereux's work dedicates one chapter to analyzing *Tess of the D'Urbervilles* and *Jude the Obscure* as proto-feminist texts.

[6]   See Exodus 17:14, Exodus 32:32–3, Deuteronomy 9:14, Deuteronomy 25:6, Deuteronomy 25:19, and Deuteronomy 29:20. The examples almost always refer to a promise to the people of Israel that they and their offspring will rise in prominence over the offspring of other tribes.

[7]   See Dale Kramer's article "Hardy and Readers: Jude the Obscure" (1999), pages 168–9, for a discussion of the importance of revision in the study of Hardy's novels.

[8]   His second wife expressed a similar sentiment when faced with the prospect of being called "Mrs. Hardy." In a letter to Siegfried Sassoon on June 30, 1922, she wrote, "I am oppressed by the thought that I am living in *her* house, using *her* things—and, worst of all, have even stolen her name" (qtd. in Tomalin *Hardy* 352).

"Man, Even to Himself, is a Palimpsest"

Before I turn to *Jude the Obscure*, I will survey moments in Hardy's earlier novels that embody the metaphorization of the palimpsest, in particular in connections between material and psychological repetitions across generations. In *Far From the Madding Crowd* (1874), Gabriel Oak must decide if he will help the newly married Bathsheba Everdene counteract her new husband's carelessness. Troy is engaged in revelry while a storm threatens his hay and wheat ricks. Hardy's first manuscript of the novel evokes the palimpsest explicitly when describing Oak's character:

> Seven hundred and fifty pounds in the divinest form that money can wear— that of necessary food for man and beast—should the risk be run of deteriorating this bulk of corn to less than half its value because of the instability of a woman? "Never if I can prevent it!" said Gabriel.
>
> Such was the argument that Oak set outwardly before him. But man, even to himself, is a palimpsest, having an ostensible writing, and another beneath the lines. It is possible that there was this golden legend under the utilitarian one: "I will help, to my last effort, the woman I have loved so dearly." (240)[9]

In Hardy's original formulation of Oak as text, he is best understood in layers (a "palimpsest" with writing "beneath") rather than as a one-dimensional code (a "cryptographic page" with writing "between," as the passage reads in the first volume edition). In the first formulation as well, Oak's work for Bathsheba is exactly that—work ("my last effort" as opposed to "my last breath" in the first volume edition).[10] Oak is a palimpsest manuscript, and in his role as text he strives to do new work in the world, but his romantic roots show through without his knowledge or will. The realist narrative mode sparked by utilitarianism has only partially overwritten romanticism.

Oak's meditations precede Troy's commentary about modernizing Bathsheba's farmhouse. Troy argues:

> A philosopher once said in my hearing that the old builders who worked when art was a living thing had no respect for the work of builders who went before them, but pulled down and altered as they thought fit, and why shouldn't we?

---

[9] The original manuscript is now held at the Beinecke Rare Book library at Yale University. It was the basis for the Oxford University Press edition of the novel, edited by Suzanne Falck-Yi. This is the edition I cite in this chapter, unless I indicate otherwise.

[10] In the first volume edition of the novel, the latter half of the passage reads with slight variations, which I indicate in italics (*Far*, ed. Morgan vii): Such was the argument that Oak set outwardly before him. But man, even to himself, is a *cryptographic page* having an ostensible writing, and another *between* the lines. It is possible that there was this golden legend under the utilitarian one: "I will help *to my last breath* the woman I have loved so dearly" (213). After Hardy completed his first manuscript copy, it was edited by Leslie Stephen and serialized in the *Cornhill Magazine* (*Far*, ed. Falck-Yi xxxi; *Far*, ed. Morgan xvii). Hardy revised it extensively after that, including for the Wessex Edition (1912–13).

"Creation and preservation don't do well together," says he, "and a million of antiquarians can't invent a style." My mind exactly. I am for making this place more modern that we may be cheerful whilst we can. (*Far* 233–4)

The Romantic Troy seems to call for utilitarianism here, yet he belies his own authority in his impulse for quotation. After Oak's valiant actions save much of the rick, Troy tries to spin his good fortune into a universally applicable maxim: "To speak like a book I once read, wet weather is the narrative, and fine days are the episodes, of our country's history—now isn't that true?" (*Far* 254). So whereas Oak imperfectly covers his romantic self with his utilitarian self, Troy tries to overwrite romantic impulsivity with borrowed practicality, ending his attempt with a deauthorizing question rather than an authoritative answer. Whereas De Quincey suggested that one can seek awareness of "the palimpsest of the brain" (136), and Watkins suggested it can be gifted through divine revelation, Hardy's characters seem unaware of the two minds they display and the two philosophies they embody. Charles Hedrick's study of Roman inscriptions compares "an allusion or quotation" to "a rehabilitation," writing that "[t]o recognize a citation is to conceive of a piece of writing as a rewriting, or reinscription" (141). The literary or cultural allusion "also works to defer the authority for its utterance elsewhere" because of its status as "the rehearsal of a statement made on the authority of someone else" (141).

Both Oak and Troy reveal the palimpsests of their brains during a discussion of concrete material inheritances, a pattern that also holds in Hardy's multiple descriptions of ancestral homes alongside the psychology of those who inhabit, inherit, adapt, or abandon them. Consider Hardy's description of Fancy Day's ancestral home in *Under the Greenwood Tree* (1872):

> The most striking point about the room was the furniture. This was a repetition upon inanimate objects of the old principle introduced by Noah, consisting for the most part of two articles of every sort. The duplicate system of furnishing owed its existence to the forethought of Fancy's mother, exercised from the date of Fancy's birthday onwards. The arrangement spoke for itself: nobody who knew the tone of the household could look at the goods without being aware that the second set was a provision for Fancy when she should marry and have a house of her own. (*Greenwood* 93)

The parental expectation is not just that Fancy will inherit the contents of the parent's house, but that her house will become a carbon copy of her parent's house. But will the new version be able to duplicate all of the things that express her parent's experience? The window ledge above the mantelpiece was

> curiously stamped with black circles—burnt thereon by the heated bottoms of drinking cups which had rested there after previously standing on the hot ashes of the hearth for the purpose of warming their contents—the result giving to the ledge the look of an envelope which has passed through innumerable post-offices. (94)

Fancy's married home can only be a perfect copy of her parent's home if behavior, including accidental behavior, transfers as easily as furniture. Fancy, however, is eager to distance herself from her father's way of being, which Hardy registers as her frustration with his way of speaking. On her wedding day, she "strictly charged her father and the tranter to carefully avoid saying 'thee,' and 'thou' in their conversation, on the plea that those ancient words sounded so very humiliating to persons of newer taste" (193). Although her house is destined to approach her father's, she is determined that her language will not. Yet, an early scene shows that at least partial display of her genetic inheritance may be inevitable. The first objects we read in the novel are not books, but boots. An early scene introduces the main protagonists by comparing the daughter's boot and the father's, with reference to the "tell-tale leather, evidencing a nature and a bias" (*Greenwood* 26). "Bias" here means the pattern on which the fabric is cut, but also the inherited or acquired tendencies of the individual. "Nature" refers both to the soundness of the leather and the "soundness" of the genetic inheritance.

A Laodicean (1881) ends with the dramatic burning of an ancestral building, after it has been carefully renovated by an architect and his lover. The manuscript of the novel met a similar end, as Hardy burned it after printing was complete (xxxv). The novel is as conscious of the passing of old things as *Under the Greenwood Tree*; in fact, *A Laodicean* begins by echoing the preface of *Under the Greenwood Tree* in its regrets about the passing of traditional church music (8–9). Hardy peppers the text with analyses of neglected family portraits, artifacts that do not fare well over time. The living Miss De Stancy is almost mistaken for one of these artifacts, as Somerset finds her "in a niche of the curtain-wall" (22). He notices that her nose offers a "defective reprint" of the "De Stancy face with all its original specialities" because "the nose tried hard to turn up and deal utter confusion to the family shape" (23). In regarding the inanimate artifacts rather than the living one, he decides that the paintings, too, are distortions, some "willfully false, no doubt; many more so by unavoidable accident and want of skill" (21). The skeptical statements about the preservation of family qualities preview Paula's failed baptism, her rejection of her "father's dying wish that she should make public profession of her—what do you call it—of the denomination she belonged to" (28). Paula's rejection of her father's religion mirrors Somerset's rejection of his father's art. On the one hand, he proclaims early in the novel that he is not interested in his father's art because he has been overexposed to it (*Laodicean* 57). On the other, he assumes transmission, insisting that "[p]eople's features fall naturally into groups and classes" and "often repeat themselves" when studied by "an observant person" (*Laodicean* 63).

The narrator concludes, upon reading the body of Captain De Stancy, that "[h]is visage, which was of the colour of light porphyry, had little of its original surface left; it was a face which had been the plaything of strange fires or pestilences, that had moulded to whatever shape they chose his originally supple skin, and left it pitted, puckered, and seamed like a dried water-course" (208–9). Those trying to "read" (209) his face could tell that he "had either been the victim of some terrible necessity as regarded the occupation to which he had devoted himself, or that he was a man of dogged obstinacy, from sheer sang froid holding his ground amid malign forces when others would have fled affrighted away (208–9). Yet Captain De Stancy worked to avoid having his interior display his past as clearly as his exterior, as his struggles "seemed to have affected him but little within" (209). Captain De Stancy's "occupation" has marked him in specific ways that belie the "Protean quality ... by means of which he could assume the shape and situation of almost any ancestor at will" (170). Bodies and artifacts intersect again in the De Stancy tattoo on Dare's chest that flaunts his connection with this formerly esteemed family (126, 140, 143). Dare himself offers, as commentary on his father, "the obtrusive memento of a shadowy period" (157) in his father's past. Without Dare, De Stancy's form may have successfully obscured that period of his life.

When Captain De Stancy chastises Dare for the shapelessness of his dependent life, De Stancy sounds like Samuel Butler's father, or like Sir Austin Feverel or Patrick Brontë as "editors" of their children's narratives:[11]

> Why are you here?—unnaturally concerning yourself with the passions of a man of my age, as if you were the parent, and I the son! Would to Heaven, Willy, you had done as I wished you to do, and led the life of a steady, thoughtful young man! Instead of meddling here, you should now have been in some studio, college, or professional man's chambers, engaged in a useful pursuit which might have made one proud to own you. (184–5)

Captain De Stancy, a character out of Romance, tries to encourage utilitarianism in his illegitimate offspring. He suggests that he will only own his son in "modern" terms, that is, in terms of work rather than great expectations. Whereas his own power over his son comes from inheritance, if his son is to have power over him, it must be "worldly power" (Mill, *Spirit* 27).

The offspring, rather than the fathers, are unduly attached to the ancestral trappings. Paula's attraction to "being a family out of date" (173) contrasts with De Stancy's question when he "regard[s] these canvas grandmothers" of the family gallery "and asks, 'Why was a line so antiquated and out of date prolonged till now?'" (173). Similarly, Somerset the younger is surprised by his father's apathy as relates to their family tree; he "reflected and said that he believed there was a genealogical tree about the house somewhere," but added "Not that I ever took much interest in it'....without looking up from his canvas; (188). It takes a while for the older Somerset, who is engaged in his current profession rather than his past ancestry, to remember that his copy "was in an iron box at the banker's," he having "used it as a wrapper for some bonds and other valuable papers" (188). De Stancy and Somerset, unlike their offspring, see "canvas grandmothers" (173)

---

[11]   As described in Chapter 5 of this book, Samuel Butler's father writes to his son, who wants to discontinue the education his father has paid for, "Do pray put life into some practical shape. You refuse the plan I had looked to—and refuse it at the 11th hour when time and education had been laid out for it. Still I don't quarrel with that but it rests with you to find a substitute" (Butler, *Family Letters* 72).

and "copies on parchment" (188) of family trees to be less valuable than texts that declare wealth and social standing in the present economy. Charlotte De Stancy is among the chorus of younger people who cling to material traces, and Sir William among the many elders who criticize them for it: "What is the utility of such accumulations? ... Their originals are but clay now – mere forgotten dust, not worthy a moment's inquiry or reflection at this distance of time. Nothing can detain the spirit, and why should we preserve the shadow of the form?" (39). The younger characters crave continuity but the unstable nature of the new material economy denies these longings. Paula *seems* to reject the romantic ending of her own story, in which she gains a "useless" "title," "fortune and castle," in favor of the freedom of modernist self and material fragmentation: "I've thought it over— quite,' she answered. 'And I quite see what the advantages are. But how if I don't care one atom for artistic completeness and a splendid whole; and do care very much to do what my fancy inclines me to do?" (*Laodicean* 309). Yet when Paula's castle has burned and she resolves to build "a new house beside the ruin, and show the modern spirit for evermore" she cannot help but add, in the final words of the novel, a desire for the recovery of the romantic text underlying the utilitarian one: "I wish my castle wasn't burnt; and I wish you were a De Stancy!" (379).

Hardy's novels abound with futile attempts to supersede or bury another's claims on paternity.[12] In *Far From the Madding Crowd*, Gabriel attempts to obscure Troy's fathering of a child with Fanny Robbin, by erasing the phrase "and child" from Fanny's coffin lid (254). Traces, of course, remain. Bathsheba, Troy's wife, quickly discovers the truth for herself by opening the coffin (258), and a repentant Troy erects a marker over Fanny's grave, in defiance of his living wife (280). In *The Mayor of Casterbridge*, Michael Henchard discovers that his supposed daughter belongs, biologically, to the paradoxically-named "Newson," the sailor who purchased Henchard's wife during a drunken exchange. The laws of "nature" and man come into conflict when Donald Farfrae explains new technologies for recovering grain. Donald Farfrae's statement about recovering grain, "to fetch it back entirely is impossible; Nature won't stand so much as that" (46–7), foreshadows Henchard's experience losing and then partially regaining his abandoned family in a series of economic exchanges. Once Henchard knows that Elizabeth Jane is not his daughter, he "could not endure the sight of her" (124) because he could see the other man's features in her face, for "in sleep there come to the surface buried genealogical facts, ancestral curves, dead men's traits, which

---

12   In her article "The Patriarchy of Class," Penny Boumelha discusses *Under the Greenwood Tree*, *Far From the Madding Crowd*, and *The Woodlanders*, arguing that in these novels the "daughter is at once the object of and the vehicle for the social ambition of the father" (134). She claims that while in other Hardy novels, such as the ones I discuss in this chapter, "the exercise of such patriarchal power, if not always by a literal father," tends to be "tragic," in her cluster of novels "it is shown in the end to be futile" (135). In Boumelha's argument, therefore, in this part of Hardy's career there are glimmerings of alternatives to the inevitability of patriarchy. By the end of his novel-writing career, I argue, the alternatives disappear.

the mobility of daytime animation screens and overwhelms" (124). Her face is like a palimpsest manuscript which, when seen in different light, offers glimpses of another author. Neglected by her stepfather after the discovery, Elizabeth-Jane tries, like Jude, to claim a more ancient inheritance. She "began the study of Latin, incited by the Roman characteristics of the town she lived in" (131), and visited her mother's grave in "the still-used burial-ground of the old Roman-British city," in which "Mrs. Henchard's dust mingled with the dust" of the original inhabitants (131). After being rejected by her father figure, Elizabeth Jane tries to locate herself in a bygone history that cannot reject her because it cannot respond to her. She tries to dig beneath her father for a different kind of inheritance.[13] Michael Henchard's entire legacy in *The Mayor of Casterbridge* is a far cry from a monument etched in stone. He leaves only a crumpled piece of paper in which he paradoxically requests "that no man remember me" (321). His would-be daughter responds, foreshadowing Jude's quote from the *Agamemnon*, "What bitterness lies there! But there's no altering—so it must be" (321).

In *Tess of the D'Urbervilles*, the discovery of the D'Urberville clan's noble past is best met with "the thought of 'how are the mighty fallen'" (3). Hardy's real-life encounter with a boastful and intoxicated father inspired the novel's opening scene (Hardy, *Thomas Hardy's Public* 116). Tess's father tries to become his own monument, or as he puts it, "living remains." Failing in his more mundane labors, he declares,

> I'm thinking of sending round to all the old antiqueerians in this part of England ... asking them to subscribe to a fund to maintain me. I'm sure they'd see it as a romantical, artistical, and proper thing to do. They spend lots o' money in keeping up old ruins, and finding the bones o' things, and such like; and living remains must be more interesting to 'em still, if they only knowed of me. (273)

Tess's father wants to become a professional relic. The death of "Prince" early in the novel underscores the folly of his ambitions. It underscores the permanence of the realization that, as with eroded stone, his name is irretrievably "worn away to Durbeyfield" (29). Hardy, himself conceived out of wedlock and childless throughout his marriages (Tomalin, *Hardy* 172–3), had personal issues at stake in investigating alternatives to heterosexual reproduction within the confines of heterosexual marriage.

The "intrinsically mobile" (Irwin 65) spaces in Hardy's novels reflect an imaginative restlessness, but also a level of indecision about the ideal social, political, or familial systems. Michael Irwin calls Hardy's final novels "peripatetic in their very design, the main characters being unable to settle in any one place

---

[13] Compare with Bathsheba's conversation with Troy in *Far From the Madding Crowd*, shortly before the ill-fated seduction. When asked if she speaks French, she replies, "No: I began, but when I got to the verbs father died" (152). It is telling that Bathsheba's education from her father ends before the verbs, at the point of action. She is left without the tools to know what an exotic seducer like Troy will do, and allows wordless passion to direct her actions.

for long" (71), and Christine Bolus-Reichert calls Hardy's literary visions "repudiations of organic historicism" that "choose revolution over evolution—they choose to return" (226).

"That Which Cannot Be Blotted": *Jude the Obscure*

Hardy's literary notebooks contain a clipping from an article entitled "The Woman of the Future."[14] The article is a critique of late-century feminists who wanted to herald a new age of "matriarchy," which required "a decay of all the delicate adjustments of relations between father, mother, and child, which form the strongest pillars of our social order" (*Literary* 2.326–7). The writer hopes that nature will eliminate such outliers, leaving only the "womanly women" to marry and procreate (*Literary* 2.330). By contrast, in a letter to Florence Henicker, Thomas Hardy described his final novel, *Jude the Obscure* (1895), as a tale of "two persons who, by a hereditary curse of temperament, peculiar to their family, are rendered unfit for marriage, or think they are" (*Collected* 2.94). The fear exhibited by those who regarded Jude and Sue was that their "peculiar" curse would spread to other families. The disintegration of Phillotson and Sue's marriage could herald the advent of "Matriarchy" (243), if it is fueled by a young woman's desire to exercise reproductive power without a legal tie to a specific man. Phillotson, the novel's middle-aged schoolteacher who has just been jilted by his young wife, muses, defensively, "I don't see why the woman and the children should not be the unit without the man" (243). His thoughts echo Angel's self-delusion in *Tess of the D'Urbervilles* (1891), when he insists, "as reasoners the only pedigrees we ought to respect are those spiritual ones of the wise and virtuous, without regard to corporeal paternity" (*Tess* 148). Yet once Angel knows of Tess's family legacy, he looks for past women in the present one, thinking that Tess's "fine features were unquestionably traceable" in the "exaggerated forms" of D'Urberville family portraits (170). Both men insist on the modern meritocracy, while secretly longing for the old ways, and punishing their lovers modern actions accordingly.

Jude cannot escape the legal bounds of fatherhood any more than Hardy's other tragic protagonists, due to law, culture, and to his nature. Jude tries to imagine Sue married with children, and is frustrated by the presence of Phillotson as the potential father of the children; the narrator writes, "the consolation of regarding them as a continuation of her identity was denied to him, as to all such dreamers, by the willfulness of Nature in not allowing issue from one parent alone. Every desired renewal of an existence is debased by being half alloy" (184). Jude's wish that children could be "collectively the children of us adults of the time" (288)—his socialist insistence that claiming children is "like class-feeling, patriotism, save-your-own-soul-ism and other virtues, a mean exclusiveness at bottom" (288)—is

---

[14]   *Nation* 1 (April 13, 1907): 255–6.

immediately negated by a conservative retreat to marriage as making "a more natural home" (289) for Little Father Time, and by the boy's insistence on calling Sue mother and then punishing her for transgressive maternity.[15]

Sue is haunted by Arabella as the biological mother of Jude's son (292). Sue's anxiety persists despite Jude's insistence that "The beggarly question of parentage—what is it, after all? What does it matter, when you come to think of it, whether a child is yours by blood or not?" (288). However, blood betrays his tentative steps toward embracing alternatives to the letter of marriage laws. He seems to concur with the author of "Woman of the Future," in assuming that traditional marriage is not likely to go extinct. He says: "People go on marrying because they can't resist natural forces ...No doubt my father and mother, and your father and mother, saw it, if they at all resembled us in habits of observation. But then they went and married just the same, because they had ordinary passions" (272). Jude's stance implies that legitimate heterosexual couplings inevitably give way to legitimate heterosexual marriages. However, the caveat "*if* they at all resembled us" highlights the most important threat to generational continuity. The seamless flow from past to present requires culturally shared affective responses. Sue, as a "phantasmal, bodiless creature" who lacks "animal passion" (272), stands as a threat to this continuity, at least in her failure to produce heirs within wedlock. When Sue is ready to marry, she must ask her cousin and lover to be her father, too. She says, "You are 'father,' you know. That's what they call the man who gives you away" (178). This designation attempts to normalize Jude's strange role as father of his lover, and father-elect of his own father-figure, Phillotson.

Jude spends the novel in search of a symbolic father to take the place of an absent real one. Early in his courtship with Sue, Phillotson acknowledges that he is "old enough to be the girl's father," duplicating the mock-paternal relationship he has with Jude, and multiplying the consequences of transgressing it (107). Thoughts of his first symbolic father, Phillotson, and his first symbolic mother, Christminster, draw him into many ghostly human relationships, in echoes of Whitman's wish in "Crossing Brooklyn Ferry" (1860). The hope expressed in a poem such as "Crossing Brooklyn Ferry" is that an emotional equivalency exists between past and future generations. The speaker insists that when a reader of "A hundred years hence, or ever so many hundred years hence" (18) picks up the poem, he will be able to accurately recover the emotions it was meant to evoke. The line "Just as you feel when you look on the river and sky, so I felt" (22) is

---

[15] This piece originally appeared in *Literature* II (April 2, 1898), page 371, under the title "Aristocracy and Anarchism." In his notebooks Hardy quotes an explicit link between patriarchal systems and systems that thwart socialist aims. Under the heading "The Family and Socialism," Hardy quotes a review of W.H. Mallock's *Aristocracy and Evolution:*

'If I had the power,' said the Italian Socialist Rossi, 'to banish the greatest afflictions of this world, plagues, wars, famines, &c., I would renounce it, if instead I could suppress the family ...' Family life, as Mr. Mallock does well to point out, presents a fatal difficulty to practical socialism. (*Literary* 2.69)

more of an aspiration than a given, and the uncertainty infuses the line with pathos. The existence of the document, at least, is meant to sustain, or even replace, the hands that composed it. In the lines "Consider, you who peruse me, whether I may not in unknown ways be looking upon you" (112), the body of the author and the body of the text are conflated. Angel quotes from "Crossing Brooklyn Ferry" in chapter 25 ("The Consequence") of *Tess of the D'Urbervilles*, seeing Whitman as a kindred spirit as he concocts "a plan for plunging into that world anew" (120). Jude and Angel attempt to capture Whitman's optimism, and fail. Angel plunges into a disastrous marriage with Tess, fueled by false feelings of sympathy for rustic life and faded aristocracy. Jude's disaster comes from trying to idealize potential surrogate fathers and mothers.

Jude says to the wind, "You ... were in Christminster city between one and two hours ago: floating along the streets, pulling round the weather-cocks, touching Mr. Phillotson's face, being breathed by him; and now you are here, breathed by me; you, the very same" (19). When looking into a well while drawing water, he thinks again of becoming Phillotson: "I've seen him look down into it, when he was tired with his drawing just as I do now, and when he rested a bit before carrying the buckets home. But he was too clever to bide here any longer—a small sleepy place like this!" (5).[16] Jude's emphasis on the difference between Phillotson's travel and his own stasis initiates a new campaign for repetition, as Jude also resolves to leave. Until then, Jude can only be a partial echo of Phillotson, because he is unsure whether he can follow his imagined father to this seemingly inaccessible Alma Mater. The hold that Christminster has on Jude, despite its "funereally dark" visage at times (17) has "a tangibility, a permanence, a hold on his life" because "the man for whose knowledge and purposes he had so much reverence was actually living there; not only so, but living among the more thoughtful and mentally shining ones therein" (18). The relationship is incestuous because the mentor, the father figure, is contained *inside* of the desired mother. Jude wants Phillotson to be the father of his ambitions, even as Phillotson is hoping that Christminster will give birth to him as well.

Jude later seeks father figures in the hymn-composer and the apothecary, only to find that his idealistic devotion is again misplaced. Eventually, he tests national inheritance as a replacement for personal family ties, but finds himself at the suicide's crossroads. As he thinks about his rejection letter from one of Christminster's colleges, he thinks "of what struggling people like himself had stood at that Crossway, whom nobody ever thought of now," how "at Fourways men had stood and talked of Napoleon, the loss of America, the execution of King Charles, the burning of the Martyrs, the Crusades, the Norman Conquest, possibly of the arrival of Caesar" (121). Here, Jude tries to place himself in a decidedly English "royal" lineage, straining to find additional layers of connection as he moves back in time. As with Stephen Dedalus, in another famous *künstlerroman*, the effort leads to a sense of

---

[16]   Compare with Whitman's "Crossing Brooklyn Ferry": "Just as you stand and lean on the rail, yet hurry with the swift current, I stood yet was hurried" (25).

disorientation rather than rootedness.[17] Jude's conscious yearning for a generational connection is tied to material objects that represent the culture he hopes to acquire. Phillotson's piano becomes one symbol of his potential as parent and mentor. It is held by "an old maiden resident" (3) at the start of the story because Phillotson does not have room for it, or for what it represents. When Jude asks Phillotson for "any old second-hand copies" (25) of Latin grammars, he sends the letter inside of the pianoforte that Phillotson, finally settled in Christminster, has just sent for (25). In exchange for the instrument, however, Jude is given "two thin books" (25), a meager inheritance and unequal exchange that foreshadows Jude's disillusioned assessment of Phillotson as "an obviously much chastened and disappointed man" (102). Their reunion "destroyed at one stroke the halo which had surrounded the schoolmaster's figure in Jude's imagination ever since their parting" (102).

Jude's first extended meditation on "the letter" comes courtesy of those Latin grammars, which he thought would be the "secret cipher" that "would enable him, by merely applying it, to change at will all words of his own speech into those of the foreign one" (26). The process of his disillusionment reveals how all documents hold within them the history of every owner. The new reader cannot always select which layers of the text to attend to:

> The book was an old one—thirty years old, soiled, scribbled wantonly over with a strange name in every variety of enmity to the letterpress, and marked at random with dates twenty years earlier than his own day. But this was not the cause of Jude's amazement. He learnt for the first time that there was no law of transmutation, as in his innocence he had supposed (there was, in some degree, but the grammarian did not recognize it); but that every word in both Latin and Greek was to be individually committed to memory at the cost of years of plodding. (26)

The economic history of texts—their status as inheritable objects—threatens their use value as transporters of information.[18] The markings in pen and ink

---

[17]   See Stephen Dedalus's schoolbook exercise in *A Portrait of the Artist as a Young Man*, when he tries to locate himself in his world:
>   Stephen Dedalus.
>   Class of Elements.
>   Clongowes Wood College.
>   Sallins.
>   County Kildare.
>   Ireland.
>   Europe.
>   The World.
>   The Universe (12)
Stephen eventually sees familial, local, and national affiliations as "nets" that he must escape rather than embrace.

[18]   Hardy's narrative of Jude's education echoes debates that reemerged in late Victorian culture about the value of classical education, especially the study of Greek and Latin, most vividly realized in Matthew Arnold's "Literature and Science" (1893–1894), written to counter challenges leveled by T.H. Huxley and others as proponents of technical, vocational training.

threaten to obscure the print that links Jude with the education he craves. Jude's dream of having the dead speak again is complicated by the question, *which dead?* Jude realizes that it will require "a labour like that of Israel in Egypt" (26) to recover classical knowledge within a 30-year-old text with 20-year-old scribbles, bequeathed to Jude by a middle-aged man. Jude's inability to decipher this multi-layered text leads him, in despair, to link the span of his life with his reading habits: "he wished he had never seen a book, that he might never see another, that he had never been born" (27).

Jude tries to counter his failure to manage one dialogic text with another. His next grammar is a "Greek Testament ... with better type than his old copy, following Griesbach's text as amended by numerous correctors, and with variorum readings in the margin" (40). The text is so littered with overwriting that he has to cover up the margin translations if he has any hope of learning from it. He also reads "the Twenty-Ninth Volume of Pusey's Library of the Fathers" in a "second-hand" copy, obtained "at a price that seemed to him to be one of miraculous cheapness for that invaluable work" (148). Jude's concept of value, centered in humanistic knowledge, clashes with market value. This acquisition is one of many instances in which Jude mistakes obsolescence for actual value in an industrial economy. His self-delusions, argues a writer in the *Saturday Review* (February 8, 1896), mirror the delusions of several of Jude's class at the time: "If the reader is one of those who have been educated from the beginning, it may interest him to learn that today in the second-hand bookshops old out-of-date textbooks are sold by the thousand" (153). The sympathetic review chastises those who see the novel as anything other than a "tremendous indictment of the system which closes our three English teaching Universities to what is, and what has always been, the noblest material in the intellectual life of this country—the untaught" (154). Hardy's focus pairs him with George Meredith, ends the review, as one who forces readers of "Wardour Street romancers and whimpering Scotch humourists" to move "from a library into a schoolroom" (154).

Sue, Jude's cousin and fellow family fatalist, also wrongly believes that she can gain mastery of the new world of men and their books. Sue says, "My life has been entirely shaped by what people call a peculiarity in me. I have no fear of men, as such, nor of their books" (152). Sue's rearranging of the Testaments, and her annoyance at the headings added to editions of the Song of Songs ("It seems the drollest thing to think of the four-and-twenty elders, or bishops, or whatever number they were, sitting with long faces and writing down such stuff" [157]) are meant to be signs of her liberation from the oppressive texts of patriarchs. Yet Sue, too, is more of a copier and compiler than an author. Imitation creeps into all of her supposed statements of rebellion. When Sue leaves Phillotson for her lover, Jude, she vows to "live by" John Stuart Mill's statement from *On Liberty* that "She or he, 'who lets the world, or his own portion of it, choose his plan of life for him, has no need of any other faculty than the ape-like one of imitation'" (34). In imitating the statement about imitation, Sue instead behaves like the masses described in Mill's "The Spirit of the Age," as he outlines the attractions of "worldly power."

"The conditions which confer worldly power are still, amidst all changes of circumstances, the same as in the middle ages—namely, the possession of wealth, or the being employed and trusted by the wealthy," he writes (26). In the face of the "three distinguishable sources of moral influence" (27)—the appearance of wisdom (traditional authority), religion (charismatic authority), or "worldly power" (27)—he proclaims, "All persons, from the most ignorant to the most instructed, from the most stupid to the most intelligent, have their minds more or less under the dominion of one or other, or all, of the influences which have just been mentioned" (27). Thus, there is a distinct irony in Sue's attempt to live by Mill's statement, as she supposedly attempts to liberate herself from patriarchal texts. After Sue achieves freedom from the marriage tie with Phillotson, she offers Jude a different kind of apish devotion, an offer to copy out a manuscript for "The Roman Antiquities of Wessex" (245). Trained as an ecclesiastical engraver by her father, Sue re-inscribes other's works rather than creating her own. Jude sees in her "strictly proper" and "lifelessly spoken" words something cribbed "from a list of model speeches in 'The Wife's Guide to Conduct" (197). Her attempts to conquer men by conquering their books ring as false as Jude's attempt to curtail new desires by reading old "sermons on discipline" and "passages in Church history that treated of the Ascetics of the second century" (199), and equally ineffective.

Drusilla Fawley fails to convince Jude to avoid the marital or intellectual aspects of the family curse.[19] Arabella embodies Jude's inability to read his way out of the limitations of his own body. Arabella becomes another of the margin scribblers in Jude's second-hand grammars. When she touches his books with her greasy hands, her fingers "left very perceptible imprints on the bookcovers" (68), reminders of the incompatibility of classical ideals with workman realities. To avoid recovering painful memories etched onto "wayside objects" on the road to Alfredston, Jude tries to read books instead (66), but that attempt at *escape* from repetition itself *constitutes* a repetition. The narrator explains, "he sometimes felt that by caring for books he was not escaping commonplace nor gaining rare ideas, every working man being of that taste now" (66).

The novel's repetitions, although inevitable in *some* form, cannot be forced into *preferred* shapes. Jude cannot will himself to drown where his mother drowned, because ice over the water prevents him; nature's overwriting obscures the possibility of exact repetition. However, despite his best efforts, a different kind of overwriting happens without him. As John Plotz writes in *Portable Property* (2008), in Hardy's novels the "characters' inescapable, untransferrable, and unavoidably diverse ways of perceiving the world travel with them" (Plotz 124). When Jude returns home from this failed suicide attempt, he finds traces of Arabella, "marks of pig-dressing, of fats and scallops," even though "the materials themselves had been taken away" (71). In a repetition of his father's abrupt abandonment of his mother, and foreshadowing Little Father Time's suicide note to the family on scrap paper, he finds his wife's note of abandonment written "on the inside of an old

---

[19]   She asserts that marriages in the family are destined to be disastrous, even deadly, and also that "[t]he boy is crazy for books, that he is. It runs in our family rather" (8).

envelope ... pinned to the cotton blower of the fireplace" (71). The novel insists on the continued relevance of parental influence on a child's social mobility and psychological stability, even when that child is unaware of what those inheritances entail. Jude discovers late in his brief life that his mother committed suicide after being abandoned by his father, setting the stage for his son's fratricide and suicide after feeling unwanted by his real and surrogate mothers.

Young Jude, Jude's son with Arabella, is heralded as the "beginning of the coming universal wish not to live" (355), a rupture from the past as well as a return. Jude and Sue hope to marry for his benefit, but he dissuades them after hearing an apocryphal family story that leads him to underscore both literary and familial ties. Sue says that the family story reminds her of the "tragic doom" of "the house of Atreus," and Jude adds echoes with the tragedy of "the house of Jeroboam" (297). If Sue is "sentimentally opposed to the horrors of over-restoration" (315) Little Father Time exists to preclude that possibility. In Patrick O'Malley's reading, Father Time represents late eighteenth-century Gothic imaginings disrupting a late Victorian text (663). In Andrew Miller's imaginings, Little Father Time, as with little Paul Dombey, both embodies and erases possibility. He writes, "The presence of a child encourages the thought that the future might be different; the presence of a dead child forces the thought that the past could have been different" (A. Miller 123). David Musselwhite calls Little Father Time "the return of all the undigested *meanings* of the text—the return of all the *de-signified* and *enigmatic signifiers* that bestrew the narrative—not least, perhaps, that admonishing pointing finger" (Musselwhite 184). If, as Hardy writes in his notebooks, quoting Walter Pater's *Appreciations,* "All art does but consist in the removal of surplusage. E.g. gem engraver" (*Literary* 2.17), then Little Father Time, who wields his lead instrument to write, "Done because we are too many" (*Jude* 355), is the ultimate artist.

Conclusion: "Broken Lines of the Original Idea"

Jude Fawley quotes the *Agamemnon,* "Things are as they are, and will be brought to their destined issue" (358), but in so doing, he distances himself from the author role in his own life. The clearest alternative to history as a straight line—history as cycle—fails him, just as matriarchy becomes, in this novel, a failed alternative to embedded patriarchal legacies. Circles are the shapes of haunting. Jude travels home "by a roundabout track" (11) when he is ashamed at being fired, and soon feels wary that the road to Christminster must repeat the path of that first failure (13–14). Jude is taking "a roundabout route which he did not usually frequent" (33) when he has his first ill-fated encounter with Arabella, and they traversed a "circular British earth-bank" shortly before she shows him the fragile eggs hidden in her bosom, the prelude to the first feigned conception and the second ill-fated one. Christminster, the place of unrealized hopes for Jude, exudes "the stillness of infinite motion—the sleep of the spinning top," a haunting phrase which, the narrator admits, is itself a borrowed idea (115).

How legible is one's own past when "man, even to himself, is a palimpsest, having an ostensible writing, and another beneath the lines" (Hardy, *Far* 240)? Jude finds it difficult to decipher a message he left for himself in the landscape without deferring to more established authorities:

> A milestone, now as always, stood at the roadside hard by. Jude drew near it, and felt rather than read the mileage to the city. He remembered that once on his way home he had proudly cut with his keen new chisel an inscription on the back of that milestone, embodying his aspirations. It had been done in the first week of his apprenticeship, before he had been diverted from his purposes by an unsuitable woman. He wondered if the inscription were legible still, and going to the back of the milestone brushed away the nettles. By the light of a match he could still discern what he had cut so enthusiastically so long ago:
>   THITHER J.F.
> The sight of it, unimpaired, within its screen of grass and nettles, lit in his soul a spark of the old fire. Surely his plan should be to move onward through good and ill—to avoid morbid sorrow even though he did see uglinesses in the world? Bene agere et lætari——to do good cheerfully—which he had heard to be the philosophy of one Spinoza, might be his own even now. (73–4)

This scene is a replay of Tess re-encountering Alec at "Cross-in-Hand," and having her hand forced by him onto a fragmented "stone pillar" of uncertain origins, "on which was roughly carved a human hand" (244). In that scene, Tess was forced to swear her allegiance to Alec, the father of her Sorrow, by linking her living hand with the imprint of that ancient one. Here, Jude redirects himself through his inscription on the back of a marker erected long before he first walked by. His inscription was meant to support the "official" documentation on the other side of the sign. The personal resolution spurred by the sign is not original to Jude, but borrowed (from "one Spinoza"). The borrowed sentiments placed on the back of the borrowed writing surface foreshadow and duplicate Jude's relationship with the products of his labor. He is a repairer rather than a creator, a "comrade of the dead handicraftsmen whose muscles had actually executed" the buildings (84). His work, as with any antiquarian working with texts, is an act of recovery, a recognition "in the old walls" of "the broken lines of the original idea; jagged curves, disdain of precision, irregularity, disarray" (85). The novel vacillates about whether the benefits of such restorations compensate for the decided lack of originality inherent in the attempt.

"Authorship," defined as one's individual ownership over new ideas, was in rapid development in Victorian Britain, as writers such as Dickens fought to maintain financial and editorial control over their works in the face of opportunistic international publishing schemes. Medieval writers did not make such a distinction. As Lauryn S. Mayer notes, citing Mary Carruthers and Elizabeth Bryan, "the medieval idea of writing did not make sharp distinctions between ... writing, copying, and compiling" (Mayer 123; see also Olson 30). Characters like Sue, who describe themselves as "more ancient than mediaevalism" (*Jude* 139), delude themselves into thinking that what they offer approaches authorship.

As with Sue's mere rearranging of the Bible—and the work of the Christminster students on the other side of the wall (Barnaby 47)—Jude's labor is merely derivative:

> Moreover he perceived that at best only copying, patching and imitating went on here; which he fancied to be owing to some temporary and local cause. He did not at that time see that mediævalism was as dead as a fern-leaf in a lump of coal; that other developments were shaping in the world around him in which Gothic architecture and its associations had no place. The deadly animosity of contemporary logic and vision towards so much of what he held in reverence was not yet revealed to him. (85)

Patrick O'Malley reads this passage as "a type of necrophilia, a desire for dead forms" that must be corrected even as it registers the narrator's "wistfulness" for what was lost (655). Michael Irwin argues, however, that the rumors of the "death" of medievalism are greatly exaggerated, and that Hardy always couples attempted erasures with attempted recoveries. As with the leaf in the lump of coal that may have itself helped to constitute the coal (O'Malley 657), the objects in the novel do not just disappear. There is always "an afterlife ... as opposed to mere dissolution" (Irwin 110).

Jude's dying body on Remembrance Day becomes a final text for the reader to examine:

> An occasional word, as from some one making a speech, floated from the open windows of the Theatre across to this quiet corner, at which there seemed to be a smile of some sort upon the marble features of Jude; while the old, superseded, Delphin editions of Virgil and Horace and the dog-eared Greek Testament on the neighbouring shelf, and the few other volumes of the sort he had not parted with, roughened with stone-dust where he had been in the habit of catching them up for a few minutes between his labours, seemed to pale to a sickly cast at the sounds. (430–31)

Jude's body has become an artifact, in line with the "dog-eared" and obsolete texts that he introduces to Hardy's readers. The "stone-dust" that covers everything encases the story of the scholar underneath that of the stonemason, and then turns the stonemason into a statue, the object of his labors.

When Sue argues, after *Jude the Obscure*'s pivotal murder-suicide, "I am glad—almost glad I mean— that they are dead, Richard. It blots out all that life of mine!" (418) or Jude says, quoting the book of Job, *"Let the day perish wherein I was born, and the night in which it was said, There is a man child conceived"* (426), their attempts at erasure fail due to the abundance of alternate documentation, as in to the marriage, birth, and death records appearing in the provincial newspapers. The novel, too, prevents Jude and those who represent his struggles from being completely "obscured," if not in his life, at least to future readers. Edward Barnaby calls realism the mode of "meta-spectacle: a making visible of the process whereby consciousness becomes distorted or concealed by the proliferation of discourses and images that objectify reality" (Barnaby 43). Barnaby describes a narrative process that performs the work of a palimpsest editor, "making visible" what a "proliferation of discourses and images" have "distorted or concealed."

Hardy writes in his preface to the first edition that the novel aims "to give shape and coherence to a series of seemings, or personal impressions, the question of their consistency or their discordance, of their performance or their transitoriness, being regarded as not of the first moment" (xxxv–xxxvi). Such an approach turns Hardy's work from a realist novel into a psychological novel, and Hardy's characters become embodiments of "impressions," given "shape and coherence" (perhaps "a local habitation and a name") by the author. By contrast, Hardy doubts that such shapes can be imposed on real human history. In a note written in 1885, Hardy said, thinking of politics in particular, "History is rather a stream than a tree. There is nothing organic in its shape, nothing systematic in its development. It flows on like a thunderstorm-rill by a road side; now a straw turns this way, now a tiny barrier of sand that. The offhand decision of some commonplace mind high in office at a critical moment influences the course of events for a hundred years" (Hardy, *Life* 179). Hardy uses the concept of the stream when describing literary inevitability as well as political exigencies. In the 1890 essay "Candour in English Fiction," Hardy calls Imagination "the slave of stolid circumstance" and rejects the possibility that literary "inventiveness" can escape being "conditioned by its surroundings like a river stream" (Hardy, *Thomas Hardy's Personal* 125).

The passages above express Hardy's attempt to "give shape and coherence" to his characters' unfortunate lives and troubled minds, but also his convictions about the arbitrariness of real "course[s] of events" *and* the author's "condition[ing]" by this arbitrariness. Together, the meditations throw Hardy's authorial control into question, or rather, his decisions about how to convey control or lack thereof to his readers. Was *Jude* crafted, discovered, compiled, birthed, or inherited? Was Hardy the writer, compiler, or copier of his own text? Hardy was vague when asked a similar question. He concluded, in a response to a review of the novel, dated November 10, 1895, "It required an artist to see that the plot is almost geometrically constructed—I ought not to say *constructed,* for, beyond a certain point, the characters necessitated it, and I simply let it come" (*Collected* 2.93). He begins with excitement that the reviewer understood his design, but then chooses to relinquish his claim as a designer. It is as if Hardy, as with George Meredith and Samuel Butler, cannot decide whether an author should present himself as a father or as a peer. His novels were composed, he suggests on the one hand, as a more open system than what cruel nature has offered to his doomed characters. Yet, another reading offers Hardy as the cleverest of parents, presenting the illusion of freedom but instead imposing his will forcefully on his creations. In writing Jude's swift and cruel decline, Hardy struck some readers as the latter. Swinburne wrote to Hardy, after struggling to complete the novel, "how cruel you are! Only the great and awful father of "Pierette" and "L'Enfant Maudit" was ever so merciless to his children" (Hardy, *Life* 288). Alternatively, one can see Hardy as subject to the same "natural forces" and "ordinary passions" (Hardy, *Jude* 272) as his protagonists.

Hardy, writing his final novel at the end of the Victorian age, but preparing to become the poetic voice of the early twentieth century, seems to straddle the roles of father and son. The act of writing itself offers him the opportunity to trouble both categories, allowing ancestors and offspring to blend into each other on one canvas.

Arabella gives her son with Jude his father's name, but everyone refers to him as "Little Father Time." He embodies the warping of "ordinary passions." He is "Age masquerading as Juvenility, and doing it so badly that his real self showed through crevices" (290). Similarly, Sue, the woman who aspires to be his adoptive mother, though she never gains this title legally, declares, rejecting Jude's label of her as "modern," "I am more ancient than mediaevalism, if you only knew" (139). The elder Jude, too, is out of time. In his youth, he was called "an ancient man in some phases of thought, much younger than his years in others" (22). When first at Christminster, he wears "a closely trimmed black beard of more advanced growth than is usual at his age" (77), and while walking its streets he begins to feel "a self-spectre ... almost his own ghost" (80). Even as a ghost, he fails to join a community of peers. Jude, Sue, and Little Father Time exist as if haunted by their past-ness, uncertain whether their spectral presences at the end of the Victorian era can sustain them into modernism. Hardy figures their status as out of time through references to reading and writing. Christminster's ghosts, the great authors and intellectuals of the past, overwrite Jude's own thoughts, yet his recovery of those voices is only partial: "As he drew toward sleep various memorable words of theirs that he had just been conning seemed spoken by them in muttering utterances; some audible, some unintelligible to him" (81–2).

Part of the novel's devastation comes in the haunting sense that the entire tragedy could have been averted had it been moved to another time. As Sue says, and as several critical reviews of the novel confirmed, "the time was not ripe for us! Our ideas were fifty years too soon to be any good to us" (422–3). [20] Despite the gap between her past and present selves, Sue expresses confidence that she, though "more ancient than medievalism" (139), can foreshadow the future. She says, "Everybody is getting to feel as we do. We are a little beforehand, that's all" (301). She claims, quoting Shelley's "terrible line of poetry" from *The Revolt of Islam* (1818), that in a few generations all will "see weltering humanity still more vividly than we do now, as 'Shapes like our own selves hideously multiplied,'" and will be afraid to reproduce them" (301). While Jude echoes the author of "Woman of the Future" in assuming that nature will reinforce the traditional family, Sue suggests that future acts of reproduction will speak to destruction of the past rather than its renovation.

---

[20]   In "On Some Critics of 'Jude the Obscure,'" (1896), Sir George Douglas offers an overview of the "united onslaught" (120) against Hardy's novel in prominent newspapers. He samples the *Pall Mall Gazette's* review of "Jude the Obscene" (120), *The World's* take on "Degenerate Hardy" (121), and the *Athenaeum's* assessment of *Jude* as "a titanically bad book" (121). Douglas is most irked by the *Guardian's* harsh review, though he does not find it surprising since that publication is "the guardian of conventional orthodoxy" (121), yet still reviewed a book Hardy warned was "not 'for use in families'" (120).

Sue's profession is "acquired from her father's occupation as an ecclesiastical worker in metal," and the letters etched by her are "clearly intended to be fixed up on some chancel to assist devotion" (89). Jude's profession, and fondness for church music, is acquired from Hardy's own father, the master mason (*Life* 12), and Jude's end is a darker repetition of the end of the elder Thomas Hardy. Hardy regretted his absence at his father's deathbed, but was glad to hear that his father's request for water from the family well was granted, unlike Jude's final request for water in the novel published three years later (262). In instilling his characters with qualities from his own father, Hardy shows awareness of a security in imagining alternative patriarchs for oneself. In an interview given while he was at the University of Aberdeen to receive an honorary doctorate (he, like Jude, never received a real one), he seemed to have other substitutes for the "letter" that "killeth" in mind (Tomalin, *Hardy* 284). He felt compelled to make a case for illegitimate children, saying that "illegitimacy—so far from being the blackest blot in a community—may be regarded in one aspect as a form of virtue" (qtd. in *Hardy* 285). Contrived relationships (Elizabeth Jane's and Jude's to the classics), are essentially illegitimate replacements for real fathers, but they allow one to have control over the shape of that inherited identity.

There are certainly echoes of Shakespeare's *King Lear* in Hardy's final novel, and also of Macbeth's "vaulting ambition" that arguably doom men to a lonely death, but the novel can also be seen as a version of *Hamlet's* play-within-a-play. Hardy's copy of *Hamlet* had "his father's name and the date of his death" scribbled beside the lines "Thou hast been / As one in suffering all that suffers nothing / A man that Fortune's buffets and rewards/ Hath ta'en with equal thanks" (Hardy, *Life* 262; Shakespeare, *Hamlet* III.ii.24–27). In the speech, Hamlet introduces his play-within-a-play, written to vindicate the father but also to shake off his ghost. In response to a friend's comment that life's meaning can be found in children, Hardy responded:

> For my part, if there is any way of getting a melancholy satisfaction out of life it lies in dying, so to speak, before one is out of the flesh; by which I mean putting on the manners of ghosts, wandering in their haunts, and taking their views of surrounding things. To think of life as passing away is a sadness; to think of it as past is at least tolerable. (Hardy, *Life* 218)

Here, Hardy sees a benefit to regarding himself as a ghost speaking to fellow ghosts, as one with Whitman's ferry-crosser rather than a descendent of him. He acknowledges, yes, that the past is past; on the other hand, he relegates himself to that very past.

Conclusion
The Father as "Type"

Notably, John Stuart Mill's delineation of "three distinguishable sources of moral influence" (*Spirit* 27) and Max Weber's outline of "three pure types of legitimate domination" (215) were left incomplete. Mill does not fulfill his promise to continue "The Spirit of the Age" after its fifth serialized installment. Weber subtitled *Economy and Society* "An Outline of Interpretive Sociology," and died before he could oversee the complete, multivolume, multiauthor series he envisioned (xxviii, lvi–lvii). Weber also knew that his pure types work only as rough models. In discussing the limits of his scheme he wrote, "It may be said of every historical phenomenon of authority that is it not likely to be 'as an open book'" (216). Yet, even as one of his "types" of authority melds with another (as charismatic authority, for example, must become traditional or legal-rational to survive beyond the first generation), the major classifications still resonate (216).

Subsequent readers of Weber have praised the usefulness of his "pure types," but have also offered suggestions. Usually, critics add a "fourth type." For example, Martin Spencer, writing in the 1970s, found legal-rational authority an insufficient category to explain extra-textual powers, as in how presidents of the United States have exercised powers beyond those delineated in the Constitution (Spencer 129). Spencer requested a distinction between legal-rational authority "as an administration of laws, not of men," as opposed to *value-rational* authority as "a government of principles, not of men" (130). Spencer was not alone in hoping for an ever "purer" and unmediated type of authority than Weber allowed—one that transcends men *and* their books.[1]

The attraction of frameworks such as Mill's and Weber's is the same as that of all systems of classification. Yet, as I close this volume, I must acknowledge that my work with Weber and Mill looks suspiciously like Sir Austin's "System" (Chapter 2), or Mr. Tulliver's demand that his son write "pretty nigh as well as if it was all wrote out for him" (Chapter 4). Perhaps I become like the "worshipper of conventualities or forms" (Chapter 1) that Patrick Brontë refused to see in himself, or as heavy-handedly didactic as Pendennis the narrator as opposed to Pendennis the character (Chapter 3). "You refused the plan I had looked to," Samuel Butler's father rails at him (Chapter 5). Perhaps he would find satisfaction in my reordering of his son's oeuvre. Maybe all frameworks resemble Casaubon's unfinished Key to All Mythologies, Sir Austin's controversial *Pilgrim's Scrip*, or Jude's illusory "law of transmutation" (Chapter 6). Thus, in my closing pages, as we leave the

---

[1]   See also Roberta Lynn Satow, "Value-Rational Authority and Professional Organizations: Weber's Missing Type" (1975), and Martin Barker, "Kant as a Problem for Weber" (1980).

Victorians and take a long view at our strategies in assessing them, I want to discuss categorization itself, especially as practiced by the "moderns" as they looked back at the Victorian patriarch.

This conclusion takes brief glimpses at an eighteenth century fictionalized autobiography, Sterne's *Tristram Shandy* (1759–1767), a Victorian fictionalized autobiography, Charles Dickens's *David Copperfield* (1849–1850), and a twentieth-century autobiography, Edmund Gosse's *Father and Son* (1907). Gosse's narrative ingests the arguments about "type" made in the previous centuries' major texts, as he self-consciously types his father as Victorian and himself as modern, and struggles to make sense of those terms. His summation of Victorian family narrative, enclosed within the refiguring of his childhood, however, seems to narrow the divide between the Victorian era, its parent, and its descendent.

The Child's Story, and the Father's Plot

The father figure who emerges from Victorian realist narrative does not resemble many figures from the previous century. He is not the gothic father of Walpole or Radcliffe, the recovered father who anchors the comic endings of Smollett or Fielding foundling narratives, or a Richardsonian patriarch, waiting at the receiving end of his daughter's epistolary effusions. Instead, he begins to resemble the patriarch of the chaotic, proto-modern novel *Tristram Shandy*. In this potentially endless—and ultimately unfinished—novel, the narratives of father and son create each other by competing for prominence. The struggle has formal implications. Tristram's opening accusation is that his parents' neurotic clock-watching at the moment of his conception did permanent damage to his physical body, his social standing, *and* his narrative. Had his parents been more attentive during his begetting, he argues, "I am verily persuaded I should have made a quite different figure in the world, from that, in which the reader is likely to see me" (Sterne 5). "Figure" has multiple meanings here: anatomical, directional, and rhetorical. The different "figure" he wants to strike, it seems, must be formed off the clock, against his father's planning. In rejecting his father's *Tristapaedia* alongside Horace's recommendations for narrative epic or tragedy, Tristram declares, "in writing what I have set about, I shall confine myself neither to his [Horace's] rules, nor to any man's rules that ever lived" (8). Yet Tristram's autobiography shares space with his father's conduct book; both works anxiously await the outcome of his body's development, just as they shape that development. The *Tristapaedia*—the book-within-a-book that guides Walter Shandy's attempts to guide his son—becomes the counterpoint to the near-formlessness of Tristram's digressive autobiography. Thus, Walter Shandy becomes both a rejected aesthetic authority and the ultimate aesthetic authority, as his text becomes model and counterpoint for the son's work. Here, perhaps, I find a way to explain the paradox underlying this book. What could have become a Bloomian *Anxiety of Influence* narrative, as sons and daughters react to fathers, is instead equally concerned with the Anxiety of the *Influencer*, as he tries, through writing and editing, to preserve himself as a living model.

My interest in this project began with Charles Dickens, specifically his 1848 novel *Dombey and Son*, the novel that bridges the divide between his freewheeling serials and his carefully planned major novels. Yet, to this point, I have only gestured toward Dickens. Critical discussions of family dynamics in Charles Dickens's novels have been so thorough and voluminous that their conclusions need only be sketched here. Catherine Waters's *Dickens and the Politics of the Family* (1997), Charles Hattens's sections about Dickens in *The End of Domesticity* (2010), Hilary Schor's *Dickens and the Daughter of the House* (1999), Goldie Morgentaler's *Dickens and Heredity* (2000), Andrew Dowling's section on Dickens in *Manliness and the Male Novelist in Victorian Literature* (2001), and Linda Zwinger's work with Dickens in *Daughters, Fathers and the Novel* (1991) have all influenced my thinking about the convener of *Household Words*.[2]

In *The Tragi-Comedy of Victorian Fatherhood* (2009), Valerie Sanders's biographies of several middle-class fathers, including Dickens, serve as counterpoints to the early twentieth-century "appetite for thrilling stories of paternal bullying" (167).[3] Dickens, the father of a large brood who named all but one of his sons after writers (69), nevertheless wrote many novels that sidestepped the father altogether (81). Holly Furneaux's *Queer Dickens* (1999) finishes this work, in emphasizing the homosocial alternatives to the nuclear family that are so

---

[2]   According to Charles Hatten, Dickens's goal was to reauthorize the patriarch—to employ "familial prescriptiveness as a central part of his effort to project his own authority as a writer" (34). Yet, Hatten admits that some of Dickens's longer pieces, such as the *Pickwick Papers*, sidestep family by focusing on "a celebration of male homosocial bonds," while works such as *Oliver Twist* and *The Old Curiosity Shop* do so by being "dominated by the grotesque and often criminal world of the city and the road" (38). In *Dickens and the Daughter of the House*, Hilary Schor claims that almost all of Dickens's fictional daughters emerge from patriarchal narratives through acts of writing, acts of "plotting" themselves. In her readings, the pattern only breaks with *Our Mutual Friend;* she writes, "the daughter, in this book, has no word of her own, and only by renouncing plotting can she fill her place, only by becoming property can she inherit" (178). She registers the shift as related to a reconsideration, by Dickens, of the power and efficacy of writing itself, saying, "only by the deepest distrust of the magic of fictions can Dickens write his last novel" (178). Linda Zwinger also contends that Dickens, as much as any other author, perpetuates the myth of the dutiful child who easily compensates for the absent mother by caring for the father. However, she claims, "In *Dombey and Son*, Dickens comes as close as he ever does to revealing the hollowness of his fictional, and his culture's ideological, daughter alibis" (37).

[3]   In contrast with books focusing on literary representations of fatherhood, Sanders offers sketches of real Victorian fathers along the lines of Smiles's *Self-Help* (1859), with the implied goal of recuperating them as real, complicated men. She gestures explicitly to authority only in her conclusion, suggesting that fatherhood "functioned ultimately as a cultural symbol, a concept of authority, in dialogue with contemporary notions of masculinity" (191). My book has worked to bridge the gap between her well-researched biographical sketches and the many studies of literary representations of families, by examining print culture itself, and the father's engagement with it, as a major source of Victorian, and modern, cultural myths.

important in his fictions, from *Pickwick* and *Oliver* onward. She discusses bachelor narratives, fostering and surrogacy, male nursing, and "homoerotically motivated intermarriage" (15). She connects such alternatives to the family romance with the freedoms of serial publication (86–7), a format that allows for perpetual deferral of the comic resolution. Thus, his novels offer a compelling push and pull, towards and away from reliance on the fathers of families.

Charles Dickens may have had Laurence Sterne's opening in mind as he penned the beginning of *Dombey and Son* (1848), his most concentrated analysis of parent-child dynamics. As with the father and child in *Tristram Shandy*, this father and son are also on differing timetables. Dombey Senior, regarding his son of 48 minutes from the perspective of 48 years, stands over him shaking "the heavy gold watch-chain that depended from below his trim blue coat" (1). Dombey Sr. wants to hurry little Paul's entrance into adulthood and business partnership, but, as Dickens's first readers found to their surprise and dismay, little Paul had other plans. Dickens may also channel Sterne in the opening of *David Copperfield*, a *künstlerroman* that begins with yet another son watching the clock. David must contrast the certainty of such timepieces with his uncertain grasp on his own story:

> Whether I shall turn out to be the hero of my own life, or whether that station will be held by anybody else, these pages must show. To begin my life with the beginning of my life, I record that I was born (as I have been informed and believe) on a Friday, at twelve o'clock at night. It was remarked that the clock began to strike, and I began to cry, simultaneously. (13)

Readers soon learn why the second David Copperfield has trouble knowing whether he is the "hero of [his] own life." He has no model in his own father, for whom he is named, because they are, yet again, on opposing timetables: "I was a posthumous child. My father's eyes had closed upon the light of this world six months, when mine opened on it" (14). David's opening sentences betray his tentative steps toward authoring himself. He begins with the beginning, because that is where one must begin. He reports facts received secondhand, and his sources are vague, faceless, and nameless. If his life is to run like clockwork—which also means, in this case, running like the typical bildungsroman, with all of its inherited conventions—then it must run on, essentially, a "grandfather" clock.[4] By chapter 2, David has embarked upon a "meandering" narrative that would make Tristram proud, deciding to rely only upon "my own experience of myself" (25).

Yet, David is not as free as he believes himself to be, because a patriarch's physical body can be replaced by his books. When young David Copperfield visits his foster guardian, Mr. Micawber, in debtor's prison, he can only think about Roderick Random's similar experience in Smollett's 1748 novel. Andrew Dowling sees the initial chapters as exemplifying Dickens's interest in the father/son relationship as one of "expulsion and return" (53). He writes, "David needs to move outside the domestic hearth, into the cold world of violence and death where his father already lies, before he can finally return as the father" (53). Ironically,

---

4   See John Maynard, "The Bildungsroman" (2002).

given Dickens's inability to write the story of his own profligate father and difficult childhood (we have only the autobiographical fragment passed to us via Forster's biography, as expanded beautifully by Clare Tomalin in *Charles Dickens: A Life* [2011]), David needs to use novels in order to access patriarchs. His attempt to access the father, and appropriate his authority, is through his father's "small collection of books in a little room upstairs" (65), which David trawls through in chapter 4 of the novel:

> From that blessed little room, Roderick Random, Peregrine Pickle, Humphrey Clinker, Tom Jones, The Vicar of Wakefield, Don Quixote, Gil Blas, and Robinson Crusoe, came out, a glorious host, to keep me company. They kept alive my fancy, and my hope of something beyond that place and time—they, and the *Arabian Nights*, and the *Tales of the Genii*—and did me no harm, for whatever harm was in some of them was not there for me; I knew nothing of it. It is astonishing to me now, how I found time, in the midst of my porings and blunderings over heavier themes, to read those books as I did. It is curious to me how I could ever have consoled myself under my small troubles (which were great troubles for me), by impersonating my favorite characters in them—as I did—and by putting Mr. and Miss Murdstone into all the bad ones—which I did too. I have been Tom Jones (a child's Tom Jones, a harmless creature) for a week together. I have sustained my own idea of Roderick Random for a month at a stretch, I verily believe. (65)

In retrospect, David is surprised that these early novels have had such an effect on his self-fashioning. It is as if the absence of his father in the flesh is alleviated by the host of literary families that he left behind. However, the contrast between David's deceased father and his surrogate, Mr. Micawber (the fictional father most closely modeled after Dickens's own) is clear by chapter 11, when David has to help Mr. Micawber sell his books in order to pay debts. And, despite his early avid reading, David becomes famously befuddled when he needs to identify "real" parent/child relationships, as with his confusion in meeting Mr. Peggotty in chapter 3 of the novel:

> Mr. Peggotty was smoking his pipe. I felt it was a time for conversation and confidence.
> "Mr. Peggotty!" says I.
> "Sir," says he.
> "Did you give your son the name of Ham, because you lived in a sort of ark?"
> Mr. Peggotty seemed to think it a deep idea, but answered:
> "No, sir. I never giv him no name."
> "Who gave him that name, then?" said I, putting question number two of the catechism to Mr. Peggotty.
> "Why, sir, his father giv it him," said Mr. Peggotty.
> "I thought you were his father!"
> "My brother Joe was his father," said Mr. Peggotty.
> "Dead, Mr. Peggotty?" I hinted, after a respectful pause.
> "Drowndead," said Mr. Peggotty. (43)

The comical conversation continues through several more iterations, as David discovers that Emily is not Mr. Peggotty's daughter (her father, Mr. Peggoty's brother-in-law, is also "Drowndead" [43]), that Mr Peggotty is childless, and that the "person in the apron who was knitting" was not Mr Peggotty's wife, but rather "the widow of his partner in a boat" (44). Surprisingly, given all of his reading, David is unable to recognize real fathers, real children, or real orphans. David instead expects to see the nuclear family at every turn. *David Copperfield* is thus less of an "orphan" narrative than one may think; instead, it is about the inescapable, though ghostly, *presence* of that father. Eventually, David experiences his father's near resurrection in the figure of Mr. Murdstone, heralded by the "unwholesome wind" David feels coming from the churchyard (Nunokawa 191).

These fictionalized autobiographies—which are as much about the difficulties of writing family narrative as living it, in that both Tristram and David present themselves as authors—have echoes in Edmund Gosse's autobiography. In *Father and Son*, Gosse describes himself, in his youthful precocity, in a way that resonates with the "old fashioned" (136) boy Paul Dombey in Dickens's 1848 novel. Mr. Dombey, with his eyes on the clock, fears his son's fascination with an early death: "'He was speaking to me last night about his—about his Bones,' said Mr. Dombey, laying an irritated stress on the word. 'What on earth has anybody to do with the— with the—Bones of my son? He is not a living skeleton, I suppose" (69). In this work, little Paul Dombey's fate is clear from the start, though the swiftness of his decline surprised early readers. In his autobiography, Gosse describes himself as the same kind of unnatural boy, detailing his mother's deathbed dedication of his soul to God, and his premature baptism into a community of adult saints. Edmund Gosse is also rushed along on his father's accelerated timetable, and his lack of childlike innocence is similarly registered through his interest in bones. Of his precocious statement that a skeleton is a "man with the meat off," Gosse writes, adding:

> I had often watched my Father, while he soaked the flesh off the bones of fishes and small mammals. If I venture to repeat this trifle, it is only to point out that the system on which I was being educated deprived all things, human life among the rest, of their mystery. (51)

Gosse's *Father and Son* is the autobiographical narrative of one man's attempt to understand his own "Victorian" father. In laying out his relationship with his father, Gosse depends on strong contrasts. He calls his story a "record of the clash of two temperaments" and "a case of Everything or Nothing'" (251). This record is not fiction, and his goal is not, he says, to write about himself. He relates, in refusing to elaborate on his unjustly undiagnosed nearsightedness, "this is not an autobiography, and with the cold and shrouded details of my uninteresting school-life I will not fatigue the reader" (217). Gosse claims for himself a kind of narrative farsightedness, even as he condemns those around him for failing to correct his vision. Ironically, in light of his aversion to cold science, Gosse describes his book in scientific terms, as "a *document*, as a record of educational and religious conditions which, having passed away, will never return" (33) and as "a study of the development of moral and intellectual ideas during the progress of infancy" (33). If Gosse writes against his father thematically, he still self-consciously speaks his father's language.

Gosse's stark dichotomies lend a rigid structure to the autobiography, as when he says halfway through, "My public baptism was the central event of my whole childhood. Everything, since the earliest dawn of consciousness, seemed to have been leading up to it. Everything, afterwards, seemed to be leading down and away from it" (156). As with the footprint that marks the center of Defoe's *Robinson Crusoe* (1719),—the turning point from a narrative of exodus to a narrative of return—this is a spiritual autobiography, a "narrative of a spiritual struggle" (34) that reveals its bones and makes its inner workings visible. At every turn, Gosse self-consciously describes his text as full of clearly interpretable symbols. Gosse turns his father into an embodiment of the passing of the nineteenth century, calling his book "the record of a struggle between two temperaments, two consciences and almost two epochs" (35).

Although Gosse adheres to a strict form, he does not do so without recording the emotional downsides of ordered narrative. When he comments on his father's journal entry for the day of his birth—"E. delivered of a son. Received green swallow from Jamaica"—he suggests that his father values his research as much as he values his new son, and also links the father with a strict adherence to time and timing (38). He writes, "The green swallow arrived later in the day than the son, and the earlier visitor was therefore recorded first; my father was scrupulous in every species of arrangement" (38). The statement recalls Walter Shandy's *Tristapaedia* and his regular clock winding, the conduct book writers' regular aphorisms, and Paul Dombey Sr.'s heavy timepieces.

The son asks himself if he can create art in this context. Edmund Gosse is not allowed to duplicate young Richard Feverel's wild scrawl, but is "forced, in deep depression of spirits, to turn from my grotesque monographs, and paint under my father's eye, and from a finished drawing of his … touch by touch, pigment by pigment, under the orders of a task master" (148). He begins to copy his father's scientific writing by the age of 10, and to keep his "uncouth handwriting in bounds, [he] was obliged to rule not lines only, but borders to the pages" (148). Since the "subject did not lend itself to any flow of language," Gosse "was obliged incessantly to 'borrow' sentences, word for word, from [his] Father's published books" (147).

In my previous chapters, the child's narrative competes not only with the father's story, but also with a marketplace full of competing versions of family life. Gosse responds to competition in arguing that since both of his parents had public biographies written about them, his autobiography will instead focus on what those texts left out (42–3). Gosse insists that the book is an alternative to mere repetition of what has been written. He wants to emphasize that he has more to say than just his parent's names. "It has been recorded that I was slow in learning to speak," he writes, "I used to be told that having met all invitations to repeat such words as 'Papa' and 'Mama' with gravity and indifference, I one day drew towards me a volume, and said 'book' with startling distinctness" (47). Gosse records what we have seen all along, that books are a way to access the father, but also, at least at first, a way to work around him. However, like David Copperfield, the young Gosse relies upon his parents even within this story of bypassing them. Gosse "used to be told" the story of his first words, presumably by the same figures who were bypassed by those words.

Gosse underscores his continued dependence on family narratives within the structure of his own, in an anecdote about the reading he completes *outside* of his father's study, in his story about finding part of a romance inside of a hatbox:

> The hat-box puzzled me extremely, till one day, asking my Father what it was, I got a distracted answer which led me to believe that it was itself a sort of hat, and I made a laborious but repeated effort to wear it. The skin-trunk was absolutely empty, but the inside of the lid of it was lined with sheets of what I now know to have been a sensational novel. It was, of course, a fragment, but I read it, kneeling on the bare floor, with indescribable rapture ... This ridiculous fragment filled me with delicious fears; I fancied that my Mother, who was out so much, might be threatened by dangers of the same sort; and the fact that the narrative came abruptly to an end, in the middle of one of its most thrilling sentences, wound me up almost to a disorder of wonder and romance. (59)

This encounter was facilitated by his father's distraction; his inability to provide a decisive answer led Gosse to construct one for himself. Again, however, as with Mary Shelley's Victor Frankenstein, who blames his father's distraction for the creation of his monster, or George Eliot's Latimer, who blames his father's distraction for his morbid sensibilities, a *lack* of instruction sends the youthful Gosse to "almost a disorder of wonder and romance" (59).[5] The youthful Gosse tries to impose fiction on the real, rather than the other way around. Richard Feverel tried to remove the constricting skin of the *Pilgrim's Scrip*, but young Gosse tries

---

[5]   Upon recalling that his father called his most fanciful reading in speculative science "sad trash" (M. Shelley 22) after only a "cursory glance" (22) and without further comment, Victor says, "If, instead of this remark, my father had taken the pains to explain to me, that the principles of Agrippa had been entirely exploded ... [i]t is even possible, that the train of my ideas would never have received the fatal impulse that led to my ruin" (22). George Eliot's Latimer, making a pitch for "a little more sympathy from strangers when I am dead" (Eliot, *Lifted* 4), blames his father's decision that "a scientific education was the really useful training for a younger son" (6) for the "uncongenial medium" that prevented his "happy, healthy development" (7). It is unlikely that readers were meant to take Victor and Latimer seriously, as they drew on a strategy for gaining sympathy that was as old as the first novel. Robinson Crusoe's father attempts to dissuade his son from going to sea with every brand of authority he could muster: "serious and excellent counsel" (Defoe 27), "tears" (29), and the economic argument that "the middle station of life was calculated for all kinds of vertues and all kinds of enjoyments" (28). Whereas Victor and Latimer blame a lack of parental advice for their disastrous paths, Crusoe sets the precedent for anticipating the necessity of reading against the son's description of cause and effect. Crusoe's final success would not be possible had he *not* ignored his father.

to wear the text that he finds.[6] One gets the sense ("ridiculous fragment") that the fiction doesn't deserve the rapturous response it receives from an innocent Gosse. In narrating his response in retrospect, Gosse uses the word "fancy" rather than "imagination," which means that in a Coleridgean sense he is participating in association rather than creation.[7] A more trained reader of romance would see this fragment as an invitation to invent the rest of the fictional story as he saw fit, but this untrained child can only immediately reinstate father and mother into what he reads.

As with Casaubon's *Key to All Mythologies* in Eliot's *Middlemarch* and Theobald's sermons on geology in Samuel Butler's *The Way of All Flesh*, so with the *Omphalos* of Gosse's father. *Omphalos* (1857) is famous for attempting to reconcile the geological record with the Bible, by suggesting that God made the earth look older than it is to test man's faith. Edmund Gosse writes that

> Never was a book cast upon the waters with greater anticipations of success than was this curious, this obstinate, this fanatical volume"; his father thought that *Omphalos* "was to bring all the turmoil of scientific speculation to a close, fling geology into the arms of Scripture, and make the lion eat grass with the lamb. (104–5)

Gosse casts his father as Casaubon or as Richard Feverel. Like them, his desire is to create a perfect synthesis. Gosse writes, "My Father, and my Father alone, possessed the secret of the enigma; he alone held the key which could smoothly open the lock of geological mystery ... But alas! atheists and Christians alike looked at it, and laughed, and threw it away" (105).

All of the narratives of father and child in this study have discussed the relationship between family fictions and families in the world, as novelists experiment with extra-literary sources of authority. *Father and Son*, a biography about a father but also an autobiography about the discovery of fiction, does similar work, but in reverse, by renovating the biography by discussing fiction within it. In its first lines, the son declares, "At the present hour, when fiction takes forms so ingenious and so specious, it is perhaps necessary to say that the following narrative, in all its parts, as so far as the punctilious attention of the writer has been able to keep it so, is scrupulously true" (33). As one expects through all of the qualifying statements in the sentence, the rest of the narrative concerns itself with trying to make room for fiction within the "scrupulously true." The young Gosse was not allowed to read any fiction as a youth because of his mother, who

---

6   The *Pilgrim's Scrip* in Meredith's *Ordeal of Richard Feverel* is analogous with the "Great Scheme" of Gosse's father to make his son into a walking example of grace and piety (212).

7   In *Biographia Literaria* (1817), Coleridge calls fancy "no other than a mode of Memory emancipated from the order of time and space" that "must receive all its materials ready made from the law of association" (Coleridge, *Portable* 516). By contrast, imagination "dissolves, diffuses, dissipates, in order to re-create ... It is essentially *vital*, even as all objects (*as* objects) are essentially fixed and dead" (516).

had "a remarkable, I confess to me still somewhat unaccountable, impression that
to 'tell a story', that is, to compose fictitious narrative of any kind, was a sin" (48).
Gosse sees this as "a very painful instance of the repression of an instinct" (49),
and opines that she should have been a novelist (49). The young Gosse faults his
parents' plans for his education. He writes that they "were in error thus to exclude
the imaginary from my outlook upon facts," a decision that made him "positive
and skeptical" rather than "truthful" (50). Thus, rejecting his father's models goes
hand-in-hand with rejecting the literalist readings that his youthful self, not having
been exposed to fiction, imposes on the hatbox. Gosse tries to gain independence
by expanding his artistic repertoire, by experimenting his way out of symbolism
and metaphor, in essence seeking to cultivate the "sympathetic imagination" (78)
that his parents lacked. Thus, for example, he worships a chair to test his father's
admonition that worshipping wood will bring down God's wrath (67). He hopes to
forge a new relationship with symbolic language.

The epilogue of *Father and Son* is telling, both in what it claims and what it
leaves out. Gosse writes, "This narrative, however, must not be allowed to close
with the Son in the foreground of the piece. If it has a value, that value consists
in what light it may contrive to throw upon the unique and noble figure of the
father. With the advance of years, the characteristics of this figure became more
severely outlined, more rigorously confined within settled limits" (236). On the
surface, Gosse performs a retreat, handing the text that only flirted with usurping
the father safely back to him. However, Gosse inherits from other children writing
about fathers a connection between describing the patriarch and reconceptualizing
his own relationship to literary history. The son claims to focus primarily on
the father, but the narrative is presented here, as elsewhere, strongly from the
perspective of the child. Gosse acknowledges, even as he tells this symbolic story
of father and son, that he stands at a juncture at which such stories can be told only
under the most extreme circumstances. Of the time when his mother falls ill, and
thus eclipses his father in his young imagination, he writes, "Everything seemed to
be unfixed, uncertain; it was like being on the platform of a railway-station waiting
for a train" (80). Of the periods in his life when he interacts with other children
he has to "record the fact, which I think is not without interest, that precisely as
my life ceases to be solitary, it ceases to be distinct" (185). He explains, "I have
no difficulty in recalling, with the minuteness of a photograph, scenes in which
my Father and I were the sole actors within the four walls of a room, but of the
glorious life among wild boys on the margin of the sea I have nothing but vague
and broken impressions, delicious and illusive" (185). This turn away from system
seems to embody the divide between Victorianism and Modernism, but, I will
argue as I conclude, fragmentation and uncertainty is its own kind of System.

Clear "Type" on Scattered Leaves

The System and the Fragment only seem to be at odds. One is structuralist, adding
order and offering answers. Others offer the imp of deconstruction, rejecting

attempts to come to conclusions about words, sentences, paragraphs, and chapters. I end this book by asking, however, cannot the fragment itself present a "system"—a strategy for making disorder itself mean something? I think back to Elizabeth Gaskell's consistently "eccentric" fathers, Meredith's return to "conduct" in his final novel, Thackeray's embrace of "fairyland" and Eliot's of abstraction, Butler's paradoxical science of disinheritance, and Hardy's recovery of "what has been blotted." The fragment inspired both fear and awe in the hearts of the Romantics. It came to represent objects and forces that were formerly unconquerable, but that can now be contained within the mind of man. The crumbled monument could elicit pity or reverence. Shelley's Romantic poem "Ozymandias" (1818) dramatizes the textual chaos that results from a chastened authority. In the poem, two wanderers attempt to access another culture through its crumbled artifact. Both wanderers are at a loss because they are at a double remove. The traveler and the poetic speaker resort to a dialogic process of improvisation and imaginative partial reconstruction. In the process, the poetic speaker loses control over his own poem. The traveler speaks all but the first ten words of the poem, and the pedestal speaks 15 more. The authorial figure standing at the pedestal, wondering what to take away from the spectacle, is at a loss. "Nothing beside remains" (ln. 12). The form of the poem complements the fragment aesthetics of its content. An otherwise perfect sonnet is broken to bits by the frequent shifts in speaker (D'Haen 113).

Just as it may seem presumptuous to look for order not only among Victorian men, but in Victorian writing, it seems presumptuous to assume that formal disorder is where Modernism breaks with the era, rather than continues some of its major preoccupations. Victorians inherited the romantic fascination with the fragment, relating it as much to their present moment as to reconsiderations of the past. The system-builders all understood the conflict between what they hoped to build, and the materials. In his work on *Heroes and Hero-Worship*, Thomas Carlyle laid out his own set "types"—prophets, priests, kings, and the "Man of Letters"—with confidence. Yet, he begins to despair when asked to find the same sense of order within the literary marketplace:

> Complaint is often made, in these times, of what we call the disorganised condition of society … It is too just a complaint, as we all know. But perhaps if we look at this of Books and the Writers of Books, we shall find here, as it were, the summary of all other disorganisation;—a sort of *heart*, from which, and to which, all other confusion circulates in the world! (171)

Here, the writer, the setter of types, is authorized and deauthorized at once. The writers of books lack coherence, just as the society they recreate lacks coherence. Yet they still manage to be the "*heart*" and "summary" of the chaos that surrounds them. In Carlyle's version of "Spirit of the Age," he finds the purest authority in "the writers of Newspapers, Pamphlets, Poems, Books" (175). That authority looks quite traditional, charismatic, and legal-rational. These men and women, he writes, are "the real working effective Church of a modern country" (175) in "preaching not to this parish or that, on this day or that, but to all men in all times and places" (172).

Carlyle, Mill, and Weber were not the only thinkers focused on "types" of authority in Victorian culture. Steve Ellis's *Virginia Woolf and the Victorians* (2007) looks to vast amounts of Woolf's fiction, essays, and correspondence to track her obsession with understanding the men and women of that age. Jane Marcus's *Virginia Woolf and the Languages of Patriarchy* (1987) emphasizes how much of that understanding was focused on the father. In an essay from 1917, Woolf wrote, "No age of literature is so little submissive to authority as ours, so free from the dominion of the great" (Woolf, *Collected* 2.38). In her review of Samuel Butler's writing in the essay "Contemporary Writers," she concluded, "The Victorian age, to hazard another generalization, was the age of the professional man" (Woolf, *Contemporary* 29). She wonders, in the essay "Ruskin," why the Men of Letters of the period, especially Ruskin and Carlyle, were so hard on themselves and their peers: "What did our fathers of the nineteenth century do to deserve so much scolding? ... if we also dip into the lives of those great men we shall find evidence that our fathers were a great deal responsible for the tone which their teachers adopted towards them" (*Collected* 1.205) Her memories of her father, the eminent Victorian, in "A Sketch of the Past," are dim where they depend on the actual man, and vivid, and renewable, in considering his textual remains: "The sociable father then I never knew. Father as a writer I can get of course in his books; the father who is related to the man's Leslie Stephen, I suppose" (Woolf, *Moments* 115). She reveals a limitation to fully understanding a father based on what he wrote of himself, or encouraged others to write about him. "When I read his books I get a critical grasp on him" (*Moments* 115), she writes, but for the man she must depend on snatches of her imperfect memory. Lytton Strachey's *Eminent Victorians* (1918) begins with a similar concession, as he tries to use individual biographies (in his case, of "an ecclesiastic, an educational authority, a woman of action, and a man of adventure" [xviii]) to challenge preconceptions about the age. He does not aspire, however, to the conclusion that his four case studies will fully account for the century, due in part to the work of the men who preceded him: "our fathers and our grandfathers have poured forth and accumulated so vast a quantity of information that the industry of a Ranke would be submerged by it, and the perspicacity of a Gibbon would quail before it" (xvii). Strachey's fragmented history does, however, despite his claim to the contrary, imply that his case studies do exemplify the spirit of the age, as he understands it. Perhaps all of our histories must do the same.

All of the authors in this book have "refigured the father" by blurring the lines between fiction and several extra-literary forms of expression. They transported fathers in and out of the literary texts they inhabit, and incorporated structural ruptures to indicate moments in which the narratives of literary history fail them.[8] Suzanne Keen's *Victorian Renovations of the Novel* (1998) argues for an

---

[8]   In *From Sketch to Novel* (2009) Amanpal Garcha discusses "forms appropriate for a market that had started valuing periodical essays, journalistic items, and descriptive pieces over longer works more suited for 'leisurely,' extended consumption" (4). These practical choices, he argued, led to works that were "incomplete, fragmented, and hurried, like modern time itself" (3). I add how fragment aesthetics are more than a pragmatic choice. A rising

overdependence on "Henry James' condemnation of multi-plot Victorian fiction," a focus that makes "modern theories of the novel ... depend on envisioning their predecessors as formally chaotic vehicles filled with unsorted rubble" (Keen 185). Keen is correct that we should not see Victorian structural ruptures as mere accidents, but instead as part of intentional acts of sorting and discarding. Keen argues, "Writing more rigourously formal fiction than that with which the modernist critics credit them ... Victorian novelists also create narrative annexes to make workspaces within fictions, without permanently disrupting the useful construct of a coherent fictional world" (Keen 64). Henry James's critique of novels such as Thackeray's *The Newcomes* as "large loose baggy monsters, with their queer elements of the accidental and the arbitrary" (James, *Portable* 477), is a window into key "continuities between Victorian and modern form" (Keen 185). I have argued that father-based fictions, because of their generational focus and investigations of authority, provide especially rich ground on which to test the consequences of struggles between order and disorder.

These novels suggest remarkable continuities between Victorian and modern ways of seeing when the Victorian realist novel embraces, rather than elides, its own discontinuities. As A.S. Kinnear writes in the 1864 *North British Review*, "The realist in fiction is careless about plot. His sole object is to describe men's lives as they really are; and real life is fragmentary and unmethodical" (372). Or, as Virginia Woolf writes in "Mr. Bennett and Mrs. Brown" (1923) about the transition into the twentieth century, "We must reconcile ourselves to a season of failures and fragments. We must reflect that where so much strength is spent on finding a way of telling the truth the truth itself is bound to reach us in an exhausted and chaotic condition" (Woolf *Collected* 1.335). If, as Peter Brooks argues in *Realist Vision* (2005), the transition from Victorian realism to modernism was a move from things to ideas (17), perhaps the modernist "idea" of the father owes much to Victorian things.

The case studies in this book lead to a major imperative for the postmodern critic of Victorian literature, an acknowledgment that Realism, as imagined by the Victorians, has both deep roots and unexpected branches. Over the course of these chapters, I've worked to describe what the varied constructions of father-narratives—as novels interact with biography, conduct books, sermons, speeches, and professional writing—contribute to our understanding of the cultural history of fatherhood. I have stressed the claim that the relationship between fictional narratives and extraliterary approaches to fatherhood is not unidirectional or uniform, but that there is some use in understanding some of its dominant "types."

---

dialogue about divorce in culture, for example, makes fictional marriage plots "more multi-voiced, more diffuse, more open-ended" (Humpherys 42). What, then, happens to the novel when the threat posed is to patriarchal authority, and subsequently to authorship itself?

Bibliography

Abbott, Jacob. *The Fire-side, or, The Duties and Enjoyments of Family Religion.* London: T. Allman, 1836. Print.

Adams, James Eli. *Dandies and Desert Saints: Styles of Victorian Masculinity.* Ithaca: Cornell, University Press, 1995. Print.

Ahern, Stephen. *Affected Sensibilities: Romantic Excess and the Genealogy of the Novel 1680–1810.* New York: AMS Press, 2007. Print.

Allott, Miriam, ed. *The Brontës: The Critical Heritage.* New York: Routledge, 2001.

Altick, Richard. *Lives in Letters: A History of Literary Biography in England and America.* New York: Alfred A. Knopf, 1965. Print.

Aristotle, *On Rhetoric: A Theory of Civic Discourse.* Trans. George A. Kennedy. Oxford: Oxford University Press, 1991. Print.

Armstrong, Nancy. *How Novels Think: The Limits of Individualism from 1719–1900.* New York: Columbia University Press, 2005. Print.

Arnold, Matthew. "Literature and Science." *The Nineteenth Century* 12.66 (August 1882): 216–30. Print.

Austen, Jane. *Northanger Abbey.* Ed. Barbara M. Benedict. Cambridge: Cambridge University Press, 2006. Print.

Bagehot, Walter. Review of *Philip. Spectator* 35 (9 August 1862): 885–6. Print.

Bamford, Samuel. *Passages from the Life of a Radical* [1842] and *Early Days* [1848]. 2 vols. London: Fisher Unwin, 1893. Print.

Barker, Juliet. *The Brontës.* London: Weidenfeld and Nicolson, 1994. Print.

———. "The Haworth Context." *The Cambridge Companion to the Brontës.* Cambridge: Cambridge University Press, 2002. 13–34. Print.

Barker, Martin. "Kant as a Problem for Weber." *The British Journal of Sociology* 31.2 (June 1980): 224–45. Print.

Barnaby, Edward. "The Realist Novel as Meta-Spectacle." *Journal of Narrative Theory* 38.1 (Winter 2008): 37–59. Print.

Barthes, Roland. *S/Z.* Trans. Richard Miller. New York: Hill and Wang, 1974. Print.

Beer, Frances. "Biographical Keys to the *Heights*." *Approaches to Teaching Emily Brontë's Wuthering Heights.* Ed. Sue Lonoff and Terri A. Hasseler. New York: The Modern Language Association of America, 2006. 75–81. Print.

Beer, Gillian. *Meredith: A Change of Masks.* London: Athlone Press, 1970. Print.

Beetham, Margaret. "Towards a Theory of the Periodical as a Publishing Genre." *Investigating Victorian Journalism.* Ed. Laurel Brake, Aled Jones, and Lionel Madden. New York: St Martin's Press, 1990. 19–32. Print.

Benjamin, Walter. *Illuminations.* Ed. Hannah Arendt. Trans. Harry Zohn. New York: Shocken, 1969. Print.

Bennett, Tony. *Pasts Beyond Memory: Evolution, Museums, Colonialism.* New York: Routledge, 2004. Print.

Bernstein, Susan David. "Too Common Readers at the British Museum." *Victorian Vulgarity: Taste in Verbal and Visual Culture*. Ed. Susan David Bernstein and Elsie B. Michie. Burlington and Farnham, UK: Ashgate, 2009. 101–18. Print.

Berry, Laura C. *The Child, The State, and the Victorian Novel*. Charlottesville and London: University Press of Virginia, 1999. Print.

Bodenheimer, Rosemarie. *The Real Life of Mary Ann Evans: George Eliot, Her Letters and Fiction*. Ithaca: Cornell University Press, 1994. Print.

Bohrer, Frederick N. "The Times and Spaces of History: Representation, Assyria, and the British Museum." *Museum Culture: Histories, Discourses, Spectacles*. Ed. Daniel J. Sherman and Irit Rogoff. Minneapolis: University of Minnesota Press, 1994. 197–222. Print.

Bolus-Reichert, Christine. *The Age of Eclecticism: Literature and Culture in Britain, 1815–1885*. Columbus: The Ohio State University Press, 2009. Print.

Bonaparte, Felicia. *The Gypsy-Bachelor of Manchester: The Life of Mrs. Gaskell's Demon*. Charlottesville: University Press of Virginia, 1992. Print.

Boumelha, Penny. "The Patriarchy of Class: *Under the Greenwood Tree, Far From the Madding Crowd, The Woodlanders*." *The Cambridge Companion to Thomas Hardy*. Ed. Dale Kramer. Cambridge: Cambridge University Press, 1999. 130–44. Print.

Bridges, Charles. *An Essay on Family Prayer*. London: Seeley, Burnside and Seeley, 1847. Print.

Brontë, Charlotte. "The Last Sketch." *Cornhill Magazine* 1 (1860): 485–98. Print.

———. *Mr. Ashworth and His Son*. HEW 1.4.16. Harry Elkins Widener Collection. Houghton Library, Harvard University. Manuscript.

———. *Villette*. New York: Bantam, 1986. Print.

Brontë, Patrick. *The Cottage in the Wood: Or the Art of Becoming Rich and Happy*. Bradford: Printed and Sold by T. Inkersley, 1815. Reprinted in *Brontëana: His Collected Works and Life*. Ed. J. Horsfall Turner. Bingley: Printed for the Editor by T. Harrison & Sons, 1898. Print.

———. *Cottage Poems*. Halifax: Printed and Sold by P.K. Holden, for the Author, 1811. Print.

———. "A Funeral Sermon for the Late Rev. William Weightman, MA, Preached in the Church of Haworth in Sunday, the 2nd of October, 1842." Printed by J.U. Walker, George Street, 1842. Reprinted in *Brontëana: His Collected Works and Life*. Ed. J. Horsfall Turner. Bingley: Printed for the Editor by T. Harrison & Sons, 1898. Print.

———. *The Letters of the Reverend Patrick Brontë*, Ed. Dudley Green. Gloucestershire, UK: Nonsuch, 2005. Print.

———. *The Maid of Killarney: or, Albion and Flora. A Modern Tale; In which Are Interwoven Some Cursory Remarks on Religion and Politics*. London: Baldwin, Chadock, and Joy, 1818. Print.

Brooks, Peter. *Realist Vision*. New Haven: Yale University Press, 2005. Print.

Browning, Robert. *Selected Poetry*. Ed. Daniel Karlin. New York: Penguin, 1989. Print.

Buckham, Phillip Wentworth. *The Theatre of the Greeks*. Cambridge: Printed by J. Smith, 1830. Print.

Buckley, Jerome. *Season of Youth: The Bildungsroman from Dickens to Golding*. Cambridge, MA: Harvard University Press, 1974. Print.

Bulwer-Lytton, Edward. "On Art in Fiction" [1838]. Reprinted in *Victorian Criticism of the Novel*. Ed. Edwin M. Eigner and George J. Worth. Cambridge: Cambridge University Press, 1985. 22–38. Print.

Burnham, Michelle. "Between England and America: Captivity, Sympathy, and the Sentimental Novel." *Cultural Institutions of the Novel*. Ed. Diedre Lynch and William B. Warner. Durham: Duke University Press, 1996. 47–72. Print.

Butler, Samuel. "The Aunt, the Nieces, and the Dog." *Essays on Life, Art, and Science*. Ed. R.A. Streatfeild. London: A.C. Fifield, 1908. 45–68. Print.

———. *The Authoress of The Odyssey*. Ed. David Grene. Chicago: University of Chicago Press, 1967. Print.

———. *The Book of the Machines*. [Cellarius]. Feltham, Middlesex, UK: Quarto Press, 1975. Print.

———. *The Correspondence of Samuel Butler with His Sister May*. Ed. Daniel F. Howard. Berkeley and Los Angeles: University of California Press, 1962. Print.

———. "The Deadlock in Darwinism." *Essays on Life, Art, and Science*. Ed. R.A. Streatfeild. London: A.C. Fifield, 1908. 234–340. Print.

———. *Erewhon*. 1872. Ed. Peter Mudford. New York: Penguin, 1970. Print.

———. *The Essential Samuel Butler*. Ed. G.D.H. Cole. New York: E.P. Dutton & Company, 1950. Print.

———. *Evolution, Old and New*. 1879. London: David Bogue, 1882. Print.

———. *Ex Voto. The Shrewsbury Edition of the Works of Samuel Butler*. Vol. 9. Ed. Henry Festing-Jones and A.T. Bartholomew. New York: E.P. Dutton & Company, 1924. Print.

———. *The Fair Haven* [1873]. Ed. Gerald Bullett. London: Watts & Co., 1938. Print.

———. *The Family Letters of Samuel Butler, 1841–1886*. Ed. Arnold Silver. Stanford, CA: Stanford University Press, 1962. Print.

———. *A First Year in Canterbury Settlement, and Other Early Essays. The Shrewsbury Edition of the Works of Samuel Butler*. Vol. 1. New York: AMS Press, 1968. Print.

———. *Further Extracts from the Notebooks of Samuel Butler*. Ed. A.T. Bartholomew. London: Jonathan Cape, 1934. Print.

———. *God the Known and God the Unknown*. Ed. R.A. Streatfield. London: A.C. Fifield, 1909. Print.

———. *The Humour of Homer and Other Essays*. Freeport, New York: Books for Libraries Press, 1967. Print.

———. *Life and Habit*. 1877. New York: Cosimo, 2005. Print.

———. *Mr. Heatherley's Holiday: An Incident in Studio Life* (1874). Oil on canvas. Tate Gallery, London. *Tate Gallery*. Web. 16 August 2013.

————. *The Note-Books of Samuel Butler*. Ed. Henry Festing-Jones and A.T. Bartholomew. *The Shrewsbury Edition of the Works of Samuel Butler*. Vol. 20. New York: AMS Press, 1968. Print.

————. *The Note-Books of Samuel Butler, Vol. 1 (1874–1883)*. Ed. Hans-Peter Breuer. Lanham, MD: University Press of America, 1984. Print.

————. "Quis Desiderio." *Essays on Life, Art, and Science,* Ed. R.A. Streatfeild. London: A.C. Fifield, 1908. 1–17. Print.

————. *Unconscious Memory*. 1880. New York: E. Dutton & Company, 1911. Print.

————. *The Way of All Flesh*. Ed. A.C. Ward. London: Heron Books, n.d. Print.

Carlyle, Thomas. "Biography." *Fraser's Magazine,* 5.27 (April 1832): 253–60. Print.

————. *On Heroes, Hero-Worship, and the Heroic in History*. 1841. Ed Herbert S. Murch. Boston: D.C. Heath & Co., 1913. Print.

————. *New Letters of Thomas Carlyle*. Ed. Alexander Carlyle. London: J. Lane, 1904. Print.

————. *Past and Present*. Ed. Richard D. Altick. New York: New York University Press, 1965. Print.

————. *Reminiscences*. 1881. Ed. Charles Eliot Norton. London: Macmillan, 1887. Print.

————. *Sartor Resartus & On Heroes and Hero Worship*. London: Dent, 1926. Print.

Carpenter, Mary Wilson. *Imperial Bibles, Domestic Bodies: Women, Sexuality, and Religion in the Victorian Market*. Columbus: Ohio University Press, 2003. Print.

Carré, Jacques, ed. *The Crisis of Courtesy: Studies in the Conduct-Book in Britain: 1600–1900*. Leiden: E.J. Brill, 1994. 1–8. Print.

————. "Introduction." *The Crisis of Courtesy: Studies in the Conduct-Book in Britain: 1600–1900*. Ed. Jacques Carré. Leiden: E.J. Brill, 1994. 1–8. Print.

Carroll, David, ed. *George Eliot: The Critical Heritage*. New York: Routledge, 2009. Print.

Cazamian, Louis. *The Social Novel in England 1830–1850*. London and Boston: Routledge & Kegan Paul, 1973. Print.

Chapman, Raymond. *Forms of Speech in Victorian Fiction*. London and New York: Longman, 1994. Print.

Chesterfield, Lord. *Letters to His Son and Others*. 1774. London: J.M. Dent, 1959. Print.

Childers, Joseph W. *Novel Possibilities: Fiction and the Formation of Early Victorian Culture*. Philadelphia: University of Pennsylvania Press, 1995. Print.

Chitham, Edward. *The Brontë's Irish Background*. Houndmills, UK: Macmillan, 1986. Print.

Cixous, Hélène. "The Laugh of the Medusa." *Signs* 1.4 (Summer 1976): 875–93. Print.

Clark, Anna. "Gender, Class, and the Nation: Franchise Reform in England, 1832–1928." *Re-Reading the Constitution: New Narratives in the Political History of England's Long Nineteenth Century*. Ed. James Vernon. Cambridge: Cambridge University Press, 1996. 239–53. Print.

Clarke, Micael M. *Thackeray and Women*. Dekalb: Northern Illinois University Press, 1995. Print.

Clayton, Jay. "Evolutionary Circles: Rivalry and the Eclipse of Darwinism." North American Victorian Studies Association. Madison, WI. 28 September 2012. Lecture.

Cogtugno, Clare. "Stowe, Eliot, and the Reform Aesthetic." *Transatlantic Stowe: Harriet Beecher Stowe and European Culture*. Ed. Denise Kohn, Sarah Mear, and Emily B. Todd. Iowa City: University of Iowa Press, 2006. 111–30. Print.

Cohen, Monica F. *Professional Domesticity in the Victorian Novel: Women, Work, and Home*. Cambridge: Cambridge University Press, 1998. Print.

Cohen, Paula Marantz. *The Daughter's Dilemma: Family Process and the Nineteenth-Century Domestic Novel*. Ann Arbor: The University of Michigan Press, 1991. Print.

Coleridge, Samuel Taylor. *The Portable Coleridge*. Ed. I.A. Richards. New York: Penguin, 1978. Print.

———. *Table Talk*. London: John Murray, 1836. Print.

Cordery, Gareth. "Foucault, Dickens, and David Copperfield." *Victorian Literature and Culture* 26.1 (1998): 71–85. Print.

Cuno, James. *Museums Matter: In Praise of the Encyclopedic Museum*. Chicago and London: University of Chicago Press, 2011. Print.

D'Albertis, Deirdre. "'Bookmaking out of the Remains of the Dead': Elizabeth Gaskell's *The Life of Charlotte Bronte*." *Victorian Studies* 39.1 (Autumn 1995): 1–31. Print.

Dames, Nicholas. "Brushes with Fame: Thackeray and the Work of Celebrity." *Nineteenth-Century Literature* 56.1 (June 2001): 23–51. Print.

Daniels, Anthony. "Butler's Unhappy Youth." *New Criterion* 23.5 (January 2005): 11–17. Print.

Davidoff, Lenore and Catherine Hall. *Family Fortunes: Men and Women of the English Middle Class, 1780–1850*. London and New York: Routledge, 2002. Print.

Davidson, Jenny. *Hypocrisy and the Politics of Politeness: Manners and Morals from Locke to Austen*. Cambridge: Cambridge University Press, 2004. Print.

Davis, Philip. "Victorian Realist Prose and Sentimentality." *Rereading Victorian Fiction*. Ed. Alice Jenkins and Juliet John. New York: St. Martin's Press, 2000. 13–28. Print.

Defoe, Daniel. *Robinson Crusoe*. Ed. Angus Ross. New York: Penguin, 1985. Print.

De Quincey, Thomas. *Confessions of an English Opium-Eater and Other Writings*. Ed. Robert Morrison. Oxford: Oxford University Press, 2013. Print.

Devereux, Joanna. *Patriarchy and its Discontents: Sexual Politics in Selected Novels and Stories of Thomas Hardy*. New York: Routledge, 2003. Print.

D'haen, Theo. "Antique Lands, New Worlds? Comparative Literature, Intertextuality, Translation." *Forum for Modern Language Studies* 43.2 (April 2007): 107–20. Print.

Dickens, Charles. *David Copperfield*. 1850. New York: Signet, 1980. Print.

———. *Dombey and Son*. 1848. Ed. Alan Horsman. Oxford: Oxford World's Classics, 2001. Print.

Dillon, Sarah. *The Palimpsest: Literature, Criticism, Theory*. London: Continuum, 2007. Print.

Disraeli, Benjamin. *Speech at the Banquet of the National Union of Conservative and Constitutional Associations, at the Crystal Palace, on June 24, 1872*. Wiesbaden: Franz Steiner, 1968. Print.

———. *Sybil: Or, The Two Nations*. London: Oxford University Press, 1926. Print.

Dooley, Allan C. *Author and Printer in Victorian England*. Charlottesville and London: University Press of Virginia, 1992. Print.

Douglas, Sir George. "On Some Critics of *Jude the Obscure*." *The Bookman* 9.52 (January 1896): 120–22. Print.

Dowling, Andrew. *Manliness and the Male Novelist in Victorian Literature*. Aldershot, UK: Ashgate, 2001. Print.

———. "Recent Approaches to Eliot." *Critical Quarterly* 20.1 (1978): 78–82. Print.

Eliot, George. *Adam Bede*. New York: Signet, 1961. Print.

———. "Address to Working Men." Reprinted in *Felix Holt: The Radical*. Ed. Lynda Mugglestone. New York: Penguin, 1995. 483–99. Print.

———. *Daniel Deronda*. Ed. Terence Cave. London: Penguin Books, 1995. Print.

———. *Felix Holt: The Radical*. London and New York: Penguin, 1995. Print.

———. *George Eliot: A Writer's Notebook, 1854–1879, and Uncollected Writings*. Ed. Joseph Wisenfarth. Charlottesville: University Press of Virginia, 1981. Print.

———. *The George Eliot Letters*. Ed. Gordon Haight. 7 vols. New Haven: Yale University Press, 1954–1955. Print.

———. *The Journals of George Eliot*. Ed. Margaret Harris and Judith Johnston. Cambridge: Cambridge University Press, 1998. Print.

———. *Impressions of Theophrastus Such*. Iowa City: University of Iowa Press, 1994. Print.

———. *The Lifted Veil and Brother Jacob*. Ed. Sally Shuttleworth. New York: Penguin, 2001. Print.

———. *Middlemarch*. New York: Penguin, 1994. Print.

———. *The Mill on the Floss*. Oxford: Oxford University Press, 1998. Print.

———. "The Natural History of German Life" *Westminster Review* New Series Vol. 10 (July/October 1856): 51–79. Print.

———. *Scenes of Clerical Life*. Ed. Jennifer Gribble. New York: Penguin, 1998. Print.

———. *Silas Marner*. New York: Signet, 1999. Print.

———. "Silly Novels by Lady Novelists." *Westminster Review* 66 (Oct 1856): 442–61. Print.

Ellis, Steve. *Virginia Woolf and the Victorians*. Cambridge: Cambridge University Press, 2007. Print.

Ellis, Stewart Marsh. *George Meredith: His Life and Friends in Relation to His Work*. London: G. Richards, 1919. Print.

Fawcett, Henry. *The Economic Position of the English Labourer*. New York and London: Garland, 1984. Print.

Festa, Lynn. *Sentimental Figures of Empire in Eighteenth-Century Britain and France*. Baltimore: Johns Hopkins University Press, 2006. Print.

Finn, Margot C. "The Authority of the Law." *Liberty and Authority in Victorian Britain*. Ed. Peter Mandler. Oxford: Oxford University Press, 2006. 159–78. Print.

Fisher, Judith L. "Ethical Narrative in Dickens and Thackeray." *Studies in the Novel* 29.1 (1997): 108–17. Print.

———. *Thackeray's Skeptical Narrative and the 'Perilous Trade' of Authorship*. Aldershot: Ashgate, 2002. Print.

Fisher, Philip. "Self and Community in *The Mill on the Floss*." Reprinted in *Mill on the Floss*. Ed. Carol Christ. New York: Norton, 1994. 520–43. Print.

Flanders, Judith. *Inside the Victorian Home*. New York: Norton, 2004. Print.

Flint, Christopher. *Family Fictions: Narrative and Domestic Relations in Britain, 1688–1798*. Stanford, CA: Stanford University Press, 1998. Print.

Foster, Joseph. "William M. Thackeray." *London Society* No. 314 (February 1888): 143–52. Print.

Foster, Shirley. "Elizabeth Gaskell's Shorter Pieces." *The Cambridge Companion to Elizabeth Gaskell*. Ed. Jill L. Matus. Cambridge: Cambridge University Press, 2007. 108–30. Print.

Foucault, Michel. *Discipline and Punish: The Birth of the Prison*. Trans. Alan Sheridan. New York: Pantheon, 1977. Print.

———. *The History of Sexuality: An Introduction*. [1976]. New York: Vintage, 1990. Print.

———. *Power*. Ed. James D. Faubion. New York: The New Press. 2000. Print.

———. "The Subject and Power." *Critical Inquiry* 8.4 (Summer 1982): 777–95. Print.

Fraiman, Susan. *Unbecoming Women: British Women Writers and the Novel of Development*. New York: Columbia University Press, 1993. Print.

Freud, Sigmund. *Civilization and Its Discontents* [1930]. Trans. James Strachey. New York: Norton, 1961. Print.

———. *Moses and Monotheism* [1937]. Trans. Katherine Jones. New York: Vintage, 1959. Print.

Furneaux, Holly. *Queer Dickens: Erotics, Families, Masculinities*. Oxford: Oxford University Press. 2009. Print.

Galbraith, John. *The Anatomy of Power*. Boston: Houghton Mifflin, 1983. Print.

Gallagher, Catherine. *The Industrial Reformation of English Fiction: Social Discourse and Narrative Form, 1832–1867*. Chicago: University of Chicago Press, 1985. Print.

Garcha, Amanpal. *From Sketch to Novel: The Development of Victorian Fiction*. Cambridge: Cambridge University Press, 2009. Print.

Gaskell, Elizabeth. *Cranford*. Ed. Patricia Ingham. New York: Penguin, 2005. Print.

Gaskell, Elizabeth. *A Dark Night's Work and Other Stories*. Ed. Suzanne Lewis. Oxford: Oxford World's Classics, 1992. Print.

———. "The Doom of the Griffiths." *My Lady Ludlow, and Other Tales*. London: Smith, Elder & Co., 1906. 237–77. Print.

———. "The Half-Brothers." *My Lady Ludlow, and Other Tales*. London: Smith, Elder & Co., 1906. 391–404. Print.

———. *The Letters of Mrs. Gaskell*. Ed. J.A.V. Chapple and Arthur Pollard. Manchester, UK: Mandolin, 1997. Print.

———. *The Life of Charlotte Brontë*. Ed. Elisabeth Jay. New York: Penguin, 1997. Print.

———. "Lizzie Leigh." *Cousin Phillis, and Other Stories*. Ed. Heather Glen. Oxford: Oxford World's Classics, 2010. 3–31. Print.

———. *Mary Barton*. Ed. Macdonald Daly. New York: Penguin, 1996. Print.

———. *North and South*. Ed. Patricia Ingham. New York: Penguin, 1995. Print.

———. "The Poor Clare." *My Lady Ludlow, and Other Tales*. London: Smith, Elder & Co., 1906. 329–90. Print.

———. *Ruth*. Ed. Angus Easson. New York: Penguin, 1997. Print.

———. "The Sin of a Father." *Household Words* 18.453 (27 November 1858): 553–61. Print.

———. *Sylvia's Lovers*. Ed. Nancy Henry. London: Everyman, 1997. Print.

———. *Wives and Daughters*. Ed. Pam Morris. New York: Penguin, 1996. Print.

———. *The Works of Elizabeth Gaskell*. 10 Vols. London: Pickering and Chatto, 2005. Print.

Georgel, Chantal. "The Museum as Metaphor in Nineteenth-Century France." *Museum Culture: Histories, Discourses, Spectacles*. Ed. Daniel J. Sherman and Irit Rogoff. Minneapolis: University of Minnesota Press, 1994. 113–22.

Gettleman, Debra. "Reading Ahead in George Eliot." *Novel: A Forum on Fiction* 39 (Fall 2005): 25–47. Print.

Gilbert, Sandra, and Susan Gubar. *The Madwoman in the Attic: The Woman Writer and The Nineteenth-Century Literary Imagination*. New Haven: Yale Nota Bene, 2000. Print.

Goldberg, S.L. *Agents and Lives: Moral Thinking in Literature*. Cambridge: Cambridge University Press, 1993. Print.

Goode, George Brown. *Museum-History and Museums of History*. New York: The Knickerbocker Press, 1889. Print.

Goodlad, Lauren. *Victorian Literature and The Victorian State: Character and Governance in a Liberal Society*. Baltimore: Johns Hopkins University Press, 2003. Print.

Gosse, Edmund. *Father and Son: A Study of Two Temperaments*. 1907. Ed. Peter Abbs. New York: Penguin, 1989. Print.

Griffin, Dustin. *Satire: A Critical Introduction*. Lexington: The University Press of Kentucky, 1994. Print.

Gross, John. *The Rise and Fall of the Man of Letters: Aspects of English Literary Life Since 1800*. Chicago: Elephant Paperbacks, 1992. Print.

4 3 2

Grosz, Elizabeth. *Volatile Bodies: Toward a Corporeal Feminism*. Bloomington: Indiana University Press, 1994. Print.

Gulick, Sidney L., ed. *Two Burlesques of Lord Chesterfield's Letters: The Graces (1774), The Fine Gentleman's Etiquette (1776)*. Los Angeles: William Andrews Clark Memorial Library, 1960. Print.

Gunn, Simon. *The Public Culture of the Victorian Middle Class: Ritual and Authority and the English Industrial City, 1840–1914*. Manchester and New York: Manchester University Press, 2000. Print.

Haack, Susan. "The Ideal of Intellectual Integrity in Life and Literature." *New Literary History* 36.3 (Summer 2005): 359–73. Print.

Hack, Daniel. *Material Interests of the Victorian Novel*. Charlottesville: University of Virginia Press, 2005. Print.

Hall, Catherine. *Civilising Subjects; Metropole and Colony in the English Imagination, 1830–1867*. Oxford: Blackwell, 2002. Print.

Hall, Donald E. *Fixing Patriarchy: Feminism and Mid-Victorian Male Novelists*. New York: New York University Press, 1996. Print.

Hardy, Thomas. *The Collected Letters of Thomas Hardy*. Ed. Richard Little and Michael Millgate. Oxford: The Clarendon Press, 1980. Print.

———. *Far from the Madding Crowd*. Ed. Suzanne B. Falck-Yi. Oxford: Oxford University Press, 2008. Print.

———. *Far from the Madding Crowd*. Ed. Rosemarie Morgan. New York: Penguin, 2003. Print.

———. *Jude the Obscure*. 1895. Ed. Patricia Ingham. Oxford: Oxford University Press, 1985. Print.

———. *A Laodicean*. Ed. John Schad. New York: Penguin, 1997. Print.

———. *The Life and Work of Thomas Hardy*. Ed. Michael Millgate. Athens: University of Georgia Press, 1985. Print.

———. *The Literary Notebooks of Thomas Hardy*. 2 vols. Ed. Lennart A. Bjork. New York: New York University Press, 1985. Print.

———. *The Mayor of Casterbridge*. Ed. Keith Wilson. New York: Penguin, 1997. Print.

———. *Tess of the D'Urbervilles*. Ed. Scott Elledge. New York: Norton, 1991. Print.

———. *Thomas Hardy's Personal Writings*. Ed. Harold Orel. New York: St. Martin's Press, 1966. Print.

———. *Thomas Hardy's Public Voice: The Essays, Speeches, and Miscellaneous Prose*. Ed. Michael Millgate. Oxford: Clarendon Press, 2001. Print.

———. *Under the Greenwood Tree*. Ed. Simon Gatewood. Oxford: Oxford University Press, 1985. Print.

Hatten, Charles. *The End of Domesticity: Alienation from the Family in Dickens, Eliot, and James*. Newark: University of Delaware Press, 2010. Print.

[Hazlitt, William.] *Sketches of the Principal Picture-Galleries of England with a Criticism on "Marriage A-La-Mode."* London: Taylor and Hessey, 1824. Print.

Hedrick, Charles W. *History and Silence: Purge and Rehabilitation of Memory in Late Antiquity.* Austin: University of Texas Press, 2000. Print.

Hennelly, Mark. "The 'Surveillance of Désirée'": Freud, Foucault, and *Villette. Victorian Literature and Culture* 26.2 (1998): 421–40. Print.

Hoberman, Ruth. "Women in the British Museum Reading Room during the Late-Nineteenth and Early Twentieth Centuries: From Quasi to Counterpublic." *Feminist Studies* 28.3 (Fall 2002): 489–512. Print.

Hodgetts, J. Frederick. *Older England: Illustrated by the Anglo-Saxon Antiquities in the British Museum in a Course of Six Lectures.* London: Whiting & Co, 1884. Print.

Homer. *The Odyssey.* Trans. Robert Fagles. New York: Penguin, 1996. Print.

Horne, Lewis. "Sir Austin, His Devil, and the Well-Designed World." *Studies in the Novel* 24.1 (Spring 1992): 35–47. Print.

How, William Walsham. *Daily Family Prayer for Churchmen. Compiled Chiefly from the Book of Common Prayer.* London, 1852. Print.

Hughes, Linda K and Michael Lund. *Victorian Publishing and Mrs. Gaskell's Work.* Charlottesville and London: University Press of Virginia, 1999. Print.

———. *The Victorian Serial.* Charlottesville and London: University Press of Virginia, 1991. Print.

Hume, David. *A Treatise of Human Nature.* New York: Collier, 1962. Print.

Humpherys, Anne. "Breaking Apart: The Early Victorian Divorce Novel." *Victorian Women Writers and the Woman Question.* Ed. Nicola Dame Thompson. Cambridge: Cambridge University Press, 1999. 42–59. Print.

Hunt, Leigh. *Men, Women, and Books.* London: Smith, Elder & Co., 1909. Print.

Irwin, Michael. *Reading Hardy's Landscapes.* Houndmills, UK: Macmillan, 2000. Print.

Jaffe, Audrey. *The Affective Life of the Average Man: the Victorian Novel and the Stock-Market Graph.* Columbus: Ohio State University Press, 2010. Print.

James, Henry. *The Portable Henry James.* Ed. John Auchard. New York: Penguin, 2004. Print.

———. *Views and Reviews.* Boston: The Brill Publishing Company, 1908. Print.

James, John Angell. *The Family Monitor: or, A Help to Domestic Happiness.* 1828. Boston: Crocker and Brewster, 1838. Print.

Jeffers, Thomas L. *Samuel Butler Revalued.* University Park and London: Pennsylvania State University Press, 1981. Print.

Jelinek, Estelle. *Women's Autobiography: Essays in Criticism.* Bloomington: Indiana University Press, 1980. Print.

Jones, Anna Maria. *Problem Novels: Victorian Fiction Theorizes the Sensational Self.* Columbus: Ohio State University Press, 2007. Print.

Jones, Mervyn. *The Amazing Victorian: A Life of George Meredith.* London: Constable, 1999. Print.

Jones, Vivien. "Mary Wollstonecraft and the Literature of Advice and Instruction." *The Cambridge Companion to Mary Wollstonecraft.* Ed. Claudia L. Johnson. Cambridge: Cambridge University Press, 2002. 119–40. Print.

———. "The Seductions of Conduct: Pleasure and Conduct Literature." *Pleasure in the Eighteenth Century*. Ed. Roy Porter and Marie Mulvey Roberts. Washington Square: New York University Press, 1996. 108–32. Print.

Joyce, James. *A Portrait of the Artist as a Young Man*. Ed. John Paul Riquelme. New York: Norton, 2007. Print.

———. *Ulysses*. New York: Vintage, 1990. Print.

Kaplan, Fred. S*acred Tears: Sentimentality in Victorian Literature*. Princeton: Princeton University Press, 1987. Print.

Keen, Suzanne. *Victorian Renovations of the Novel: Narrative Annexes and the Boundaries of Representation*. Cambridge: Cambridge University Press, 1998. Print.

Kinnear, A.S. "Mr. Trollope's Novels." *North British Review* 40.80 (May 1864): 369–401. Print.

Klein, Julius Leopold. *History of the Drama*. 12 vols. Leipzig: T.O. Wiegel, 1865–1876. Print.

Knezevic, Borislav. *Figures of Finance Capitalism: Writing, Class, and Capital in the Age of Dickens*. New York and London: Routledge, 2003. Print.

Knight, Charles, ed. *Old England: A Pictorial Museum of Regal, Ecclesiastical, Municipal, and Popular Antiquities*. 2 vols. London: James Sangster and Co., 1850s. Print.

Knoepflmacher, U.C. *George Eliot's Early Novels: The Limits of Realism*. Berkeley: University of California Press, 1968. Print.

———. *Laughter and Despair: Readings in Ten Novels of the Victorian Era*. Berkeley: University of California Press, 1971. Print.

Kramer, Dale. "Hardy and Readers: *Jude the Obscure*." *The Cambridge Companion to Thomas Hardy*. Ed. Dale Kramer. Cambridge: Cambridge University Press, 1999. 164–82. Print.

Krueger, Christine L. *The Reader's Repentance: Women Preachers, Women Writers, and Nineteenth-Century Social Discourse*. Chicago and London: University of Chicago Press, 1992. Print.

Lacan, Jacques. "The Signification of the Phallus" [1958]. *The Routledge Language and Cultural Theory Reader*. Ed. Lucy Burke, Tony Crowley, and Alan Girvin. London, England: Routledge, 2000. 132–8. Print.

Lenard, Mary. *Preaching Pity: Dickens, Gaskell, and Sentimentalism in Victorian Culture*. New York: Peter Lang, 1999. Print.

Levine, George. "Intelligence as Deception: *The Mill on the Floss*." *PMLA* 80.4 (September 1965): 402–9. Print.

Lewes, George Henry. "The Condition of Authors in England, Germany, and France." *Fraser's Magazine for Town and Country* 35.207 (March 1847): 285–95. Print.

———. "The Lady Novelists" [1852]. Reprinted in *The Victorian Art of Fiction*. Ed. Rohan Maitzen. Toronto: Broadview, 2009. Print.

———. *On Actors and the Art of Acting*. London: Smith, Elder, & Co., 1875. Print.

Liddle, Dallas. *The Dynamics of Genre: Journalism and the Practice of Literature in Mid-Victorian Britain*. Charlottesville: University of Virginia Press, 2009. Print.

Lincoln, Bruce. *Authority: Construction and Corrosion*. Chicago: University of Chicago Press, 1994. Print.

Linehan, Katherine Bailey. "Mixed Politics: The Critique of Imperialism in *Daniel Deronda*. *Texas Studies in Literature and Language*, 34.3 (Fall 1992), 323–46. Print.

Linton, E. Lynn. "Candour in English Fiction." *New Review* 2.8 (1890): 10–14. Print.

Lock, John and W.T. Dixon. *A Man of Sorrow: The Life, Letters and Times of the Rev. Patrick Brontë, 1777–1861*. [London:] Nelson, [1965]. Print.

Lucas, Samuel. Review of *The Ordeal of Richard Feverel*. *The Times* (14 October 1859): 5. Print.

Mansfield, Harvey C. *Manliness*. New Haven: Yale University Press, 2006. Print.

Marcus, Jane. *Virginia Woolf and the Languages of Patriarchy*. Bloomington and Indianapolis: Indiana University Press, 1987. Print.

Mayer, Lauryn S. *Worlds Made Flesh: Reading Medieval Manuscript Culture*. New York: Routledge, 2004. Print.

Maynard, John. "The Bildungsroman." *A Companion to the Victorian Novel*. Ed. Patrick Brantlinger and William B. Thesing. Malden, MA: Blackwell, 2002. 279–301. Print.

Mayo, Robert D. "*The Egoist* and the Willow Pattern." *English Literary History* 9 (1942): 71–8. Print.

McAleavey, Maia. "The Plot of Bigamous Return." *Representations* 123.1 (Summer 2013): 87–116. Print.

———. "Soul-mates: David Copperfield's Angelic Bigamy," *Victorian Studies* 52.2 (Winter 2010): 191–218. Print.

McClelland, Keith. "England's Greatness, the Working Man." *Defining the Victorian Nation: Class, Race, Gender and the British Reform Act of 1867*. Ed. Catherine Hall, Keith McClelland, and Jane Rendall. Cambridge: Cambridge University Press, 2000. 71–118. Print.

McCormack, Matthew, ed. *Public Men: Masculinity and Politics in Modern Britain*. New York: Palgrave, 2007. Print.

McDonagh, Josephine. "Writings on the Mind: Thomas De Quincey and the Importance of the Palimpsest in Nineteenth Century Thought." *Prose Studies* 16.2 (1987): 207–24. Print.

McMaster, R.D. *Thackeray's Cultural Frame of Reference: Allusion in The Newcomes*. Houndmills: Macmillan, 1991. Print.

Melville, Herman. "Bartleby." *Billy Budd and Other Stories*. New York: Penguin, 1986. 1–46. Print.

Meredith, George. *The Adventures of Harry Richmond*. 2 vols. 1871. New York: Russell & Russell, 1968. Print.

———. *The Amazing Marriage* [1895]. New York: Russell & Russell, 1968. Print.

———. *Beauchamp's Career*. [1876]. New York: Charles Scribner's Sons, 1897. Print

———. *Bibliography and Various Readings. The Works of George Meredith*. Vol. 27. London: Constable and Co., 1911. Print.

———. *Diana of the Crossways*. [1884]. New York: Russell & Russell, 1968. Print.

————. *The Egoist*. [1879]. Ed. Robert M. Adams. New York: Norton, 1979. Print.

————. "Essay on the Idea of Comedy." *Collected Works*. Vol. 23. New York: Russell and Russell, 1968. 3–58. Print.

————. *Letters of George Meredith*. Ed. C.L. Cline. 3 vol. Oxford: Clarendon Press, 1970. Print.

————. *Miscellaneous Prose. Works of George Meredith*, Vol. 23. New York: Russell and Russell, 1968. Print.

————. *One of Our Conquerors*. London: Chapman and Hall, 1891. Print.

————. *The Poetical Works of George Meredith*. London: Constable and Company, 1912. Print.

————. *The Ordeal of Richard Feverel* [1859]. Ed. Edward Mendelson. New York: Penguin, 1999. Print.

————. *Selected Letters of George Meredith*. Ed. Mohammad Shaheen. New York: St. Martin's Press, 1997. Print.

Meredith Now: Some Critical Essays. Ed. Ian Fletcher. London: Routledge, 1971. Print.

Meyer, Susan. "'Safely to Their Own Borders': Proto-Zionism, Feminism, and Nationalism in *Daniel Deronda*. *ELH* 60.3 (Autumn 1993): 733–58. Print.

Mill, John Stuart. *Nature; The Utility of Religion; and Theism*. London: Longmans, Green & Co., 1923. Print.

————. *Spirit of the Age, On Liberty, and the Subjection of Women*. Ed. Alan Ryan. New York: Norton, 1997. Print.

————. *Utilitarianism*. [1861]. Ed. Oskar Piest. New York: Liberal Arts Press, 1957. Print.

Miller, Andrew. "Lives Unled in Realist Fiction." *Representations* 98 (Spring 2007): 118–34. Print.

Miller, Lori. "The (Re)Gendering of High Anglicanism." *Masculinity and Spirituality in Victorian Culture*. Ed. Andrew Bradstock, Sean Gill, Anne Hogan and Sue Morgan. Houndmills, UK: MacMillan, 2000. 27–43. Print.

Miller, Lucasta. *The Brontë Myth*. London: Jonathan Cape, 2001. Print.

Miller, S.M. *Max Weber*. New York: Thomas Y. Crowell, 1963. Print.

Milton, John. *Areopagitica*. [1644]. Oxford: Clarendon Press, 1874. Print.

"The Morality of the Church and the Drama." *Theatrical Journal* 12.602 (June 1851): 206-207. Print.

Morgentaler, Goldie. *Dickens and Heredity: When Like Begets Like*. New York: St. Martin's Press, 2000. Print.

Morse, Deborah. "The Half-Brothers." *"The Facts on File Companion to the British Short Story*. Ed. Andrew Maunder. New York: Facts on File, 2007. 247–48. Print.

————. "Lizzie Leigh." *The Facts on File Companion to the British Short Story*. Ed. Andrew Maunder. New York: Facts on File, 2007. 176–7. Print.

————. "Stitching Repentance, Sewing Rebellion: Seamstresses and Fallen Women in Elizabeth Gaskell's Fiction." *Keeping the Victorian House: A Collection of Essays*. Ed. Vanessa D. Dickerson. New York and London: Garland, 1995. 27–74. Print.

Muggeridge, Malcolm. *The Earnest Atheist: A Study of Samuel Butler*. New York: Haskell House, 1971. Print.

Musselwhite, David. *Social Transformations in Hardy's Tragic Novels: Megamachines and Phantasms*. Houndmills: Palgrave, 2003. Print.

Nanni, Giordano. *The Colonisation of Time: Ritual, Routine, and Resistance in the British Empire*. Manchester: Manchester University Press, 2012. Print.

Nelson, Claudia. *Family Ties in Victorian England*. Westport: Praeger, 2007. Print.

———. *Invisible Men: Fatherhood in Victorian Periodicals, 1850–1910*. Athens: University of Georgia Press, 1995. Print.

Netz, Reviel and William Noel. *The Archimedes Codex: How a Medieval Prayer Book Is Revealing the True Genius of Antiquity's Greatest Scientist*. Philadelphia: Da Capo Press, 2007. Print.

Newman, John Henry. *Apologia Pro Vita Sua*. [1864]. Oxford: Clarendon Press, 1967. Print.

Nicotra, Jodie. "The Seduction of Samuel Butler: Rhetorical Agency and the Art of Response." *Rhetoric Review* 27.1 (2008): 38–53. Print.

Nielsen, Danielle. "Samuel Butler's *Life and Habit* and *The Way of All Flesh*: Traumatic Evolution." *English Literature in Transition* 54.1 (2011): 79–100. Print.

Norrman, Ralf. *Samuel Butler and the Meaning of Chiasmus*. New York: St. Martin's, 1986. Print.

Nunokawa, Jeff. "Death with Father in *David Copperfield*." *Paternity and Fatherhood: Myths and Realities*. Ed. Lieve Spaas. Houndmills: Macmillan, 1998. 186–92. Print.

Olson, Mary C. *Fair and Varied Forms: Visual Textuality in Medieval Illuminated Manuscripts*. New York: Routledge, 2003. Print.

O'Malley, Patrick R. "Oxford's Ghosts: *Jude the Obscure* and the End of the Gothic." *Modern Fiction Studies* 46.3 (Fall 2000): 646–71. Print.

Otis, Laura. *Organic Memory: History and the Body in the Late Nineteenth and Early Twentieth Centuries*. Lincoln and London: University of Nebraska Press, 1994. Print.

"Palimpsest Manuscripts." *The Literary Gazette* 377 (10 April 1824): 234–5. Print.

"Palimpsests." *The Saturday Magazine* 19.607 (December 1841): 238–39. Print.

Palmer, Sally. "Projecting the Gaze: The Magic Lantern, Cultural Discipline, and *Villette*." *Victorian Review* 32.1 (2006): 18–40. Print.

Palmeri, Frank. "Cruikshank, Thackeray, and the Victorian Eclipse of Satire." *SEL* 44.4 (Autumn 2004): 753–77. Print.

Parker, Pamela. "Constructing Female Public Identity: Gaskell on Brontë." *Literature and the Renewal of the Public Sphere* (2000). Ed. Susan V. Gallagher and M.D. Walhout. New York: St. Martin's Press, 2000. Print.

Penn, William. *Fruits of a Father's Love: Being the Advice of William Penn to his Children, Relating to their Civil and Religious Conduct*. 1727. 9th edition. Philadephia, 1774. Print.

Perry, Ruth. *Novel Relations: The Transformation of Kinship in English Literature and Culture, 1748–1818*. Cambridge and New York: Cambridge University Press, 2004. Print.

Peterson, Linda. *Becoming a Woman of Letters: Myths of Authorship and Facts of the Victorian Market*. Princeton: Princeton University Press, 2009. Print.

———. "Elizabeth Gaskell's *The Life of Charlotte Brontë*." *The Cambridge Companion to Elizabeth Gaskell*. Ed. Jill L. Matus. Cambridge: Cambridge University Press, 2007. 59–74. Print.

Philmus, Robert M. "H.G. Wells as Literary Critic for the *Saturday Review*." *Science Fiction Studies* 4.2 (July 1977): 175–93. Print.

Picker, John. *Victorian Soundscapes*. Oxford: Oxford University Press, 2003. Print.

Pinion, F.B. *A George Eliot Miscellany: A Supplement to Her Novels*. Totowa, NJ: Barnes & Noble Books, 1982. Print.

Plotz, John. *Portable Property: Victorian Culture on the Move*. Princeton: Princeton University Press, 2008. Print.

Polhemus, Robert. *Lot's Daughters: Sex, Redemption, and Women's Quest for Authority*. Stanford, CA: Stanford University Press, 2005. Print.

Poovey, Mary. *Making a Social Body: British Cultural Formation, 1830–1864*. Chicago: University of Chicago Press, 1995. Print.

———. *Uneven Developments: The Ideological Work of Gender in Mid-Victorian England*. Chicago: University of Chicago Press, 1989. Print.

Price, Leah. *The Anthology and the Rise of the Novel*. Cambridge: Cambridge University Press, 2000. Print.

———. "The *Life of Charlotte Brontë* and the Death of Miss Eyre." *SEL* 35.4 (Autumn 1995): 757–68. Print.

Raby, Peter. *Samuel Butler: A Biography*. London: Hogarth Press, 1991. Print.

"Reading as a Means of Culture." *Sharpe's London Magazine* New Series 31 (December 1867): 316–23. Print.

Reed, John R. *Victorian Will*. Athens: Ohio University Press, 1989. Print.

Reed, John S. *Glorious Battle: The Cultural Politics of Victorian Anglo-Catholicism*. Nashville: Vanderbilt University Press, 1996. Print.

Review of *The Codex Zacynthius: Greek Palimpsest of Fragments of St. Luke*. *Dublin University Magazine* 59.351 (March 1862): 303–8. Print.

Review of "*Daily Family Prayer for Churchmen*." *The English Review* 17.34 (July 1852): 456. Print.

Review of "*Form of Family Prayer, for Sunday and Daily Use*." *Christian Remembrancer* 21.9 (September 1839): 534–5. Print.

Review of "Jude the Obscure." *Saturday Review* 81.2102 (8 February 1896): 153–4. Print.

Review of *The Life of Charlotte Brontë*. *The Athenaeum* 1536 (4 April 1857): 427–9. Print.

Review of *The Life of Charlotte Brontë*. *Examiner* 2567 (11 April 1857): 228–9. Print.

Review of *The Life of Charlotte Brontë*. *The Leader* 8.368 (11 April 1857): 353–4. Print.

Review of *The Mill on the Floss*. *Spectator* (7 April 1860). Reprinted in *The Mill on the Floss*. Ed. Carol Christ. New York: Norton, 1994. Print.

Review of *The Ordeal of Richard Feverel*. *The Critic* 19.469 (2 July 1859): 6–7. Print.

Review of *The Ordeal of Richard Feverel*. *Saturday Review* 8.193 (9 July 1859): 48–9. Print.

Roberts, Neil. *Meredith and the Novel*. New York: St. Martin's Press, 1997. Print.

Robertson, Linda K. *The Power of Knowledge: George Eliot and Education*. New York: Peter Lang, 1997. Print.

Rogers, Helen. "In the Name of the Father: Political Biographies by Radical Daughters." *Life Writing and Victorian Culture*. Ed. David Amigoni. Aldershot: Ashgate, 2006. 145–63. Print.

Roscoe, W.C. "W.M. Thackeray, Artist and Moralist." *National Review* 2 (January 1856): 177–213. Print.

Rubery, Matthew. *The Novelty of Newspapers: Victorian Fiction After the Invention of the News*. Oxford: Oxford University Press, 2009. Print.

Ruth, Jennifer. *Novel Professions: Interested Disinterest and The Making of the Professional in the Victorian Novel*. Columbus: Ohio State University Press, 2006. Print.

Ryan, Vanessa. *Thinking without Thinking in the Victorian Novel*. Baltimore: Johns Hopkins University Press, 2012. Print.

Sanders, Valerie. *The Tragicomedy of Victorian Fatherhood*. Cambridge: Cambridge University Press, 2009. Print.

Satow, Roberta Lynn. "Value-Rational Authority and Professional Organizations: Weber's Missing Type." *Administrative Science Quarterly* 20.4 (December 1975): 526–31. Print.

Scarry, Elaine. *Resisting Representation*. Oxford: Oxford University Press, 1994. Print.

Schiller, Friedrich. *The Death of Wallenstein: A Tragedy in Five Acts*. Trans. Samuel Taylor Coleridge. London: G. Woodfall, 1800. Print.

Schor, Hilary M. *Dickens and the Daughter of the House*. Cambridge: Cambridge University Press, 1999. Print.

Scott, Sir Walter. *The Lay of the Last Minstrel: A Poem*. [1805]. London: Printed for Longman, Hurst, Rees, Orme, and Brown, 1908. Print.

Sedgwick, Eve Kosofsky. *Between Men: English Literature and Male Homosocial Desire*. New York: Columbia University Press, 1985. Print.

Sennett, Richard. *Authority*. New York: Knopf, 1980. Print.

Shaffer, Elinor. *Erewhons of the Eye: Samuel Butler as Painter, Photographer, and Art Critic*. London: Reaktion, 1988. Print.

Shakespeare, William. *Hamlet*. New York: Signet, 1998. Print.

———. *King Lear*. Oxford: Clarendon Press, 1974. Print.

Shaw, Marion. "*Sylvia's Lovers* and Other Historical Fiction." *The Cambridge Companion to Elizabeth Gaskell*. Ed. Jill L. Matus. Cambridge: Cambridge University Press, 2007. 75–89. Print.

Shelley, Mary. *Frankenstein*. Ed. J. Paul Hunter. New York: Norton, 2012. Print.

Shelley, Percy. *Shelley's Poetry and Prose: Authoritative Texts, Criticism.* Eds. Donald H. Reiman and Sharon B. Powers. New York: Norton, 1977. Print.

Sherman, Daniel, and Irit Rogoff. "Introduction." *Museum Culture: Histories, Discourses, Spectacles.* Ed. Daniel J. Sherman and Irit Rogoff. Minneapolis: University of Minnesota Press, 1994. ix–xx. Print.

Shirley. "Charlotte Brontë." *Fraser's Magazine for Town and Country* 55.329 (May 1857): 569–82. Print.

Siskin, Clifford. "Novels and Systems." *Novel: A Forum on Fiction.* 34.2 (Spring 2001): 202–14. Print.

Skelton, John Henry. *My Book; Or, the Anatomy of Conduct.* London: Simpkin and Marshall, 1837. Print.

Smiles, Samuel. *Self-Help: With Illustrations of Character and Conduct.* 1859. New York: John W. Lovell Company, 1884. Print.

Smith, Adam. *The Theory of Moral Sentiments.* 1759. Ed. Knud Haakonssen. Cambridge: Cambridge University Press, 2002. Print.

Solomon, Robert C. *In Defense of Sentimentality.* Oxford: Oxford University Press, 2004. Print.

Spacks, Patricia Meyer. *Novel Beginnings: Experiments in Eighteenth-Century English Fiction.* New Haven and London: Yale University Press, 2006. Print.

Spencer, Martin E. "Weber on Legitimate Norms and Authority." *The British Journal of Sociology* 21.2 (June 1970): 123–34. Print.

St. John, Ian. *Disraeli and the Art of Victorian Politics.* London: Anthem Press, 2005. Print.

Stephen, James Fitzjames. "The Relation of Novels to Life." *Cambridge Essays Contributed by Members of the University* [1855]. Reprinted in *Victorian Criticism of the Novel.* Ed. Edwin M. Eigner and George J. Worth. Cambridge: Cambridge University Press, 1985. 95–6. Print.

Stephen, Leslie. "The Heroines of George Eliot" [1925]. *George Eliot: the Mill on the Floss and Silas Marner: A Casebook.* Ed. R.P. Draper. London and Basingstoke, UK: Macmillan, 1977. Print.

Sterne, Laurence. *The Life and Opinions of Tristram Shandy, Gentleman.* Ed. Ian Campbell Ross. Oxford: Oxford University Press, 1983. Print.

Stevenson, Richard C. *The Experimental Impulse in George Meredith's Fiction.* Lewisburg: Bucknell University Press, 2004. Print.

Stone, J.S. *George Meredith's Politics.* Ontario: P.D. Meany, 1986. Print.

Stoneman, Patsy. "The Brontë Myth." *The Cambridge Companion to the Brontës.* Ed. Heather Glen. Cambridge: Cambridge University Press, 2002. 214–41. Print.

———. "Gaskell, Gender, and the Family." *The Cambridge Companion to Elizabeth Gaskell.* Ed. Jill L. Matus. Cambridge: Cambridge University Press, 2007. 131–47. Print.

Strachey, Lytton. *Eminent Victorians.* New York: Barnes and Noble, 2003. Print.

Streatfeild, R.A., ed. *Samuel Butler: Records and Memorials.* Cambridge: Printed for private circulation, 1903. Print.

Sussman, Herbert. *Victorian Masculinities: Manhood and Masculine Poetics in Early Victorian Literature and Art.* Cambridge: Cambridge University Press, 1995. Print.

Swafford, Kevin. *Class in Late-Victorian Britain: The Narrative Concern with Social Hierarchy and its Representation.* Youngstown, NY: Cambria Press, 2007. Print.

Taylor, D.J. *Thackeray.* London: Chatto and Windus, 1999. Print.

Thackeray, William Makepeace. *The Adventures of Philip; To Which Is Prefaced, A Shabby Genteel Story.* 1862. Ed. Walter Jerrold. London: Dent, 1903. Print.

———. *The Book of Snobs.* [1846–1847]. New York: St. Martin's Press, 1978. Print.

———. *The English Humourists of the Eighteenth Century.* Ed. Hannaford Bennett. London: John Long, 1906. Print.

———. *Henry Esmond.* London: Smith, Elder, & Co., 1852. Print.

———. *The History of Pendennis,* Ed. Robert Morss Lovett. New York: Scribners, 1917. Print.

———. *The Letters and Private Papers of William Makepeace Thackeray.* Ed. Gordon N. Ray. 4 vol. Cambridge: Harvard University Press, 1945. Print.

———. *The Luck of Barry Lyndon.* [1844] Ed. Martin F. Anisman. New York: New York University Press, 1970. Print.

———. *The Newcomes.* London: Everyman, 1994. Print.

———. *The Paris Sketchbook; The Irish Sketchbook.* New York: Caxton, [prev. 1840]. Print.

———. *The Paris Sketch Book of Mr. M.A. Titmarsh; and, Eastern Sketches.* Boston: Estes and Lauriat, 1883. Print.

———. "Reminiscences and Anecdotes of Thackeray." *Arthur's Home Magazine* 48.10 (October 1880): 572–3. Print.

———. Review of Disraeli's *Sybil: Or, The Two Nations. The Morning Chronicle* 13 May 1845. Reprinted in *Thackeray's Contributions to the Morning Chronicle.* Ed. Gordon Ray. Urbana: University of Illinois Press, 1955. 80. Print.

———. *Sketches and Travels in London* [1847–1850]. New York: Leypoldt & Holt [etc., etc.] 1867.

———. *Some Family Letters of W.M. Thackeray: Together with Recollections by his Kinswoman, Blanche Warre Cornish.* Boston: Houghton Mifflin, 1911. Print.

———. *Vanity Fair.* New York: Penguin, 1968. Print.

———. *The Yellowplush Papers.* [1838]. New York: D. Appleton, 1853. Print.

Thornton, William. *The Householder's Manual of Family Prayer.* London, 1853. Print.

T.H.W., *A Street I've Lived in: A Sabbath Morning's Scene.* London: Wesleyan Conference Office, 1858. Print.

Tilloston, Geoffrey, and Donald Hawess, eds. *Thackeray: The Critical Heritage.* London: Routledge & Kegan Paul, 1968. Print.

Tomalin, Claire. *Charles Dickens: A Life.* New York: Penguin, 2011. Print.
————. *Thomas Hardy.* New York: Penguin, 2007. Print.
Tosh, John. *A Man's Place: Masculinity and the Middle-Class Home in Victorian England.* New Haven: Yale University Press. 1999.
Trollope, Anthony. *Thackeray* [1879]. London: Routledge/Thoemmes Press, 1996. Print.
Uglow, Jenny, *Elizabeth Gaskell: A Habit of Stories.* London: Faber and Faber, 1993. Print.
Vickers, Nancy. "'The Blazon of Sweet Beauty's Best': Shakespeare's Lucrece." *Shakespeare and the Question of Theory.* New York: Methuen, 1985. 95–115. Print.
————. "Members Only: Marot's Anatomical Blazons." *The Body in Parts: Fantasies of Corporeality in Early Modern Europe.* New York: Routledge, 1997: 3–21. Print.
Voskuil, Lynn M. *Acting Naturally: Victorian Theatricality and Authenticity.* Charlottesville and London: University of Virginia Press, 2004. Print.
Ward, James. "Heredity and Memory." *Essays in Philosophy.* Cambridge: Cambridge University Press, 1929. 253–76. Print.
Warhol, Robyn. *Gendered Interventions: Narrative Discourse in the Victorian Novel.* New Brunswick, NJ, and London: Rutgers University Press, 1989. Print.
————. *Having a Good Cry: Effeminate Feelings and Pop-Culture Forms.* Columbus: The Ohio State University Press, 2003. Print.
Watkins, M.G. "The Palimpsest." *Quiver* 9.421 (January 1874): 206. Print.
Weber, Max. *Economy and Society: An Outline of Interpretive Sociology.* Ed. Guenther Roth and Claus Wittich [1920]. 3 vols. New York: Bedminster Press, 1968. Print.
Wells, H.G. "The Method of George Meredith." *Saturday Review* 80 (Dec 21, 1895): 842–3. Print.
Wharton, Edith. *The Writing of Fiction.* New York: Touchstone, 1997. Print.
White, Allon. *The Uses of Obscurity: The Fiction of Early Modernism.* New York: Routledge & Kegan Paul, 1981. Print.
Whitewell, Elwin. "*The Newcomes.*" *Quarterly Review* 97 (September 1855): 350–78. Print.
Whitman, Walt. "Crossing Brooklyn Ferry." *Norton Anthology of American Literature,* 6th edition, Vol. C. New York: Norton, 2003. 79–83. Print.
Wilde, Oscar. "The Decay of Lying." *The Complete Works of Oscar Wilde.* New York: HarperPerennial, 1989. 970–92. Print.
Williams, Ioan. *The Realist Novel in England: A Study in Development.* London: Macmillan, 1974. Print.
Wilt, Judith. *The Readable People of George Meredith.* Princeton: Princeton University Press, 1975. Print.
Woolf, Virginia. *Collected Essays.* 4 vol. London: The Hogarth Press, 1966. Print.
————. *The Common Reader, Second Series.* London: Hogarth Press, 1986; 1932. Print.

————. *Contemporary Writers*. New York: Harcourt Brace & World, 1966. Print.

————. *Moments of Being*. Ed. Jeanne Schulkind. Orlando: Harcourt, 1985. Print.

————. *A Room of One's Own*. New York: Harcourt, Brace and Company, 1929. Print.

————. "Sketch of the Past." *Moments of Being: Unpublished Autobiographical Writings*. Ed. Jeanne Schulkind. Sussex: The University Press, 1976. Print.

Wordsworth, William. *Lyrical Ballads* [1800. Repr. 1802]. Ed R.L. Brett and A.R. Jones. London: Methuen & Co., 1963. Print.

Zwinger, Linda. *Daughters, Fathers, and the Novel: The Sentimental Romance of Heterosexuality*. Madison: The University of Wisconsin Press, 1991. Print.

Index

For Product Safety Concerns and Information please contact our
EU representative GPSR@taylorandfrancis.com Taylor & Francis
Verlag GmbH, Kaufingerstraße 24, 80331 München, Germany